MW01231391

Allow The Children

SUSAN COOK

ISBN-13: 978-0692597453
ISBN-10: 069259745X

CONTENTS

ALLOW THE CHILDREN

ACKNOWLEGEMENTS

Over the years, as I have told the stories in this book, so many individuals have urged me to record and preserve them. "Write a book!" is a phrase I heard over and over until I decided to do it. Thanks so much to all of you who encouraged me.

Special thanks to Janice Delong, Lynn Laughlin and Lisa Taylor for proofreading and editing.

Special thanks to my wonderful daughter-in-law, Liz Cook (www.liz-cook.com) for the cover photo, design and formatting of the book.

The greatest thanks of all goes to my husband, Michael Cook, who walked through all of these adventures with me.

Section I

THE STORY OF ALLOW THE CHILDREN

"How did you get started in this mission work?" is a question that often comes from someone who has just met me. It also comes from folks who remember ours as a very ordinary family working our way through life without anything that set us much apart from others. Back then, I did not make international flights nearly every month. I did not have the responsibility for hundreds of orphaned children. I did not know anyone in Nepal or Bangladesh… or Pakistan.

In the year 2013, our little mission agency bought 100+ international air tickets. Fifteen of them were for me, and the others were for various individuals and groups who served on mission projects with Allow The Children. I am amazed when I ponder where this ministry is and all that is going on around me. It reminds me that Michael and I certainly did not plan it or even imagine it. We are thankful that the Lord has allowed us to be part of this, which is only one of His many projects in bringing about His plans for His world. I hope this book will answer the questions of *how we started* as well as *what we are doing* and the most important question, which is *WHY we do it.*

When did Allow The Children start? This is a question I often struggle with as I describe the beginnings of the ministry to those who ask. The simple answer is June 2003. That is the time when the United States government recognized us as a valid non-profit organization and allowed us to receive and receipt donations for tax exemption. June 2003 would certainly be the business or financial beginning of Allow. It is the date we mark when we celebrate an anniversary. Of course, no one wakes up one morning and accomplishes a launch for a non-profit on the same day. Allow The Children started long before 2003 and even before we chose that name or formed a plan in our minds.

Building a house or a business or a ministry begins with the thought or the idea. For me, the "thought" might have begun when I was in the eighth grade. We (students) were given a class assignment to research a career of interest to us and to do a major project based on it. The assignment covered a whole semester. We were to gather brochures and all kinds of printed information about the chosen career and mount them in a display. We needed to learn about the educational and occupational requirements. Interviews with those in the chosen field were expected. A major paper was required which would describe all aspects of the career, including how we could move toward it and why the identity with that life purpose was desired.   Finally, we each presented our career research to not only our own class, but the entire eighth grade of the school, which I believe was four classes of about thirty students each.   The desire was in my heart and mind much earlier, but as I search my memory, I think this was the first time I shared my personal aspiration towards mission work with anyone.

I think all eighth graders should do a project like this. It certainly made me think and ponder my future. I did not attend a Christian school.   I was in a rough, secular environment with very liberal ideals.   Presenting a faith-based career project was not going to be "cool", and I knew it. I wanted to choose something else, but I just could not. "Missionary" went on the top of my display board and a number of my fellow students called me "Missy" for the rest of the school year, some out of affection and some from contempt. In the eighth grade, I had no thought of founding a mission agency. My project was on *being* a missionary. One would need to "qualify" under a mission board and of course, a missionary needed to have a plan to do something and a place in mind to do it. I never settled on a target place or a specific missionary task. I was interested in going anywhere and had the opportunity for short term mission trips been available then as it is today, I am sure that I would have worked hard to raise the funds to participate in them. The memory of my great desire to be some part of mission work, and no opportunity to do it, is still with me today. It is one of the things that drives me to plan short-term trips to give young people, and old people and in-between people a chance to be part of reaching the world with the gospel.

Sometime during my teen years, I privately and publicly committed my life to missions, though still without any specific direction. I knew that I wanted to be part of evangelism in some way. I wanted the world to be different-*better*-because I was here. My plan was to take one step and then the next step towards this goal.

What would I actually *do* as a missionary? In my experience, Bible college was for men. Church planting and preaching were for men. Women could contribute if they married a man doing these things, but as an individual, the choices seemed to be teaching or nursing. With no intention of spending days of my life trapped in a room with a bunch of children, I decided on nursing. As early as my ninth grade year, I was studying the entrance requirements for nursing schools and planning my high school classes to include the math and science needed for entrance.

Virginia Baptist Hospital School of Nursing was the reason I came to Lynchburg, Virginia, after growing up in northern Virginia with the diverse mix of military families that surround Washington, DC. Lynchburg was and is very different from northern Virginia, but I learned the culture, and it became home. I graduated from nursing school in 1977 and found great satisfaction in my job as an emergency department nurse.

I enjoyed interaction with co-workers and patients from many different cultures and socioeconomic groups. I loved the "cutting edge" and the gratification of helping to turn a medical emergency around to a good solution. I came to understand that our best efforts and doing everything right does not always bring about the desired objective. I banked valuable experience dealing with some of the most horrific events of life, and I saw some terrible things become better because of skills and efforts I was able to apply. One of the most difficult and necessary experiences I had was coming to accept the fact that I could not do *everything*. If, for example, multiple victims of a major accident came through our doors, I could help one person immediately. I might be able to move between two patients, but someone else was going to have to help the others. Some of them might suffer or die without help, if there were too many for our staff to manage. I might even need to decide whether my patient was less likely to survive than another and therefore, I should leave the first one to minister to the other.

One more lesson I learned from the emergency department was that the patient who received my best efforts might not respond with gratitude. The person I was trying to help—because of emotions, misunderstanding, drugs, contagion or even purposeful intent—might hurt me in some way. It was a fact and a necessary risk. The Lord was preparing me for what was to come.

After the years of study and training, I did not settle into a lifetime in the field of nursing. I loved emergency nursing, and it is part of who I am today, however it was not the work the Lord had for me. I originally intended to move towards a nursing career somewhere in an international missionary setting. It did not happen.

The plans and dreams I had in the 70's were shattered by life events. Some of those events were out of my control, and there were some that I could have managed better than I did. With the advantage of maturity and hindsight, I can see some different decisions I might have made, nevertheless history stands as it is. I was off the path of becoming a missionary according to my own definition, but the Lord used all of the circumstances to bring about His plan.

I married Michael Cook and spent the 80's as the wife of a businessman. My nursing career ended when I decided to focus on homemaking and motherhood. It would have been an emotional event for me, had I known on my last day of full-time employment that I would never return. I left nursing for a completely different life—to raise five children and be as actively involved in our local church as it was possible to be. I still loved missions and missionaries. I spent many hours doing projects and writing letters to help and encourage the missionaries sent out by our church. We took every opportunity to have missionaries in our home and often talked about making a trip to visit them on the field—but the possibility of that seemed as far away as the moon. I was not really planning to do anything like that, and I was not nurturing any such dream. I was mostly trying to keep up with our children's music lessons and sports schedules, doctor and dentist appointments, family activities, church responsibilities, and raising Chihuahua puppies. To this list, I later added managing rental apartments, which was a task for which I had no preparation, experience or particular interest. I was surprised to find that I really enjoyed it.

One way to become a property manager is to buy an apartment building or seek employment with an existing company. Another way is to be drafted into the role when one's father-in-law buys an apartment building and another and another. Michael and his father were slowly moving out of the fast food restaurant business. As they sold the restaurants, they invested in duplexes, quadplexes and sometimes larger buildings with multiple units. They did the real estate work and the accounting and the taxes. I did anything involving the tenants, including screening prospects, conflict resolutions, collections, evictions, marketing vacant units, arranging for repairs. All of a sudden, I was responsible for legal and financial decisions that were beyond my experience, and I was researching to find out what to do. Some of these decisions were far-reaching with potentially high stakes. There might be answers in a book for documents and government regulations, but there were no set answers for the people issues. I just needed to pray and work through those. It was the best experience possible for times still in the future when I would be alone in countries far away, facing other high stake decisions.

I enjoyed the good will of tenants (customers!) who were happy with my management, and I tolerated the angst of those who were not pleased when I (for example) enforced a late fee or started the eviction process. I spent many hours counseling young people (and some older people too) that food was the only thing that was a higher priority in their personal finances than their rent.

Anyone who is working and getting a paycheck is spending it for something. It should be spent for food first and the very next thing is housing. I often told a tenant that if he lost his job and needed food, he should tell me and I would bring some groceries, but if he was getting a paycheck, food was the only priority ahead of his rent.

This discussion usually occurred during the signing of the lease, before any problems came. Occasionally, in our well churched area, the new tenant would suggest that his tithe was his first priority. I would not disagree with that, but I told him that I had never seen anyone who was faithful with his tithe who failed to pay his rent, and to this day, I still have not. If they did not pay their rent on time, they would certainly be charged the late fee—a policy that applied both to the Christian and the heathen, to those with whom I had a prior relationship as well as the new acquaintance, to those who had a sob story and those who did not offer any excuse. If they did not pay their rent by the set date of the month, I would ask them to leave the apartment. If they did not leave, I would start eviction proceedings. In some cases, I filed evictions against tenants who were fellow church members or the sons/daughters of good friends. In those cases, I told them that they could move into my house for a time, if necessary, but they could not stay in the apartment. None accepted the offer. They usually found a way to pay the rent.

From a few hours a week, the apartment management grew into more than a full time job, complete with frequent after hours demands. During more than ten years of apartment management, I left my warm bed many times to open a door when a tenant was locked out. I once stayed the night with a woman whose husband was away, when she came home to find someone had broken into her apartment. I broke up parties that were loud and with amazing numbers of (often drunk) people packed into the unit. I worked through the aftermath of fires and floods, criminal activities, legal threats, and some illegal threats. I captured wildly barking dogs and confined them so that a repairman could work. I had to research laws and procedures. I learned to "nurture" the client relationship. I provided parenting for college students and daughtering for some elderly tenants. I climbed on a roof (in a skirt) and "fixed" a clanging attic fan by tying it closed. I boosted my children up onto roofs to clear out gutters. I killed insects for adult men. (No, I am not kidding.) I learned to use a computer and developed organizational structures. It was incredible experience, both the good times and the difficult. The Lord was preparing me for the ministry work that was to come.

During the same time period, Michael was working with various business and financial endeavors. He was teaching part-time in a community college. He was chairman of the missions committee at our church. He was also gaining experience that would be needed in the ministry that was coming. As Michael spent days with business, financial, and teaching tasks, the Lord was preparing him. His missions committee responsibilities kept both of us involved with church leadership and developed our knowledge and interest in mission work.

Where was Allow The Children during all of this time? We had no thought to join or start a mission agency, but through my emergency department days and the property management, raising five children and serving in children's ministries in our church—the Lord was preparing me. By the time we founded Allow, I had developed some confidence in dealing with life situations that (perhaps) I could not have handled in my twenties. I do not know whether we could have successfully launched Allow at an earlier time, but I can look back now and see some of what God was doing and it looks like a plan was in progress.

The 90's was the transition period. A number of circumstances converged together that dramatically changed our lives. The *first circumstance* was that we began making short-term trips to various mission fields. Michael felt that his responsibilities as missions chairman should include visiting the different missionaries sent out by our church—to encourage them, to see how we could help them, and to report back to the church concerning the ministry work being accomplished. We traveled for two to three weeks at a time. Michael's role was the more important one on these trips. Mine was basically whatever I made it to be. Sometimes I did some teaching or medical work. It was mostly a time of gaining experience in travel, learning cultural diversities and managing life in varied situations. Perhaps most importantly, my love for the work took roots and grew. I saw physical and spiritual needs that I could fill, and I wanted to help. During this time, we visited Germany, Hungary, Austria, Vietnam, Cambodia, Laos, India, Nepal, Russia, France, Australia, New Zealand, Mexico, Cuba and Israel, and some of these countries multiple times. Most of the trips were very project-oriented and some had a very light agenda, but I saw the Lord fill the schedule with worthwhile tasks that I could not have planned from the United States. My work was usually divided between medical clinics and Bible teaching. Michael's work was mostly teaching with some administration tasks. We learned important lessons about air travel, food, and communication without a common language, changing money, predicting expenses, and living from a suitcase with life constantly changing around us. I was learning a method of mission work that was different from the one I saw as an eighth grader.

The *second circumstance* that changed in the 90's was our business responsibilities. I was a full-time, very busy property manager. Michael had a demanding fast food business, and he was still teaching for the community college. Both of us were planning and managing our responsibilities in order to be out of the country for at least two trips a year. In between trips, I could not imagine that life would be any different.We did not have jobs that we could quit or take any kind of extended leave. The restaurants and the apartments would not just go away and stop their demands on our time. But miraculously, they did. Michael and his father sold the restaurants, one by one, investing the money into (usually) more apartments. Sometimes they kept the building and land as an income investment, but over a few years' time, they backed out of day to day restaurant operation. More apartments increased my work load, and I was running hard during those years, but it all stopped almost overnight. Michael placed the apartments with a property management company. Quite suddenly, I was no longer showing vacancies, resolving conflicts, sitting in court waiting for my cases, collecting rent and looking for people to cut grass. My business career, which I really did enjoy (most of the time) had ended. Hiring the property management company meant that they took a deep cut of the income, *but we had enough* coming in and now I also had my life back, with some choices about what I wanted to do with it.

Michael's business career had not ended. He still had some monthly accounting and investment management to do, but his time was remarkably free compared to previous years. Some missionaries spend years raising their faith support. Ours was raised with business investments. We could have retired, but neither of us wanted that. We could have kept managing the apartments personally and built more wealth, but neither of us wanted that either. By the end of the 90's, the foundation for our ministry was in place. We had some international experience. We had enough (abundant) personal support income and no personal debt. We had a great desire to serve in some kind of mission work, and we had some ideas about how our individual gifts could be used.

The *third circumstance* of the 90's was that the active period of our parenting was winding down. At the end of 1999, our three oldest children were adults and already leading independent lives. Our youngest son was in college, out of state. Our youngest daughter was sixteen in January of 2000. Though still under our support, she was making good decisions for herself and managing her life well. With our children "launched" or close to it, we increased our travel and began to identify ourselves more with missions and less with business.

As the century turned into 2000, we were still making several short project trips each year. We did not feel any specific "call" to a certain country or even a certain task. We were responding to invitations or opportunities to teach. Many times one trip brought contacts and invitations for the next. We never seemed to be looking for a place to go or a project to do. We were looking for the time in our schedules to do one of the projects that was waiting. We made trips to many different countries, and I enjoyed them all. Cambodia was my favorite place, the country where I first experienced the passion and sacrifice of the Asian believers. It is not easy to be a Christian in a Hindu or Buddhist culture. Those who name the Name of Christ pay a price that an American can only imagine. Believers are purified by the process, and a great devotion to God is a common result. Nepal was no different, and though my love for the country was not born immediately, the doors kept opening. The invitations for teaching, medical clinics, and ministry of various kinds kept coming. Nepal was soon the most common destination of our mission work.

We frequently visited a certain children's home in Nepal. The children of the home were orphaned or abandoned and always hungry when they first arrived. They were damaged by experiences in their very short lives that would surely seem to leave them emotionally crippled forever, but God brought them to a place where they could heal. Perhaps for the first time, their physical needs were met. They learned the meaning of love and safety. They received education, which for most of them, was beyond reach in their previous circumstances.

All of these things are important and make for a worthy life work, but here is the sweet part: the children came from a geographic area and culture that was devoutly Buddhist. They spoke and understood only one language, one that few outside of their own people ever mastered. Through the ministry of a children's home, they learned of a Savior who created them and loves them and wants to spend eternity with them. Many of the children had come to faith and were remarkably committed. Some had stood strong for Christ even when beaten during visits to relatives because they refused to worship the Buddha. *Wow!*

There was a story about one small orphan boy, in the Christian children's home, who had a brother being raised in a Buddhist monastery. He was taken to the monastery to visit his brother for a few days. The monk who picked him up and returned him, reported that during meal times he was always present. During the daily times when they worshiped the Buddha, the boy ran and hid. He was only about five years old, but he wanted to worship only Jesus.

I did some small projects for the children's home—collecting clothing, blankets, school supplies, vitamins—whatever they needed. I had the delightful experience in our church of asking the people to STOP bringing things. I had all that I could carry, but the family support and encouragement from our church was incredible and a major factor of our ministry development. People often gave me money to take on the trip to spend for the children if I learned of something they needed. They always needed something. I took photos of the children, keeping track of their names and ages. I distributed the photos, not for money, but for prayer and pen pal writing. When all the children's photos were placed, people were still asking for them, so I made another set and then a third set. I collected letters before each trip and brought back answers from the children. After a year, it seemed that we should take new photos and update the information. That was a challenging job, but it seemed important, and I experimented with different ways to accomplish it. I was learning to manage a sponsorship program, step-by-step. The Lord was providing the training I needed for the work that was coming.

Without ever making the decision to do so, we became focused on one country. We had developed good relationships in Nepal. Nepal was where the children's home was that we loved so much. We usually had a plan and a project with approximate dates for the next trip before we left the country each time. We were no longer visiting the different mission areas for our church. My mind and heart was on our own work, which was developing, and it was in Nepal.

Still, we had no plan to confine our work to any one country. Nepal was simply the country we were in most of the time. We received regular invitations to return. We were working with one children's home and no specific ambition to ever be involved in another. We held teaching conferences and medical clinics there. I made trips into Nepal, sometimes with no agenda at all, just allowing the Lord to fill my schedule once I arrived, and it always happened. Michael and I traveled together sometimes, but we discovered that it was more efficient in many ways to travel separately. One issue was speaking opportunities. If we were together, almost all of the speaking invitations went to Michael. But if I went alone, my speaking schedule stayed as full as I was able to manage. There were some times when Michael was teaching men, and I had the women in a different part of the building. At other times, there might be only one translator available or the meeting was in a one-room church, and I was part of the audience. Likewise, if I was doing something medical, Michael might be off to the side sitting and waiting. Both of us preferred the active roles. If one of us stayed in the United States, it also helped to have someone with the family and the dogs and the property management business—and so we developed that pattern.

One of the things we did to help the children's home was to present the ministry to a large agency for support consideration. They provided child sponsorship in many different countries, and after seeing the presentation on this home, they included it into their program. Since we were making regular trips into Nepal, they asked us to manage the funds and collect the materials they needed. The "materials needed" were new photos and information sheets and a variety of other paper work to be filled in and submitted on a regular schedule. From their instructions, I learned how to take the photos, mark and track them. I had the children write to the sponsors. I labeled each envelope and carried the letters back and forth each time I made a trip. As I prepared the sponsorship package each year for the larger organization, I was learning. The Lord was providing the training for running a sponsorship program of our own.

When I traveled alone in Nepal, I was usually busy during the day and settled for an early bedtime. On some occasions, I decided to go to Thamel, the tourist area, for an American style dinner and some shopping. Thamel was not particularly close to the area of the city where I stayed; the ride was about thirty minutes by taxi on a good day. After dark, the traffic often backed up, and the trip might take well over an hour to return. Traveling alone in the city at night may not be the best idea for a woman, but I rarely entertained such thoughts. *Whether I wanted to go* was the only issue.

On one occasion, when I went to Thamel, I enjoyed a nice dinner and then walked about the souvenir shops. Most shopkeepers open early in the morning and operate their shops all day long. They might own their space, but more likely, they rent it, and they need to make sales in order to pay what they owe each month and have some profit for themselves. They often have family members who work with them and they can take short periods of time off, but much of the time they all work in hopes of interacting with as many customers as possible.

The evenings are the busiest times. Tourists walk along the streets. Shopkeepers maintain a watchful eye for any potential customer who shows an interest in their goods. Lights are bright. Tables are spread with all kinds of trinkets and handcrafts. At ten minutes to nine, everything is still bustling and busy. At nine o'clock, as if by special agreement among them, all of the shops close, and it happens in an instant. The shopkeepers are tired from working since early morning. If a customer is still bargaining in their store, they will wait for the possible sale, but nine is the closing time.

This is what happened with me one night. I was not watching the time. I was bargaining for a scarf, and the owner showed no sign of closing, nor of being in any hurry to do so. When the transaction was made and I stepped outside, the garage type door slammed closed behind me, and in the next moment the lights were off. All of the other shops on this street had already closed. There were no street lights. All light and sound came from the shops that were now closed. Thamel is a busy place with many intertwining streets. A short walk should take me to some civilization once again. There was a drainage ditch, on the side of the street, deep enough to twist an ankle and was impossible to see in the pitch dark. I walked up one street and then another. Everything was closed. An occasional feral dog was the only sign of life. I kept walking, very aware of how vulnerable I was and wondering how to find the way back to my hotel. Taxis pack in and wait in a certain place, and I did find the spot, but the lot was completely empty now. Taxi drivers waited for one last fare of the night and would not return, because the shops were closed and all of the tourists, who had good sense, were already back in their hotels. If I could not find a taxi, the next good idea was to find a hotel there in Thamel, book a room and just stay there for the night. Although that was a good plan, I kept walking without finding any hotel. There are a lot of hotels in some areas of Thamel, but I was not in the right area. I saw only long, dark, deserted streets and dirty archways that might become my shelter for the night. The more time that passed, the less likely a taxi would come.

I began to pray, asking the Lord to give me some shelter, either a taxi or a hotel with a vacancy. As I spoke the prayer, a vehicle slowly turned onto the same street where I walked. Evidently, the Lord was simply waiting until I asked. Yes, it was a taxi, and it stopped beside me. Was it safe to get into the vehicle alone with this man in this deserted place? It seemed safer than the street, and I was convinced that the taxi came in answer to my prayer. I climbed into the back seat and spoke with confidence. I did not know which way to go, but anywhere except here was my plan. I began directing him along. We soon came to a main street and eventually to my hotel.

This incident might seem to be inconsequential. I did not get hurt. I was not traumatized or even as afraid as I probably should have been. It all ended well, and it describes a very significant event in my life. It might have been the first time that I was lost and alone in the dark with no way to help myself. All of the familiar tools I use to manage my life and solve my problems were absent. I could not see where I was stepping in the dark. I did not know which way to go. An animal or a person might appear and hurt me at any moment, and there was little I could do in defense. I had money, but my money did me no good. It made me a target. I was helpless and vulnerable and there were no options to improve my situation. I was in a situation where I had nothing but prayer. There were many more experiences like this one to come as I traveled alone to many places in the world for Allow The Children. I think this was a training session. When I called to my God, He answered. He was teaching me to depend on Him and trust Him.

In the early years when we went to Nepal, we stayed in a certain hotel. The quality of the facility was modest, but it was clean and safe and convenient to the places we needed to go. The relationships were wonderful. I came to know the Buddhist owners and staff well. An older man, a guard, snapped to attention and saluted as I rounded the corner onto the property. The waiters knew that I do not drink coffee or tea. The desk clerks held the corner room on the second floor for me when they knew I was coming. I preferred it because of the window that looked out over the entrance. The small lobby was not usually busy, but rarely empty. Lodgers or staff were usually loitering about, but on one particular day, there was no one around except the desk clerk and me. I was familiar with the desk clerk from previous visits, but I cannot recall ever having had a personal conversation with him. I did not know his name. Seeing that we were alone in the lobby, he addressed me.

"Madam, can you give me a book about the Jesus?" he asked quietly. Asians tend to assume that Americans are Christians, but he had seen further evidence. I often carried a Bible. He had seen me meeting with Nepali pastors and leaving the hotel with them. I felt guarded, because it is common among the poor of the third world to feign interest in Christianity with the hope of receiving some financial benefit. I also felt ashamed, because my life had passed that of this man multiple times, and I had never spoken any word or questioned to see if he might be interested in spiritual things.

"You would like a book about Jesus?" I repeated back to him.

"Yes," he said. "My wife is very interested in that."

"I would like to meet your wife," I answered. He perked up at this idea and immediately asked me to come to his house to meet his family. I wondered how far away he lived, but I knew that if I asked him, the answer would not be meaningful to me. I knew that he rode a bicycle to work, so that meant it was not within walking distance.

We decided on a day that I would go with him after his shift, to meet his family, and have dinner, and they would be expecting me to talk about "the Jesus." The day came. I entered a taxi with the desk clerk and marveled at the time which passed and still we had not arrived at his home. I was hopelessly lost, unable to even estimate which part of the city or what direction we had traveled. Fortunately, I do not scare easily—at least personal safety issues are seldom a reason that I experience fear. As I think back, I realize that I did not really know this man. I did not know where I was going. No one else knew where I was. I did not have a mobile phone. I carried a bag that he would correctly assume carried a large sum of money. Even if robbery was not his motive, we were moving into a very poor area of Kathmandu, a place where foreigners rarely visit. I was totally dependent on this man to get me back to the hotel.

My mind was on the gospel and how I would share it with this family. As Hindus living in a strong Hindu culture, they might not have any frame of reference for Christianity. This man's English was very good, but he might not know the meaning of words like "repentance" and "sin." The word, "God," would have a totally different meaning to him than to me.

The taxi left, and before me was a mud and brick building with people at every window and across the street as well, all watching to see the foreigner coming to visit their neighborhood. It was necessary to step down to a dirt floor that was below street level that seemed to be part of someone's home. From there, we moved to a wooden ladder with incredibly small slats leading to the next level which was definitely the middle of someone's living room. People were sitting about, drinking tea, watching as I continued to ascend. They did not seem surprised that I was there, but they were certainly curious. Maybe my host had told them that he was expecting a guest. I did not feel any sense of threat, rather I felt that I could stop at any point I wished and would probably be welcomed and given a cup of tea. The last flight to the flat I was to visit was—I do not jest or exaggerate—a straight up wooden ladder less than one foot wide with barely room to place a foot on each rung. It did not seem strong enough to support me, but I had no choice but to continue the climb. (To go to the toilet, one must reverse this process. There was one toilet and shower room, shared by the whole building, and it was on the very bottom level. If a light was desired, it must be carried in hand.)

When I came to the top of the ladder, I was in a small room that contained a bed slightly larger than a twin size, one chair, and a wooden cabinet full of small possessions. All kinds of items were hanging from the walls and perched on any brick jutting out to form any kind of shelf at all. The ceiling had some solid parts, but a blue tarp was stretched over most of it, probably to catch any leaks. A family of four, almost five, lived in this place. I took the chair. A small dog begged for my attention. A woman, great with child, sat on the bed with her twelve-year-old daughter beside her and on the floor, another smaller girl, six years old. The desk clerk sat next to his wife and introduced me to his family. I was pleased to know that both parents and the oldest girl were all English speakers. I greeted them and took out a little photo book of my children. Sharing pictures and talking about family is often a good way to begin a relationship and a conversation with people at a first meeting. I think I was talking about my third child (of five), when the woman interrupted me.

"Are you going to tell us about the Jesus?" she asked in a voice that was almost a cry. If I had been anxious about presenting the Word before I arrived, the emotion drained off me now, and I felt quietly confident in what I was about to say. The Holy Spirit was working here in advance of my arrival. I knew that my words would be completely directed, and at least one heart was ready to hear.

"Yes, I can do that," I said, and I smiled at the woman and daughter. I could feel their full attentiveness. I snapped my little photo book closed and opened my Bible. "I would like to tell you the whole story," I told them, and I was rewarded with encouraging nods. "It is going to be a little long."

"We want to hear the whole story," the woman said.

And so, beginning at the beginning, I read the very first verse of the Bible and I stopped to explain. "When I say, *God*, I mean the God who created all that there is, the One who created you and me. He loves us and wants us to love Him as well." I have no expertise in Hinduism. I know that the Hindu is familiar with gods who claim all kinds of power and influence, but not one who loves. The Hindu worships for a variety of reasons; often hoping for some benefit or avoidance of some suffering, but his motivation is not love. If they hear of a (G)god who loves them, they might check that one off the list. There is no need to appease that one, so the thinking is to direct worship to the ones who might have been angered by some word or action and might send some harm in response.

I went through the first chapters of Genesis, talking about creation and the sin in the garden which resulted in the separation of the man and woman from God. I continued on to the story of Cain who tried to worship God in his own way and Abel who pleased God by worshiping in the way that God taught them—with the death and the sacrifice of a perfect lamb. At this point, I had been talking for quite a while, and I stopped. It was gratifying that the attention of the two adults and the older girl did not waver at all. I played with the little dog for a moment, who was trying so hard to attract me. The man was studying his folded hands, but the two women exchanged glances at one another and back to me.

"What about Jesus?" the woman asked.

I flipped over to the book of John and began the story of Jesus, Who was born as a baby, the Son of God, fully man, but also fully God. I was not searching for words. As I spoke each sentence, the next one came to me. It was almost as if I was one of the listeners, waiting to hear what I would say next. This is an experience I have had several times since, always in Asia. It is a beautiful moving of the Spirit—just using my voice, and I love my role in it. I worked through the story of Jesus, tying it in with the lamb that Abel sacrificed, and I stopped again after describing the resurrection. I played with the little dog. The women went back to anxious glancing about. The man was still staring at his hands.

"How can we be Christians?" the woman cried out.

Wow! What a privilege it was to be part of this very, very special day. I remember continuing the pause for a few more moments, thanking the Lord for it and just basking in the certainty that this was one of those God appointments. I knew that one and perhaps more individuals in this family was passing from death to life right before my eyes. I also had the very clear understanding that I had not brought this about. What happened here had already started before I ever met this family. I was a tool in the Lord's hand to accomplish what He was doing. The beauty of the whole thing was that just as I had not been the one to bring it about, I also could not mess it up.

I looked at the girl and asked, "What do you want to do?"

"I want to follow Jesus," she said in a firm confident voice. It was the first words that I had heard her say. I do not think that I will ever forget them.

I looked at her father. "What do you want to do?" I asked him. He was breathing too fast and his hands trembled as he spoke. Was he under conviction or was it something else? The two women were settled for eternity. There were deeper things they needed to know, but their faith was already visible. They were redeemed and set apart, though they did not know it yet. The man was still very lost.

"We are Hindu," he said, "our families will be very upset if we become Christians."

"I guess that is true," I said, and I went back to playing with the dog. The women were silent with eyes wide. If the husband/father remained a Hindu, it would be very difficult for them.

"Tomorrow is a festival day. We need to put the tika on our foreheads. If we do not do that, the neighbors will ask why."

"I guess that is true," I said. The little dog was thoroughly enjoying my attention. The man's breathing became even more labored. The women were watching him with great concern, but I think not for his physical health.

"This will make many problems for us," he said, with more anxiety rising in his voice. I do not know what his objectives were for bringing me on this visit, but I do not think it was going as he planned.

"I guess that is true," I said again. I had already said all that there was to say. Now it was between him and the Lord. He was obviously in distress at this point—sweating and struggling for breath. It was not an easy decision for him, and I appreciated that he was counting the cost. I simply waited and watched him. His wife and daughter were watching silently as well. They were coming to the Lord with or without him, but I thought about what it was going to mean for them if he did not come. Christian wives of Hindu men often suffer much in Nepal. Is that what was ahead for these two precious ones? If that is what happened, what could I do? *And what should I do?* For now, I was quite sure that I should do nothing. I waited. We all waited. Even the little girl, playing on the floor, was quiet and waiting. The man was writhing spiritually, and eternity for him depended on his decision. Of course, the Lord might give him another chance on another day, but it was difficult to imagine ever being closer than now.

"Okay," he finally said. "we will be Christians." He said the words with great emotion and finality about the decision. His rigidity melted away and his breathing returned to normal. His face was calm.

"We will be Christians," he said again and then said it a third time. Now three (or maybe four, including the littlest one) sets of eyes rested, waiting on me.

"The Lord hears what we say," I told them. "Tell Him that from this day forth you will follow Him and only Him. You cannot be partly Hindu and partly Christian. To follow Jesus means that He is your only God." They all nodded in understanding and I was privileged to hear the first words that they said to their Savior.

Somehow the evening continued on. It was not a normal day, but normal things were happening. They understood that they should now attend a church, but they did not know how to find a church. They wanted to attend a certain one where the pastor was from the same tribal background as they were. The man knew this pastor from his visits to lodgers in the hotel. I knew exactly how to find the church, but I could not explain it to them. There are no street names in Nepal. One must simply know which road to take. I told them that I would call the pastor in the morning and ask him to send someone to show them the way to the church.

"Tell him we are Christians now," the man said, and I agreed that I would.

They had several questions, and I answered as best I could. They had more understanding than I did about the behavior of the Christian believer in the Hindu culture. They understood that a Christian did not participate in Hindu holiday celebrations, which all involve Hindu worship in some way.

The father told me that he had a Bible question. *"Oh no,"* I thought, *"what if it is some deep theological thing?"*

The question was, "Did Jesus go on a picnic, and He made food for everyone?" It was so wonderful to think of the familiar stories of Scripture from the perspective of one who was hearing them for the first time. I learned that they had a gospel of John. The mother and daughter had read it before I arrived and the father had read at least the part about the picnic.

We moved into the only other room of their home for dinner. It was a little kitchen built under the eaves of the house. A curtain hung in the doorway. It was necessary to crawl or bend very low to go into the adjoining room. The only seating was on the floor. A small propane cook stove was against one wall. Dishes and a few pans were stored next to it. A surprisingly small amount of food was stored against the adjoining wall. There was a single mattress in the room which was the bed for the two sisters. We ate a simple dinner and then it was time for me to go.

"Tell the pastor that we are Christians now," the man reminded me once again. "We need to go to the church," he said. He left to find a taxi for me. "Tell him we are Christians now," he instructed me again as I entered the taxi.

"Yes Brother. I will tell him."

This evening was before the time when we were setting up the sponsorship program; before Allow was launched. It was one of many home visits I made. I have always been grateful that the Lord let me have this experience. I am glad that I was not afraid to go—or too busy to go—or too tired to go—or any of many other possible hindrances that I know had caused me to miss opportunities in the past. I purposely did not give the family any financial help at the time when they came to the Lord. Their need was obvious, and it would have made me feel good to give them something, but I wanted to see what they would do without financial help. Would they go to the church? Would they begin to grow? Or did they invite me to their home hoping for money, and would they fall away quickly if they did not see that benefit?

I called the pastor and told him about the events of the evening. He promised me that he would follow up on them, and he did. He was pastor of a church of over two thousand members, but when I next came to Nepal, about six months later, he had been in their home three times. The pastor and the church received this family and set them on the road to spiritual growth and discipleship.

It was Michael's "turn" to travel in May 2003. He flew to Nepal, and I remained in the United States. He visited the children's home that we loved so much and then attended one of the churches that we knew well in Kathmandu. After the worship service, the pastor talked with Michael.

"Can you help us with our children?" he asked. "Some of them are from families so poor that they cannot enroll in school. Some of the church members are helping, but there are so many children in need."

"I do not know whether we can help," Michael answered. It was something that he would need to talk to me about after returning to the United States. There were several possible directions we could take. For example, we could "sponsor" one or more of the children ourselves, which is probably what the pastor was intending at the time. We could give a generous one time gift and perhaps challenge some others to do the same. We could pray for them, without taking on any ongoing responsibilities ourselves. After all, we were already busy with all kinds of ministry work.

The very next day, Michael happened to be talking with the pastor of another church. "Can you help our children who need to enroll in school?" came the question and the same problem as described by the first pastor. Of course, there are poor children throughout Nepal, but what was being offered (and requested) was a partnership to help some specifically identified children. The churches knew which children within their body were in genuine need. Helping them meant educating a child from a Christian family who could become a strong leader and witness for the Lord as an adult. The church had the means to receive, distribute, and account for the funds. This was an important piece. Without it, we could give money, but we would be back in the United States with no means to watch how it was being used. Both of these were pastors and churches that we had known and trusted for years. If the churches were willing to manage the funds for the children and choose the neediest situations, then our part (logically) was to find the money. Sponsorship was a natural answer to the situation. Michael was already pondering the project. That the very same question came from two very different, trusted sources seemed significant. Was it an assignment from God?

After he returned home, I can only remember parts of the conversation about it. Had I known that it was a pivotal point in my life, I am sure that I would have given it closer attention. I remember that Michael related the questions of the two pastors to me. I cannot remember whether he suggested that we start a sponsorship program or if he just planted the idea of "doing something" to help the children, and I thought of sponsorship later. In any case, my idea was a small "contained" project. I thought that many of the people who were writing letters regularly to the children in the home might want to sponsor them. We could add a few children from each of the two churches. They would need to be in separate lists according to where the money would go, so we would have three lists, therefore three sub-programs. I would send out a newsletter on this new opportunity and see what would happen. I never intended to become a fund raiser. I do not like that term or those kinds of tasks. I would never have chosen that direction and am quite sure that I have no natural skills in that area—but here we are.

I was not yet calling myself a missionary, but I did not hesitate to say that I was doing "mission work." It seemed to me that a missionary was someone who gave her life to another country, endured separation from family, left the security of America and depended on faith support. In contrast to that, we were continually popping back and forth between countries. We were with our children and parents regularly and could arrange the schedule around holidays and major events. We still lived in our comfortable American home and we were paying for it all from our own income. The church commissioned us and put our picture up on the wall with the other missionaries, but I felt no sense of qualification at the same level as the others.

A critical issue at this point was to apply and receive registration as a 501c3 non-profit organization, which would give us the ability to issue tax receipts for donations. This is important for reasons other than attracting people who want credit on their taxes. It is a statement to the public and friends alike that the government has examined Allow The Children and determined that we are a legitimate ministry, and that we have committed to giving the required accountability for the use of funds that flow through us. We studied the regulations very carefully and resolved that we would never ignore or stretch one of them. Every tax receipt that we issued would be fully supportable and clearly allowed under the government rules, and then we would carefully use the donation exactly as the donor requested. This has been a core value for us from the beginning, and we continue to carefully honor it today.

Government registration required that we form a board of directors, a constitution and by-laws, schedule regular meetings and create various reports. This is Michael's area, and he carefully worked through each step. We were forming and founding a mission agency, though that specific thought had not come to me yet. To me, it was just government paper work to make us legal. I am forever thankful for Michael's interest and aptitude in areas of finance and government compliance, which were so important as we prepared for the birth of Allow The Children. I do the largest share of the ministry development and sponsor-finding and the daily work generated by these things, but our personal ministry would never have made the jump to become an officially authorized mission agency without Michael's contribution.

Our board of directors was made up of trusted friends who had known us for years. From the time we qualified as a 501c3 non-profit organization and had the commissioning from the church, Allow The Children was truly a mission agency, and we were truly missionaries. The day that all of these things came together was in June 2003. It was an anticlimactic letter that came in the mail just as the mail came every day. It was a very important letter that we keep safe and have used many times, but it was just a piece of paper. I went about my routine in the same way on the day after receiving that letter as I did on the day before, but my life was making a very big turn. If I had that day back, it would be rich in poignant meaning for me, but at the time I missed the significance of it.

One government requirement was to choose a name for the organization, which would need to be completely unique in the United States—that is, a name different from all other registered organizations. The name for our ministry comes from a line found in Mark 10:14. The King James Version quotes the Lord saying, "Suffer the little children to come to me...." We understand the word "suffer" in this context to mean "allow" or "let" but would rarely use the word in this way. The Allow The Children ministry received its name on that day. Michael was the one who first thought of it, and I liked it immediately. I cannot remember discussing any other possible name. We did understand that the name seemed to restrict us to children's work. With our small drop of faith, we never considered a ministry which included all of our teaching, medical and village evangelism work. In the beginning, we only thought to seek donations to help the children.

Obtaining 501c3 status is said to be a long and tedious process, but for us it was quickly approved. Michael loves legal workings, and so his careful attention to the details might have been a factor, but we consider it nothing short of the *hand of the Lord* as this work was coming to birth—just as what happened next was His hand. Sponsors and project donors seemed to have been waiting for the day when we would officially launch. The ministry blossomed almost on its own and almost overnight. People who had been writing to children became their sponsors. Every newsletter I sent out brought more sponsors and more project donors. Soon we were able to give some significant support for the children's home and more people were joining with us almost every day. It did not happen without some work and some cost. I went to sleep every night and woke every morning with the ministry on my mind and heart. I talked with everyone I knew. Our church friends sponsored children. Our community friends sponsored children. My dentist became a sponsor. The girl who cut my hair took a child.

A few other churches allowed us to come and present and then became supporters. We always made it clear that the Lord had provided for us personally, so donations were used directly for the ministry. One church voted on support for us right after we spoke and in our presence. One pastor told us that a week after we had presented the ministry, he tried to lead the people in choosing whether to give a flat monthly donation for our work or to sponsor five children. He kept trying to call for the vote, but they would not vote. The people wanted to do both, and that is finally what was decided. A number of individuals in the same church sponsored children, too.

We had a warm, encouraging start for the ministry, and I was pedaling hard to keep up with it all. Records had to be kept. Sponsor packets needed to go to each new sponsor. Structure had to be created to track *everything*. Tasks that are fast and easy for me now, were time-consuming in the beginning. I was setting up computer folders and creating documents needed for one issue after another as I became aware of them. I completed all of the work, every day—receipting for checks that came in the mail, packets for new sponsors, letters answering questions, or giving new information. No matter what else I did in a day, I caught up all of the ministry tasks before I allowed my day to end. If I did not, I feared it would swallow me up and overwhelm me.

Every month we added more names to the mailing list, and the work involved in sending out the newsletter grew. We applied for a bulk mailing permit. We printed envelopes. We scheduled a board meeting. We made an outdoor sign. We developed a website.

Allow The Children was born. The intensity of attention and care the ministry required was not unlike the experience of adding a newborn to a family. Suddenly, everything in our lives revolved around the new baby. My emotions also followed the pattern of a new mother. I felt a little overwhelmed, especially considering the long-term commitment and the abrupt change in my life. I also felt an intense love and protectiveness for this thing that God had created through my husband and me. It was now our joy and responsibility to raise it for His glory. It would grow and develop and others would be involved as we went along, but for good or ill, we were (are) the parents.

I planned the first international trip of the newly formed official ministry, happily experienced with travel agents and air fare, and logistics on the ground. Today we have a partner in Nepal who picks us up at the airport and does tasks like planning for where we will sleep and transportation to the different places we need to go—but in the beginning, I needed to do all of these things myself. It is strange to remember that I arrived at the airport at night, usually alone, struggling with luggage, haggling with a taxi driver, but finally making my way across the city and into a hotel room. I loved the challenge of being in Nepal. I had to learn how to use the local currency (and how to get more of it from the bank). I needed to find my way to various places I needed to go without a map or street names and without knowing the language. There was no heat and often no electricity. There were times when political strikes stopped all transportation and sometimes internet and phone communication were down. I learned to trust and rely on the Lord in ways I never knew before. I am still learning these lessons, but I can look back and see huge steps in my walk of faith during that time.

Today I have a strong support system of friends and ministry co-workers in Nepal. Though it is difficult to explain, being in Nepal, for me, is not much different from being in Virginia. When I am in Nepal now, the things I see and hear are familiar. I know how to get to the places where I need to go. I know the money well and generally what things should cost. I know where food and medicine are, and it just feels like home. But in the early days, though I loved it, it felt like a foreign country.

When we started our sponsorship program, some of the first children I processed were the daughters of the desk clerk. He was managing to send them to school, but the condition of their home showed their great need. I visited the family almost every time I came to Nepal. I came to know that both of the girls ranked at the top of their classes. They both worked hard and showed huge potential academically. Sponsorship provided the school fees, books and consumable supplies. Sponsorship meant that their place in school was secure. A special computer class was covered. Broken eye glasses for one girl were replaced. Extra test fees were paid. It made a difference in their lives, and I loved doing it.

The first official Allow The Children trip was for the purpose of intake for the sponsorship program. We needed a good photo of each child. We needed an information sheet with the full name, age, any health or social issues that helped to describe the child or set him apart. I planned a code system so that each photo or piece of information could be identified and connected with a specific child. I needed to decide how much personal information to put into our records. We wanted to tell the sponsors that the child was an orphan or abandoned, but how much of a painful history needed or should be included? The more detailed and graphic the story, the more likely to draw a sponsor, but the child should have some privacy when the circumstances were abuse or tragically painful. It had to be a separate and individual decision for each child.

I met with the pastor of one of our churches who had requested help for the children. I had taught women's conferences with this pastor and traveled with him to do some projects in their daughter churches. He took me to a tiny rented room, and I can still remember the few furnishings and possessions. There were two small beds, each with a blanket folded upon it. Two jackets and two school uniforms hung from hooks on the wall. There was a small rice cooker and a half full bag of rice, probably the only food for the young occupants. Two little boys sat looking at us with anxious attention. I was told that the oldest boy was twelve, but he looked younger. His brother was ten. Both were thin and pale, and they were alone, but they were not orphans. They had parents in a village about six hours away. The father brought the boys to the capital city, rented the room for them, bought a bag of rice and enrolled them in school. Then, he returned to the village and left them alone. He came from time-to-time to see to their needs, but they had no way to reach him between visits. There were no cell phones at that time, and the parents did not have a landline either. If the rent was late and the landlord put them out, they were helpless children with no resources. What if they became sick? *Wow, how vulnerable they were.* I snapped their photos and filled in history papers. We could not solve all of the problems, but sponsorship would give them some security. It would cover their school fees and provide more and better food. I hoped the father would keep up the rent. It was difficult to walk away and leave the boys without solving more of the problems.

Each of the two churches had children for me to see and process into our new program. Some were orphans or half orphans (one parent deceased). Some had parents who worked very hard, but received only enough salary for survival. Some of the children were nine or ten years old and had never been enrolled in school because the parents could not pay the fees or buy the required uniform. Some of the children had parents who were handicapped or seriously ill. As I took the photos, I saw ragged clothing and bare feet, dullness in the hair and eyes that I now know comes from hunger, and hopelessness. Our monthly sponsorship would make a difference for them, though it was not going to meet every need. Some of the children needed clothing, a coat and shoes, and a visit to a dentist. Should I try to meet *more* needs for a few children or continue taking additional children to help as many as possible?

I shed some tears, but there was enough suffering to bring a flood if I had let it come. If I allowed the emotion to overwhelm me, it could stifle my ability to do anything at all. I remembered my emergency nursing days and the important principle that I would not be able to do everything for everyone. *"Suffer the little children to come to me..."* says the verse we have chosen for this ministry.

For all the physical need before my eyes, the spiritual needs were just as great. The children I processed into our program were attending good churches. With enough nutrition and education, they had the chance to grow up into culturally prepared witnesses who could multiply and help many others hear the gospel. They would know the language and the customs of this country. What an amazing opportunity we had—to be part of what the Lord was planning and preparing. Missionaries go to many different countries, and they preach and plant churches. This is an important work; but consider the chance to develop leaders within the churches and among Christian families. These kids will be the church someday. Helping to educate them and prepare them for the future was hugely important for the future of the Nepali church. I hoped that we could be part of preparing pastors and evangelists and Bible teachers, but Nepal also needs committed believers who keep shops, drive trucks, dig ditches and rock cradles. I had found my fit, fully sold into the passion and purpose of this ministry.

Some of the children had fathers who were pastors or evangelists. If we could take some of the load of meeting their family's needs, it would allow the pastor to give more time to ministry among his people. Some children were from families so poor that they were right on the verge of being sent "out to work." Some families sent children to work, especially girls, just to get the money. Some families loved their daughters very much, but it was the only choice they could see for their survival. If the girl, who might be as young as eight, was placed in a good home to work, the "employer" would feed and clothe her, provide medical care when needed, and there would be some money each month for the family to pick up. So one mouth to feed was covered and they had a little bit of money to help those who were left. The price was a daughter who would work every day, all day, cleaning floors, washing clothes by hand, and cleaning up after meals. The girl would have no chance for education or to be anything other than a house servant. She would be vulnerable and helpless to abuse of all kinds, and even if the man and sons of the house were honorable, there were the relatives and neighbors who visited, and she had little means of protection.

One such situation came up early in the formation of the ministry. I had already completed the sponsorship work for one church, but the pastor called asking me to return and consider one more little girl. When I arrived, a very sad mother and three ragged, dirty children were there with him. The mother had cancer. The father was a day laborer and unable to take off even a day of work, so great was the need of the family. The pastor was looking for a children's home to take the smallest boy. The little girl, eight years old, was about to be sent "out to work" for survival. Our sponsorship would mean that she could stay with her family and be enrolled in school next term. I cannot imagine being in the situation of this family—choosing between food for the children or medicine for the mother. She was certainly going to die, but what hope she had for more life and pain relief was in the medicine. Our sponsorship meant that a little eight-year-old girl could stay with her family during her mother's last months of life. Even after her mother's passing, her place in school was protected.

I returned to the United States to find more sponsors and to make this kind of difference for more children. I have not lost sight of the fact that the Lord draws the heart of the sponsors and provides for the needs of His people. But I love my role in the plan. I actually lay my eyes and hands on the children who will receive the help. I see them turn from no hope to a new purpose. I know that they are in school and not scrubbing floors. They have a chance for a life of their own choice.

Because all of the children in our sponsorship program are under discipleship of some kind, they also receive teaching from God's Word. One church reported to us that they tripled their number of children within the first year of our program. Certainly it was because of families hoping to enroll their children in sponsorship, but people were attending faithfully, and they were hearing the gospel. What we were doing in America was helping to bring the gospel to people in Nepal, and I wanted to do it over and over again.

When did Allow The Children start? I think the answer to this question is June 2003, the time when we were recognized and registered as a non-profit by the United States government, but the Lord was using us and preparing us years earlier.

How did we get started in this ministry? Maybe it started when we responded to that first opportunity to make an international mission trip, or maybe the answer is when we successfully obtained a 501c3 registration.

What are we doing? We are evangelizing by bringing orphaned and abandoned children, from all kinds of backgrounds, into children's homes where they hear the gospel. We are meeting needs and providing education for children of impoverished believers who will grow up as leaders and witnesses among their own people. We are planting churches by enabling and equipping national believers who have proven their hearts and effectiveness in reaching their own people for the gospel. We are making disciples by teaching and training pastors who will multiply what they learn among many others. We teach and train women who are the most effective in reaching other women. We teach, train, and support children who will grow up to be witnesses for the Lord in many different walks of life. Finally, we are providing the means for other Americans to become involved in missions.

Why are we doing this? From the heaven side, we fully believe that the Lord called us to this ministry. We believe He was preparing us and planning this for us for years—for our whole lives. From the human side, we saw needs that we could meet, both spiritual and physical. We want to be part of His work on the front lines. Allow The Children has developed into an effective tool for carrying out the Lord's commission to *make disciples in every nation.* We are joyfully serving Him.

Section II

AND THE LORD GAVE THE INCREASE

The Sponsorship Program

When Allow The Children was founded, we intended to help one children's home and two church programs. We thought we would gradually add some children to these three programs. We would return home, find sponsors and then be ready to add a few more children on the next trip. The growth of the project would be slow and manageable. I would enjoy working with it in my spare time. When we made trips to Nepal, we would have the satisfaction of seeing an on-going project and good changes in the lives of some children. As more sponsors joined us, we could help more children, but we would reach the limits of our circles soon and that would be the boundary.

I happily made lists of children and the sponsors for each. When I left for the next trip to Nepal, most of the slots were filled and I was expecting to take a few more children. Yes, each of the three ministries we started had new children to add. I felt confident and efficient as each new photo went into my camera and history sheets were completed.

One of the partners had a special request. In his hand, were fifteen more history sheets with photos. They were from a church in another small Nepali city and the surrounding villages. I had no plan to take another group of children. One children's home and two churches would keep me busy enough. As I read through the stories on these new children and looked at the photos, I wanted to help them as well. It meant that I would need to go to a different city, about six hours away from the other areas where I was working, to manage the program. It also meant looking for more sponsors, to have the regular flow of money to support the additional children. If the history sheets had not been in my hand, I might have declined, but I just could not say no. The Allow The

Children sponsorship program was going to grow by another fifteen children and we would have four separate ministries in addition to the original three. I would just trust the Lord to bring in what we needed. We were the channel between the Resource and the need. I liked that role. I could just relax and let the Lord work. I was sure that was the right thing to do. So why was I constantly thinking about how and where to find more sponsors? I resolved myself to the idea of receiving the fifteen new children (along with new children from each of the other three ministries).

The next day I received a request from Anand Neupane for children in *another* new place to be admitted to our program. Saying yes this time would mean taking Anand as a new partner and adding still another area in Nepal where I would need to travel. Anand was not a new acquaintance. I had known him for a while, and he was well recommended. Because of his relationship with our original partner, he had made copies of our child history forms. He also had fifteen completed histories with photos attached. As I read through the stories and circumstances of the children, I realized that these were the neediest of any children that we had received thus far. Their faces were thin and drawn. Their clothes were rags. Most of them had never been to school for lack of the fees and the required uniform. Our sponsorship would make life better for them. Each child sponsored could go to school with enough support left to help with food. I did not know how I could find sponsors for all of these new children, but I could not refuse to try. Yesterday, I was trusting the Lord for fifteen additional children. Now it was thirty children, five ministries, and five partners.

I returned to the capital city with only a few days left before my flight to the United States. While the sponsorship program was beginning, I still had the work that we had been doing for years. I needed to visit a church about forty minutes away, just outside of the capital city. The purpose of the visit was something about a project involving their roof. When I arrived, they had children running about in the church building. I learned that a village nearby had experienced a mudslide. Slides of all kinds are, unfortunately, common in Nepal. It is such a mountainous country and the poor often build homes in unstable areas. When the rains come, the ground loosens and land slides, mud slides, rock slides all occur with devastating results. A village, connected in some way to this church, had experienced a mudslide. Homes were destroyed, leaving children orphaned and devastated families, even among those who survived. The church was sheltering about ten children, asking church members to bring rice for them. Being poor themselves, the church members could provide no more than basic needs. Some of the children did not have shoes or a coat and the calendar was rapidly moving towards winter. The church had provided beds, but the children did not have enough blankets. School was out of the question, and I am sure the food was minimal. I looked at small faces that had seen more than any child should ever see. Some of them had lost their whole family, perhaps everyone who loved them. They were probably hungry and in less than a month, they would be cold. The pastor and the church were doing the best they could to help, but they had nowhere near the resources available to me, even though I was feeling over extended. I bought blankets and coats and shoes. I took photos and filled in history forms.

I felt a little dazed, but no other choice was possible. This time, we had taken on not only ten more children, but a children's home, rather than a church program. In a church program, the children live with a family—their own or a foster arrangement. The family already has some kind of shelter and some means of obtaining food. Our sponsorship is a significant blessing, but there is no intent to provide *everything*. For a children's home, we need at least three sponsors for each child. One sponsorship covers school (tuition, uniform, books, consumable workbooks, test fees). A second sponsorship covers food and whatever is left over from the school sponsorship is needed for food as well. The third sponsorship provides everything else, which would be clothing, medical, a portion of the rent and utilities, and transportation. Ten children, in a children's home, meant a need of thirty sponsors to take care of them, though I mercifully did not know all of these structural details at the time. I just knew I needed to raise some funds to help these orphaned children. Allow The Children could not help all of the needy children of Nepal, but the Lord had put these directly in front of me.

Our program could be overwhelmed—which would lead to its collapse—if we did not move forward carefully and wisely. I knew that I was going to need to say no sometimes and that it would be difficult. I was also convinced that every child I had taken this trip had been brought by the Lord. I needed to wait and work and pray and trust and see what would happen.

Building Support

More sponsors did come, and each one meant a difference in the life of a child. Every newsletter brought a few more. I kept talking to people. The increase was steady, but painfully slow. I had no other ideas for finding sponsors.

A nearby church invited us to come to present the ministry. We knew the pastor and some of the people well. Though small in numbers, it was a strong mission-minded church, and I was looking forward to signing on some more sponsors. It was our first speaking opportunity outside of our own church.

We had seen a lot of missionary presentations, but had never created one ourselves. It is more difficult than we thought. We put some slides together in presentation. We wrote in the notes section of the program. There was no screen at the church, but we managed to aim at a wide place on the wall. The pictures were too small and too light to be seen by all. Michael read the notes in a deadpan tone of voice. We both stumbled over words and forgot big chunks that we had intended to say. One slide was out of order and several other small glitches occurred. It was the absolute worst presentation in most every way that could be evaluated, and I still cringe to think about it.

When we were finished, the pastor said a few kind words and then asked the people what they wanted to do. *"Wanted to do about what?"* I wondered. Someone called for a vote on support for us. There was a statement or two of positive discussion. Then the vote was taken and passed by spoken word— an enthusiastic exclamation that left us incredibly encouraged. I turned to a friend behind me and asked, "What just happened here?" And I remember her smile in answer. It is one of my favorite memories from the beginning of our missionary journey.

The church sponsored five children from the new children's home and individuals in the congregation committed to almost all of the other sponsor slots. The needs of the new children's home were covered and no one could say that it was due to our amazing and persuasive presentation. *His strength is made perfect in weakness.*

We have done a lot of presentations since then and certainly made some slips, but never one as poorly done as the performance on that night. Like everything else, we improved as we went along, both in skill and confidence. Even when we have felt that we have done a competent job, I remember that night and how bad our presentation was, yet how the Lord worked in spite of it. No other church ever voted in our presence. The Lord sent the sweet encouragement and affirmation just when we needed it.

We still needed more sponsors. It was getting close to time to wire the support to Nepal and I would need to send a list of names of those who had a sponsor. The children whose names I sent would get support and the others would just need to wait a little longer.

People often asked which were the most needy? It was a difficult question to answer—impossible really. Some children seemed deeper in poverty than others, but perhaps the father had a different priority and was managing to keep them in school. Another child would not be enrolled until a sponsor was found. It was common for a family to protect a son's education at the expense of a daughter. Should I try to compensate for that by assigning a sponsor to a girl when I had a choice? It was also more likely that a sponsor would choose a photo of a girl over a boy, so should I compensate for that by assigning a boy? When a sponsor asked for "any child" and let us choose, should I send one who seemed more difficult to sponsor or one who seemed in greater need? Or should I choose one who was from a family I knew well over one who was new? Sometimes it was agonizing, but this was all part of my "on-the-job" training. The child whose photo and story went into the envelope to the sponsor would have a great change in life circumstances and there was no way to know how long the others—the ones I did not choose—would have to wait. The child whose photo was in my hand would be securely enrolled in school. A child whose photo was not chosen might be working all day in the hot sun, or scrubbing floors, or the family might have sacrificed to pay the school fees, but was not able to get a uniform and the child could not attend school without one.

I printed the photos of all the children who were waiting for sponsors. In the mornings, I carefully worked through the stack, praying purposely for each child and specifically for a sponsor. I carried them with me to church and anywhere I went. If I talked to someone about sponsoring, I could hand them some of the photos and let them choose one. Sometimes as one potential sponsor was flipping through the photos, others would join our conversation and also look through them, possibly choosing one.

Another church invited us to come and present the ministry work. A few members took pictures and pledged to sponsor a child. We officially heard from the church about ministry support a few weeks later. The church had decided to sponsor five children and the pastor's (adult) daughter wanted to come to our office to choose the children. We set the appointment and I separated out some of the photos and stories of children waiting for sponsors. She arrived and excitedly began reading through the stories, looking at pictures. I had known the girl for a long time and we had a good chat. She kept looking and looking, but after a time, she still had not chosen even one child. I knew the symptoms. She was suffering from the dilemma that whichever ones were chosen meant others were left un-chosen. She held two photos of children who had been abandoned and were now in one of our children's homes. She picked up another of an orphan who could not enroll in school until a sponsor was assigned. The orphan had a little brother. Take both of them or only one? If only one, which one? She considered a sweet little girl, daughter of a widow, or an older boy child from a poor farm family. If the little girl was not chosen, how long would she have to wait and what would her life be like until a sponsor helped? The boy was not so sweet and attractive, so would anyone else pick him?

She dropped all of the photos from her hand and broke into tears. "I can't do it!" she cried out. I tried to comfort her and assured her that I would make the choices, but it was difficult for me too. After she left, I attached five children to the church in our database, crying as I did it, and prepared the sponsorship packets to go into the mail. This was only one of many, many times that I made such choices. I did not cry every time, but the significance of the choice in the life of some child is still with me today.

The Angel Donor

One day a check for thirty-seven dollars and fifteen cents arrived by mail from someone we did not know. We still do not know how the contact happened or whether this donor had any connection at all that led him to our web site. He lived several states away. He never shared that he was in one of our church meetings or had a common friend with us. Evidently the thirty-seven dollar check was a test of some sort to see what kind of receipt he would get or just looking for evidence that we were a legitimate ministry. After a week or two, the donor called and talked to Michael. He asked some questions about our ministry and was evidently pleased with the answers. A check for ten thousand dollars came soon after the call. We could use it in any way we felt was most needed. Generous checks began coming on an irregular schedule and usually with no designation. Occasionally, he would call or email, usually asking one or two questions and then a blessing would follow.

His most common question was, "Sue, what do you need?" I did not want to take any advantage of this dear man's generosity, but I came to know that I could mention just about anything and enough funding for it would come. I almost came to expect a call or an unannounced check to arrive when we had a special need. We have never met this man, even to the day that I am writing, but the Lord certainly used him to help launch this ministry both financially and as an emotional encouragement for us. He was an angel donor, sent by God.

Our giving friend had a deep, musical voice and I sometimes imagined that he actually was an angel messenger from the Lord calling. In the first few years, before we had ever seen a photo of him and his family, it was even easier to indulge the fantasy. He seemed to have an uncanny knack for calling when I was feeling stressed or down about some financial issue and before the call ended, the problem was solved. As far as I know, angels do not have checking accounts, therefore, I do believe that he is flesh and blood. I am also convinced that our friend is a faithful follower of our Lord who serves Him with his wealth and responds when the Lord moves his heart. What an encouragement it always was when the phone calls came and the reminder once again that this ministry belongs to the Lord. He will draw the funding for what He gives us to do. The phone conversations were usually short, but occasionally we had a longer one. On one such occasion, our friend kept asking questions about the different ministries, what each one needed, how many children were waiting for sponsors? My answers were estimates without looking up the exact numbers, and I told him that, but I had an idea because of my morning prayer routine. When we finished talking, he listed a few project needs that he would cover. This was the usual way the phone calls went. He often gave generous gifts that we could use for needs like a short fall in sponsorship or a children's home budget, but to this point, he had not specifically sponsored children.

I was surprised at his next words. He said, "Sue, I am going to cover the sponsorship for all of those children for a year. There were fifty of them?" I could not even answer for a few long moments. He was lifting the pressure of the sponsorship from me—all of it—and I did not realize how heavy it was until it was gone. I would still need to find a long-term committed sponsor for each one. Once we begin sponsorship, the family would come to depend on it and we needed to keep it coming faithfully. The thought struck my mind and heart that I might not find so many sponsors and what if we failed those children after the year was up? But the same Lord that was sending this blessing would send another solution. I knew that I should trust that, but I was still in the process of learning to walk where I could not see. A second struggle was that I did not know if the number was actually exactly fifty. He intended to meet all of our sponsorship need, and of course, I wanted the number to be accurate. At the same time, I could not accept funds for fifty children if there were fewer than that. I was stunned by the blessing and anxious for the exact integrity of my words. As I replaced the phone receiver, my first act was to pick up my stack of photos and count them. The number was exactly fifty and some of them got wet as I was sobbing.

Maranatha

"Maranatha" is a word that I personally like very much. *O Lord, come!* It means hope and joy and fulfillment of the longing to be with the Savior we love and serve. When it was time to choose a name for the very first children's home that we started ourselves, that was the word that immediately came to my mind.

I was in Chitwan, doing the administrative work for our sponsorship program. I was snapping new photos of the children, filling in update forms and processing information on some new children. One of the pastors shared a problem with me. Schools in the villages offered classes only through the fifth grade. Students who wished to continue their education must come into the city to enroll in grades six and higher. Only those students with a place to live, such as a relative's home, are able to continue education beyond the fifth grade. This was a sad situation in itself, but considering the whole picture and our desire for evangelism in this unreached area, I started to ponder it. What if we provided a way for some of these children from believer families to complete their education and receive solid discipleship at the same time? If we chose children who were excellent students with a strong desire to continue studying, could we reap a crop of leaders who already spoke the tribal language and had important ties to the area? The hope would be that some graduates would continue on to a Bible college and become pastors and evangelists. Strong Christ followers in any kind of work would be valuable in planting churches. Consider the influence of producing Christian teachers and medical workers, businessmen and mothers for this place. It was exciting to think about, but I did not even know how to start such a project. It would take a lot of money and I had no idea how to get it. I smiled at the pastor and promised to pray about it. According to my custom when I promise prayer to anyone, I make a point to mention the issue to the Lord that very night. I kept my word to pray and planned to continue if the Lord brought it to my thoughts. This time, however, I checked it off my mental list, and then I gave my attention to ways of finding sponsors for the new children.

Back in the states, we went out to dinner with a couple who had been friends and fellow church members for years. We discussed the ministry work, but also several other topics. It was a social occasion, not a "business" dinner, or so I thought. At the end of the evening, they handed us a check for an amount that left me stunned. We should apply it to an area of special need, they said, whatever we saw as the priority.

Maranatha dinged in my mind. Maranatha was not tangible. It did not exist. There were plenty of needs that *did* exist, for example, we could have covered the new sponsorships for quite a while. We had need of some office equipment. The money would make a nice "emergency fund" which is something every ministry needs. It could also provide the startup for the children's home in Chitwan—the one we would call, Maranatha. Once it was launched, we would need on-going sponsorship support. I did not know where that cash flow would come from, but we decided to trust God for one step at a time.

The Nepal Country Director

Anand was just another member of the partner group we worked with at first, but our relationship with him began to change and develop into something deeper. He was an evangelist who kept a home base in Kathmandu and traveled to various areas around the country to do outreach and to plant churches. His personality is quiet and gracious, never claiming credit to himself for anything. Today, we consider him the most effective evangelist/church planter we had ever known. Our work blended well with his until today they are one and the same. He gradually began helping us in all kinds of ways, with logistics, translation, and cultural counsel. We funded outreach projects for him and began the process of finding support for the village pastors under his leadership. He arranged to take us to his own ministry areas, but also took us to the other places we needed to go. Anand is much more than a driver and translator. He advises us, especially on cultural and political issues. He sets up conferences where we would teach. He began planning a schedule for us before we arrived in country and then made it happen. He stored donated supplies such as clothing and vitamins, in his home. We stayed in a guest room in his home when we were in Kathmandu and came to feel that his family was like our own. We talked for hours about strategy and plans for the future. Many of the new directions Allow The Children took were by Anand's suggestion. Anand was the one who urged us to register with the government as an NGO (Non-Government Organization). He was the one who labored for months to fulfill all of the requirements and bring us to the point of legal recognition and authorization to bring funds into the country. Anand is our friend and co-worker. He has cared for our personal needs and has made our ministry work possible in a multitude of ways.

Anand appreciates the child sponsorship ministry, but his special calling is to provide holistic training, pastor training, and Bible training of all kinds. He worked in villages as a community health evangelist, providing physical and spiritual training according to the specific needs of the village. Building relationships by giving help with health issues, Anand develops a core group who will hear the gospel and through repeated visits and discipleship, eventually form a little church. When one man shows a special interest in the Lord, Anand tries to get some Bible training for him, but the programs are a significant distance away. The money needed for tuition and travel is not readily available and there are other issues. The men cannot leave their crops for long periods. They need training where they live and in harmony with the agricultural seasons.

Anand's long time desire was to have a training center, a building where the village pastors and church leaders could gather regularly for Bible training. The same could be used for women's training and children's conferences, medical clinics; it would have many possible uses. None of the little churches were large enough to hold such a meeting. They needed a place to sleep and prepare food together for a number of days of training. To have a training center meant buying land, raising a building, and hiring someone to live in or near it to "guard" the property. We talked about Anand's vision, but it just seemed too far out of reach.

When the special gift came in, I contacted Anand to discuss starting the children's home. The money was not enough to buy land, but it would have made a nice start on a fund for that purpose. However, it was enough to start the children's home. We could rent a house, buy what was needed and support the children for a few months. The success of the project depended on finding enough sponsors for an operational budget. After several discussions, we sent the money to Nepal and trusted the project into Anand's hands. Our part was the smallest of many who worked together to make Maranatha possible. The couple who gave the original donation was an important piece. The Nepali leaders in Chitwan were an important piece. Anand, with the role of making the arrangements, was an important piece. Our part was to receive, receipt, and deposit the check. The next step was to wire the donation to Nepal, nothing too difficult or time consuming, especially considering that the Lord was the One who had raised the fund.

Anand carried the main responsibility for the project. He had to find a house to rent, collect the needed furniture and supplies, and communicate the plans to the leaders in Chitwan. The most difficult part was to choose which children, among many who longed to continue school, to come and have a completely different life than what they had thought possible. It was decided that we would bring ten boys from the villages, all sons of church or cell group leaders, all of whom had completed the fifth grade level with good class standing.

The Strike in Chitwan

My next visit was during a time of political turmoil for Nepal. Small, poor countries like Nepal, fighting within themselves, do not get a lot of news coverage in the United States, but a true civil war among political factions raged for several years. It was a very difficult period. Many people died, many children were orphaned, and the whole country was constantly disrupted. To say that Nepal was dangerous was unfortunately true, but our partners knew where the fighting was and it was easy to avoid dangerous areas.

I needed to go to Chitwan to meet with the committee about plans for Maranatha. Chitwan district was closed. *Closed or strike* meant that a political group has some grievance or desire for change and until they are satisfied they simply announce a closing within a certain area which might be a district or even the whole country. Only the largest, strongest groups could close the whole country. There had to be enough men on the ground to enforce such an action.

Any school or business which dared to open might be targeted for vandalism or could even be burned down. Schools always closed in compliance. No one wanted to risk the safety of their children. This was a huge disadvantage to the children because school sessions and exams are scheduled country wide. Exam day comes whether or not the students have had the instruction. Government offices, including banks, usually closed. Most businesses closed, but the *back door* might be open, especially for regular customers. The owner did not want those involved in the strike to know he was conducting business, but those he knew and trusted might get in. Foreigners might be able to get in. The main inconvenience for me or any foreigner was transportation. Walking and bicycling were allowed, but no motor vehicles moved. If someone decided to drive, there was risk that rocks would be thrown. Another possibility was that a group might capture the vehicle, remove and beat the driver and then set it ablaze. Army trucks carrying armed soldiers generally drove freely and, if hindered, gunfire might erupt. A foreigner could ask the driver of an army truck for help to get to a hospital or to the airport and he might help, or he might not. Ambulances were usually allowed to move, but they could be stopped and checked to see if the patient was genuine. If the hospitals had difficulty getting their employees in, ambulances might be sent out to provide transportation. One person would need to lie down in the back and prepare to feign illness if stopped.

The visit to Chitwan was not the only item on my agenda. I completed the tasks in Kathmandu and other parts of Nepal first because of the strike in Chitwan. Closings or strikes usually lasted only one or two days, but Chitwan was a hotbed for one of the strongest, most militant groups. The strike was moving into its third week. An ambulance had been burned, reportedly for being caught without an injured or sick person. Strikers were cutting off the hands of drivers who dared to defy them. Yes, they took an ax and amputated the hand. This was effective in preventing that specific man from driving in the future and also discouraged others from doing so. We continued to wait, hoping for the strike to end, until time was running out and we were forced to make a decision about whether or not to go under the less than desirable conditions. The meeting was important—so important that we might not be able to move forward with the project if I did not get there, but it was not important enough for someone to lose a hand. We could take a domestic flight to an airport within about forty minutes of our destination. Airports remained open during strikes because of the heavy army guard. Anand booked a hotel within walking distance of the airport. The only remaining piece was how to get from the airport to the church. There was a very good chance that we would not find any way to travel and there was no way to plan for it in advance. We would need to go and see what could be done after we arrived.

We landed in Chitwan with no luggage. We were staying one night, but it was important to be able to move quickly and easily. I added a toothbrush to my shoulder bag and that was it. We walked the short way to the street and the situation was obvious. The road which passed by the airport was busy with walkers and bicycles, ox carts and army vehicles. No busses or taxis, no motor bikes, no private vehicles at all. A young man on a bicycle hurried to meet us. Anand knew him. He had pedaled the whole distance to meet us and to help. We needed him to show us the way to the church where the others were waiting.

Suddenly, a small jeep twisted around the corner and hurried its passenger to the airport entrance. The jeep sported a big sign in front and back with the word, "TOURIST" in English and Nepali. The sign was no guarantee of safety, but it helped. The country depended heavily on tourism and none of the political groups wanted to be singled out as opposing or damaging it, and individuals within these groups did not want to become involved with an injury to a tourist. So although there was certainly risk in what we were trying to do, there was also a reasonable chance of success.

Anand waved the jeep down and stepped to the window to attempt to hire him. He glanced back at me for my agreement with the amount he wanted to charge. It was the equivalent of twenty dollars. For that amount, he would take us to the church, about forty-five minutes away, wait while we had our meeting, and return us to the nearby hotel. I was delighted and quite willing to pay it. The two men lifted the bike into the open back of the jeep and I tried to climb in there as well. It was important that any bad guys along the way could clearly see the tourist. The men in the back would be clear and easy targets for anyone shooting from the jungle, but they would not want to shoot a tourist. Anand insisted that I ride in the cab, which was more comfortable and a little safer. I usually followed his suggestions immediately, but I argued this issue with him a bit. It seemed safer for everyone if I was clearly visible. He would not agree and I settled into the cab. We traveled along briskly and without incident. There were very few other vehicles of any kind. I carefully watched the tree line, especially on the isolated stretches, which were many, but no sign of men or guns. I glanced at the young man who was driving at risk of his hands to get me to the place I needed to go. (Actually, he was doing it for twenty dollars.)

Army checkpoints were very common during the war years. They checked for weapons, bombs, suspicious individuals or anything unusual. With the strike, their vehicle inspection work was presumably slow in recent days. The soldiers on this duty were usually expressionless, stoic and bored. Until now, I had never seen one with his lower jaw dropped. But this guard's jaw was positioned thus and remained so as he was questioning Anand. I did not understand the Nepali conversation, but he must have been saying, "WHAT ARE YOU DOING?? DON'T YOU KNOW WE ARE IN THE MIDDLE OF A DANGEROUS

STRIKE??" or something similar. Eventually, he let us go.

We arrived at the small village church, finding it nearly full of pastors waiting for us. They had gathered on foot and by bicycle. Well aware of the danger, they had been constantly in prayer for us during the last few hours. We made some important decisions during the meeting, lined up our various expectations and set some guidelines for the ministry. As I look back on it now, I feel certain that the Maranatha project would have failed if not for that meeting. I needed to be there and the Lord moved to let it happen. What if I had stayed back in Kathmandu and worried about the danger?

In the capital city of Nepal, one might be able to find an empty flat available to rent. Outside of the capital, it is a rare thing to find an unoccupied space. The goal was to find a house that the owners were willing to move from in return for the rent money. Maranatha began in such a home. It was a big house and the family was willing to give us three rooms in the front. Each of our rooms opened to the outside and could be individually locked. The family still lived in the house, on just the other side of the walls, but there was a sense of separateness as if renting an apartment within a house rather than living in the house "with" them. The outdoor facilities were all shared, which included the toilet and the water pump. We bought five bunk sets for one room because the plan was to receive ten boys. Another room was the "gathering" room and storage. The third room was the kitchen and the sleeping space for the house parents. As it turned out, the house parents who were chosen had a small daughter. The budget was for ten children, so they brought nine boys and included the little girl in the total count. She slept in the room with her parents. That left one bunk open and Anand was pleased to have it to sleep on when he visited.

The situation was not ideal. The landlord family was Hindu. They were not pleased to hear the praise and worship from our rooms every single night. They did not forbid it, perhaps for fear of losing their rent money, but it made for a strained relationship.

After two years, we moved Maranatha to a larger house, this time, renting the whole building and increasing the children to twenty—ten boys and ten girls. We had indoor running water, two floors, a big gathering room, a nice porch, a well-equipped kitchen, and a guest room that I enjoyed. It was wonderful to have the time with the children and having the guest room helped with expenses when we visited the children's home. Living with twenty teens might seem like a nightmare, but these were incredibly well-behaved young people from the villages. They all helped with the work of the home. Each one was grateful for regular food and the chance to study. They did not take those blessings lightly and they certainly did not want to risk losing their place in the home. The operational support had risen steadily and we were well able to manage the increase in the number of children. The house parents were doing a good job in their care and training. The children's home "plant" was successful.

We kept talking about land and constructing our own buildings—a permanent children's home and another building which would be used as both a church and a pastor training center. Anand's dream was to have a piece of land that was big enough to plant crops and raise some animals. This was important to give Marantha some self-support and also to enable us to train the children in life skills they would need when they returned to their villages. It was just a dream. There was no visible way to make it happen. Funds were coming into Allow The Children, but almost all of it went right out again for sponsorship support, various small projects, and occasional urgent needs. We were not accumulating funds and even if we did, it seemed that it would take a lifetime before we would have enough even to start such a plan. However, every project, large or small, begins with the first step. I could start presenting Maranatha and see what the Lord would do with it.

The Maranatha project went into newsletters, website, church presentations and it even had a flyer of its own. We began receiving small gifts for it and we were thankful for each one. The Maranatha Building Fund slowly grew from ten to one hundred dollars and then another month would go by and maybe another twenty would be added to it. I think we (Michael and I) put a few hundred in personally, just so it would not look so pitiful. I held the flyer and prayed over it. I talked to a few potential donors, and as I recall they smiled and nodded. We needed thousands of dollars to buy even a small piece of land and Anand wanted *a big piece*. There would be bank fees and lawyer fees, "closing costs" just as we have in the United States. The project was too big for our little ministry, but we continued to promote it and the building fund slowly grew.

Five Village Churches

Anand took me to Butwal to meet the children and the program leaders there. We processed a few new children. This program included children from the mother church, daughter churches and a leprosy camp. When the tasks were complete, the pastors wanted to take me out to see some daughter churches. I quickly learned that we were going to see the rented meeting places for five little daughter churches in five different places and that each needed a building. Each church needed three thousand dollars to build a small one room structure of brick covered with plaster. The money would be spent only for materials. The men in each congregation would raise their building. Four of the churches had purchased or donated land for the project. One church had identified some land for sale, but needed help to buy it. Each church had between twenty-five and seventy-five adult baptized believers. All were very poor and many were women who had no control over the giving in the family. I could easily see that there was no human hope that any of the little churches could raise three thousand dollars among its people. If every member brought everything that s/he had and sold every belonging, they would not have three thousand dollars. I could understand the importance of a church building in these cultures. Two churches were in Hindu communities. One was in a predominately Muslim village. Two were working among *an unreached tribal group* and those called out for His Name were growing.

The first church we visited met in a tiny rented room, perhaps eight by eight. If all of the people came at one time, they would not even be able to stand together in the room. They were already taking the children out to meet together under a tree. As more people came to the Lord, how could they manage? The next church was meeting in the pastor's home, in his sitting room. And so the circumstances went, similar situations for them all.

I wanted so much for them to have the church buildings. I really ached to see the testimony of five little village churches standing in communities that had very little light. I wanted the people to have the blessing and the encouragement of a building dedicated to the worship of our God and the teaching of His Word. The desire to help with this project was overwhelming, but I simply could not. I was not a building fund raiser. If there was any question about that, I could remember the Maranatha project which had taken absorbing prayer and frustration as I helplessly wondered how to raise so much money. I was in Nepal to administrate a child sponsorship program, to teach God's Word when I had that opportunity and occasionally to do a little medical work. These were things I was prepared to do. We all need to do our part in the Kingdom and do it well. Building projects needed to go to someone else. An important issue was that I could not choose only one or two of the churches; all five had the same need. It was impossible for the Nepali leaders to choose among them and I certainly could not. If we started with one, we needed to commit to completing all five churches. Three thousand dollars times five churches is fifteen thousand dollars. One church needed another three thousand to buy their land, so the total was eighteen thousand! If we had eighteen thousand dollars or somehow it came into our hands, I would need to put it towards our Maranatha project. A good administrator has to choose projects wisely. We should not take a new project while Maranatha was waiting and growing so slowly. Nobody can do everything. We *could not* fund the building of five churches, no matter how much I wanted to do it. I must not lead the men to hope that we would.

I told the pastors that the project was just too big for Allow. I would search for monthly sponsors for the new children they had brought, but I just could not accept such a huge building project. I would happily consider myself successful if I was able to find enough sponsors to get all of the children assigned. They were disappointed. They asked me to pray with them for it and I assured them that I would. They asked me to "make one try" for the money. I answered that I would put it into a newsletter and we would "see what God would do with it," but I needed to give my time to finding sponsors for the children.

When I returned to the United States, I did pray regularly for a period of time about the project. I truly wanted to build the churches. I just did not think it was our assignment. I prayed that the Lord would send someone to take that project. I promised to put it in a newsletter, so I did that. It was only one or two lines. *Five village churches in Nepal need three thousand dollars each for a permanent church building.* It was not the title of the newsletter or the main focus of it. It was only a line under "prayer requests" or maybe it was "current needs."

Before the newsletter ever went out, we received a gift of three thousand dollars from one of my relatives, to be used "wherever we need it." The giver was not wealthy and not given to large gifts. Nothing similar had happened before or since. But it was three thousand dollars, the exact amount needed and no other urgent projects were waiting. We would not send it unless we somehow got four more churches funded and I still did not expect that to happen. If not, we could use this gift for something else, but for now, it was set aside for one little village church. *The first church was funded.*

A few days after the newsletter went out, we received another check for three thousand dollars, designated for "village church building in Nepal." This was from a faithful donor who occasionally went into four digits, so it was not a huge surprise. *The second church was funded.*

Within another few days, I received a call from the pastor of one of our partner churches. His church was taking the project of raising three thousand dollars for one village church. This was a pledge, not funds in hand, but it was a strong church and I knew the money would come. *The third church was funded.*

We regularly receive gifts from dear people who do not designate them. These gifts can be used for whatever we need at the time. We often use them to make up a children's home budget or a medical need. Gratefully, there were no other pressing needs for a few months. Someone gave one thousand dollars for a village church and a number of smaller checks were received. We grouped these together with some undesignated gifts to make another three thousand. *The fourth church was funded.*

I prayed and waited for a phone call. Yes, our angel donor called and would give enough for the last church, the one that needed double the amount in order to purchase land. *The fifth church was funded.* The Lord was teaching me how to walk by faith. I was as surprised as everyone else when I sent the email to Nepal saying that we would fund all five of the churches.

Construction was well underway when I made my next trip to Nepal. I have rarely felt so great a sense of satisfaction, especially to know the wonderful investment a church building is for the Lord's kingdom. Once again, our role was the smallest one. Other people had given the money that we received, receipted and wired for this purpose. The Nepali pastors and evangelists had done the soul winning and nurturing that resulted in the people who would worship and serve in these churches. The men of the churches were out in the blazing heat doing some of the hardest work that there is—digging and laying concrete blocks, mixing cement by hand, breaking rocks for "fill." I snapped some photos and went on my way.

On that visit, I learned that three thousand would indeed build the church as I had been told, but if they had five thousand each, they could have a metal roof, instead of thatch, and add a toilet. Both of these additions seemed necessary and wise to include. This time, I did not hesitate. I knew that the Lord was drawing the funds for these churches. I immediately committed to the pastors that we would raise that money. Another ten thousand was needed. I knew it would come, and it did.

Land Purchase

Some farm land in Chitwan was for sale. It was big and flat and in the right area for the Maranatha project. It is difficult to compare it to acres. Nepal uses different units of measure. It was divided into Nepali units, marked by drainage ditches into rough squares. One could buy any number of squares. This was exciting. Perhaps it would be within our reach to buy enough "squares" for a house and then later on, after raising money, we could buy more, eventually getting to the amount of land we wanted. Of course, the more we bought together, the better the price. The cost would go up later, when the owner would know that we would pay more because we wanted more adjoining land. There was always the risk that someone else would come along to buy the land we wanted, but we could only buy what we could afford. A bank loan in Nepal is possible, but we did not want to put the ministry into debt. We drove out to see the land, walk it, and pray over it. *What was the Lord's desire for us?*

I was leading a group of Americans and we planned a time to take them out to the land. It was not primarily a presentation to them and it was not new information to them either. Anyone who was on our mailing list knew that we were praying for land to build a permanent home for the Maranatha children and we also wanted a training center for pastors. We were going because it was on my list to go. I wanted to see it again, to talk about how many squares we would try to buy and to agree with Anand and the other leaders that this is what we wanted to do.

Our land was a rice field recently harvested. It was easy to see the drainage ditch dividers. How many squares of land would we need as a minimum for the children's home and how many could we afford to buy? Those two numbers did not match, did not even come close, but maybe someday. I intended to snap some photos of the land (which looked like rice fields anywhere) and create a newsletter for the project when I returned to the United States. We looked, we walked, and we prayed. The next stop on our agenda was a restaurant for dinner. As we waited for our meal to be served, a member of the group took me aside privately. With steady eye contact and a completely casual expression, he told me that he was going to fund the land for Maranatha. He had prayed about it and was joyfully settled that he wanted to do it. He was going to give forty thousand dollars. The check would come as soon as he returned to the United States. We should proceed to negotiate as much land as we could get for that amount.

"Is that enough?" he asked. *Enough?* We had never decided on a "dream" number of squares or a target amount for the land purchase. It seemed so theoretical, still so far away that there was little point. But I do not think we would ever have imagined as much as forty thousand dollars. If we had raised the land money bit by bit, we would probably have happily settled for half that amount of land. I felt too stunned even to thank the man. I do not remember whether I said anything at all. He smiled and returned to the table.

Land purchases in Nepal are complicated and time-consuming. Our men wanted to give careful stewardship to the task. Some squares of land were a little larger than others and some were positioned in a more desirable place. Of course, we wanted all of our squares to adjoin one another. We needed proof that the seller truly owned the property. Both parties wanted a careful survey of the land that was to change hands. We wanted to buy as much land as we could, as the donor wished, but some of the money needed to be used for the fees involved.

The day that I knew the land was ours was almost as amazing as the day I learned of the gift that made it possible. While we waited for the processing of the purchase, several more generous gifts came for the project, and we still had the money we had been accumulating for land. A contractor was hired, and the building plan was in place by the time of the closing. We broke ground as soon as we could for the children's home. We did not have enough money to complete the construction, but we planned to do it the Nepali way—just build until the money runs out, then stop until more money is available. We never stopped. As expenses came, so came the resources. The construction was slow and tedious as it always is in Nepal, but it continued steadily along and was fully paid for when it was finally finished.

Overwhelming Ministry Demands

Allow The Children grew a little more every time I made a trip to Nepal. There was no shortage of children in need or projects to be done. Gratefully, new donors and churches seemed to grow along with us. More children and more sponsors meant more receipting, more photos to print, more email to answer, more thank you notes to write, more envelopes to stuff, more errands to run, more meetings to attend, more computer skills to learn, more paper to buy. The monthly newsletter needed to be created and packaged and mailed out every month. I was investing huge amounts of time in learning computer moves that are second nature now. I was getting overwhelmed. I remember thinking that if it were not for the international travel, I could keep up with the office work. If I was leaving for three weeks, I needed to have the newsletter ready and a list of other tasks covered for the time away. When I returned, I brought more tasks, plus what was accumulated and waiting.

My life was swallowed up by the demands of the ministry. I loved it. Even when I was attached to my office chair for hours on end, I loved it. My time for anything else was slowly (or sometimes quickly) melting away. It was not unlike the startup of a small business. Actually, it *was* the startup of a new business, a non-profit business.

Allow The Children had been born and was now in its very dependent infancy. It was not one baby, but a multiple birth, and I was trying to take care of most of it alone. Just like the birth of a baby (or twins or triplets!) my life had changed completely and I was becoming exhausted trying to meet the demands. Allow needed to be fed and protected and kept clean. It could not be left alone for long. I needed to learn a variety of parenting skills and the very life of the baby depended on how well I practiced them. There was some sick time and some diaper changing to be done—yes, some messes that had to be cleaned up. At the same time, I loved and embraced my new identity. It was incredibly satisfying to see the ministry healthy and growing and making a real difference.

Michael was working on Allow issues as well, but doing things that I could not do, such as accounting and government compliance. The things that were keeping me so busy were things that he could not do because much of the data that I was trying to enter existed in my head and nowhere else, and because I was doing the planning and organizing of the ministry programs and tasks as I went along. It was difficult to explain to someone else, and by the time I came to the point where he *could* have helped, we had already formed our separate roles. Some of the tasks were too simple and clerical for him such as stuffing the envelopes, and to be fully transparent about it, Michael and I are just not compatible when working on the same task. We learned that during our years of apartment management and it is still true today. Oh yes, it is still true.

I stopped cooking dinner and doing the laundry regularly during that time. Michael picked up some of these tasks, but we moved into a lifestyle of fast food or quick sandwiches for meals and minimum only care of the house. I worked at my desk until two am almost every night, sometimes because of time pressure, but other times simply from habit. The late night hours were the best for me, quiet and uninterrupted, although it meant dragging in the mornings. I did nothing at all for recreation. I even stopped attending church activities, other than the Sunday worship services. It was not a healthy situation for me or our family or our lives.

I was out of balance, stressed and exhausted, with the only relief being to get out of the country, so I came to long for that more and more. My life was completely different when I was out of the United States. I was not sitting at a desk all day long. I was walking a lot. Junk food was difficult to find in Nepal and my consumption of it plunged. With little to do in the late evenings, I went to sleep early and usually got more than eight hours of sleep. I felt wonderful, physically and emotionally, when I was out of the United States and it is not difficult to understand why. I dreaded the return flights, because of the physical drain of the travel, but also because my desk would be piled high and multiple demands would be slammed upon me as soon as I arrived. I also knew that the wonderful health that I enjoyed would soon be back to the achy, dragging "normal."

Staff Needed

It was very true that the young, growing ministry needed the travel and Allow might have sunk without it. It was also true that my mental and emotional health needed the travel and Allow might have sunk without it. It was also true that I needed some help with the office work and Allow might have sunk had the Lord not intervened and provided it.

The need for regular help in the office weighed on my mind and I could see no answer for it. One possible solution was to pay an employee from a percentage of our donations. Most non-profits do that. Michael and I did not need salary and we gave our time freely, but of course, not everyone could do the same. We wanted to send our donations to the field—as much of the funds as possible—100% to the field for as long as it was possible. We used our own funds for the necessary things such as paper, printing and postage, bank fees and website maintenance. We worked from our home, so we also provided office space, electricity and internet. We could not cover salaries in addition to everything else. Missionaries who came to work with us would need to raise their own support.

Another issue was succession. While Allow was an infant and young child, we would provide full support, but it would need to grow to the place where it could support itself and we needed to guide it towards that goal.

I often spoke of the need for help in our office. As a result, many kind volunteers came on a one-time basis or regularly on some loose schedule to keep the ministry moving. We had a volunteer group who came to stuff the envelopes for the monthly mailing. One lady came two days a week for months to help with the data entry, receipting and sponsor maintenance. It is no exaggeration to say that Allow would not have survived without these hands and hearts giving their time. I just do not know what we would have done, but of course, the Lord was watching and providing what we needed at the time we needed it. I was praying for someone to join us as a regular, committed part of the team, someone I could count on who would learn the work and take some of the regular load.

Govinda

Govinda Awale was one of our ministry partners in Nepal. He was the administrator of a large, active church and he managed our largest sponsorship program. When the children are in a home, there are not many problems managing our program. The children need to be gathered when I come into the country, but that is no issue, if they are all living in the same place. I expect our partners to confirm that each child is enrolled and progressing in school, attending church, receiving the money, and spending it properly. Again, this is not much of a problem for house parents who are with the children daily and handling the funds. But Govinda managed a church sponsorship program. The children lived with their families. Some of these families were pastors or evangelists who were in regular contact with the church, but many were children of widows or very poor families, which meant that contact was difficult. Some of them lived in Kathmandu and attended the mother church, but others were members of daughter churches all over Nepal. I am not sure I ever fully appreciated how much work was involved in handling the Allow program for so many children, spread across so large an area. Govinda did it with a calm grace and efficiency. I never had a question about the distribution of the support when he was in charge. When I was due to meet with a group of children, they were all there or he knew why not. When Allow was ready to take four more new children, he brought four children—not five—and they all met the criteria we had agreed on in advance. He was precise and reliable. I knew that he had many responsibilities at the church, but he was faithful with anything I ever needed him to do. He was just good, really good, as a ministry administrator. He honored the Lord with the quality of his work.

My need for office help was constantly on my mind. I talked about it in Nepal, just as I did in the United States. Govinda quietly mentioned that he would like to come to America and work in our office. It was an interesting thought, but not practical. Govinda had a wife and two children. It was a common thing for a Nepali man to go "abroad" for work and leave his family in Nepal. They did it for the good salary and to provide a better life for their loved ones. I explained to him that our ministry does not pay a salary. He would need to raise his support, which would be difficult since he would not know many people. Our ministry was not large enough to have a "list" of supporting churches that might help. I would not agree to take him without his family and we could not support them all. Govinda did have good office skills. He would be a blessing to us, yes, but I just could not see it working. Even if we decided to move forward with it, immigration was so complicated and expensive and I knew nothing about it. From that time on, Govinda would occasionally mention it again, and in answer, I would describe the salary problem again, or the medical insurance problem, or the immigration problem, or the family of four problem. He was always gracious, and if he was greatly disappointed, he did not express it. I actually started to ponder the idea of bringing a Nepali over to help in our office, but I was thinking of a single man, not one with a family. We could keep one person in our home, but a family of four would need their own place. We could not bring four and I would not bring him alone long-term.

Tamara

Tamara Mock was one of many volunteers who gave time to help me with the office work. Her parents were our good friends of many years. I often said that I knew Tamara since before she was born and it was true. I was the one who came to the Mock home in the early hours one morning to stay with the older children while Tamara was being born. When they brought her home, I sat holding the newborn girl whose life would be such an important part of our work, a ministry I could never have imagined at the time.

Tamara came regularly for years, sometimes both the morning and evening on the same day, with her paying job in between. I could see the heart in her work and that she was motivated by love for the Lord and for missions. I knew that she would jump at the chance to travel and there was no question that she would be a valuable team member. But Tamara had a few problems. One problem was financial. She did not have any visible way to pay or to raise the needed amount for the trip costs. Her job was not enough and she was fully volunteer with us. She attended a good mission-minded church and they were likely to help, but not likely to provide the full amount. I watched her day-by-day as she lovingly handled the children's photos and all kinds of other tasks so faithfully. I longed to show her our ministry field, though it did not seem possible.

A second problem was Tamara's father. Tim Mock was a gigantic, strong man with a booming voice. He loved his daughter fiercely and I think it is fair to say that he was beyond the ordinary in protectiveness. He fully approved of Tamara volunteering in our office, but I had heard him declare many times at top volume, that his daughter would *never* travel to Nepal. Nepal was dangerous and she was his little girl and NO, not Nepal for her, and I think that at the times he said it, he was quite serious, not in jest.

We were preparing for a women's trip to Nepal. The plan was to visit the different children's homes and other ministry programs to teach Bible, to take new photos of the children and update the information about them. Just as the time came to buy the air tickets, one woman had to drop out because of a health issue. She felt that she had committed to the team and was letting me down. Though I tried to reassure her otherwise, she insisted on paying the full amount for the trip and she wanted me to find someone to "take her place." So financially, Tamara had a chance to go, but I struggled with the issue of her father. If she knew of this blessing and that she was my choice to go, but he said no, well, I just did not want her to be in that situation. I called Teresa, Tamara's mother and my good friend, and asked for her husband's cell phone number. I did not tell her why and she did not ask. I shared the information with her father that someone was donating money designated for someone to go on this specific trip to a participant of my choice. I wanted to take Tamara on our trip to Nepal, but if he was not comfortable about it, she would never know of the opportunity. I expected that he would want to think and pray about it, but his answer came immediately. The strong voice was very gentle and firm this time and I remember the words of faith, *"If the Lord has provided this for her, I do not want to stand in her way."* It was a pivotal moment, both in Tamara's life and our ministry.

Tamara went with us on that team and survived. She snapped photos and hugged little ones and did some teaching. Before the trip was over, she told me that she wanted to be a missionary with Allow The Children. Joining our ministry full time meant that she could raise some monthly support and travel funds, but she knew she was coming with no immediate salary at all—only faith that the Lord was directing.

Tamara went through all of the steps to join our ministry without the slightest pause. Our board approved her enthusiastically. She had committed the summer to her present employer and wanted to keep her word. She was giving up a paying job, not knowing how much or even if she would have any support through us. She was still living at home with her parents, but she had a car and personal bills to pay like all of the rest of us. It was a beautiful step of faith that she was willing to make. We knew that Tamara was coming for a few months before it could actually happen. It was a difficult wait. We needed her, almost desperately so, but the delay gave some time to work on her support.

Tamara could not be called a strong fund raiser, but she had a God who intervened. Her church voted and set up some support for her. Some individuals in her church and a few others, pledged some monthly support. Two of our board members started giving for her monthly.

Tamara went with us to a church as we were giving a ministry presentation. She did not say a word. I do not remember whether we even introduced her. She quietly busied herself setting up a table with our pictures and ministry literature.

"Is that girl with you raising support?" the pastor asked and we answered that she was. "Well, we will take her on," he said. "Our church has the budget for another missionary." And so, without knowing her name or anything about her other than that she worked with us, Tamara had another church donor.

Finally, our angel donor made one of his well-timed calls. "Sue, what do you need?" I do not think I was able to talk about anything other than our office help need. It weighed so heavy on my mind, not just because of all the hours I worked, but because I knew that I could not keep it up much longer and the ministry would suffer for it.

"Sue, you are going to have to have some help," this businessman said. I told him about Tamara, that she was coming in another month or so, but we needed to raise missionary support for her. The board had set a target amount of support and our friend asked how much it was. *He pledged to send half of Tamara's budgeted salary for a year.* He had never met Tamara, never even talked to her. He was doing it for me and for the ministry. This was only one more of many times that this man stepped in and "rescued" us—*that the Lord rescued us*—and confirmed once again that He knows and can meet our needs. He was drawing Tamara for us and He would meet her needs too.

Right about the time that Tamara started with us full time, we were able to arrange taking our monthly mailing to a nearby company that would fold our newsletter and insert our envelopes. This blessing alone reclaimed perhaps as much as thirty hours a month for me, even considering the contributions of the volunteers. With this task lifted and Tamara working at her desk, I could finally relax and start to see some normalcy in my life once again. I took a day off occasionally. I tried to stop staying up so late at night, but that habit was difficult to break. Tamara learned quickly. Before very long, she could do almost anything I could do once the directional decisions had been made. The difference for my life was incredible and the ministry was safe.

Immigration

With Tamara full time, it seemed to end the thought of bringing Govinda to the United States. When I told him, he nodded and seemed genuinely glad that the ministry had Tamara, but gave no sense at all that she had taken the position he wanted. He somehow seemed to know that his unique place was still there. He was fully committed that Allow The Children was God's direction for him and he was willing to wait for the Lord's timing for it to come. I had to admire his faith and the beautiful combination he was of strong leadership and submissive spirit.

Govinda was valuable in the position he held and would be so for any ministry. He had traveled internationally several times, therefore he was familiar with functioning in another culture and dealing with air travel. He had years of experience in leading groups of foreigners from a variety of countries when they came to Nepal. He made ministry and logistical arrangements for them and dealt with the emergency changes necessary when something like a strike or gunfire in the place they planned to go interfered with the plans. His church was mother to over forty daughter churches and cell fellowships probably doubled that number. Govinda had contacts all over the country. He had proven skills in dealing with people, both Nepali and foreigners, and he could speak Nepali well, which none of the rest of us could do. There were many times when we needed a Nepali document translated or clarification with a Nepali speaker on a phone call. The question was not whether we needed more office help, but whether the Lord would give us another valuable missionary staff member. My attitude towards bringing Govinda to the United States began to change from casual thought to serious consideration; from too complicated to think about to what exactly do we need to do?

I thought the first step would be to bring him for a short time on a tourist visa. I was in Nepal in May and invited him to return to the United States with me for two or three months. For that to happen, he would need to apply and be approved for a tourist visa, which is known to be a difficult task for a Nepali and the pastor and church committee would have to agree to the leave time for him from his job in Nepal. He would also have to resolve his personal commitments for the time away. The time was short, but all of the pieces came together. By the time I was ready to leave, Govinda had accomplished all of these issues and we had a plane ticket for him.

Govinda spent about three months with us. He saw what life in America was like and what life in our ministry would be. There were so many aspects to show him—food, transportation, housing, medical care, children's education. He never wavered in his resolve to come. The list of problems was still there—support, immigration, family of four—but as we stepped forward, the Lord answered every one.

I may never have begun the immigration procedure had it not been for our home church. Our pastor's encouragement and offer to help was a huge part of the plan. There were several significant areas of help from the church, but one big one was the mission house. Govinda could live with his family in the mission house on our church property for some unspecified period of time. This meant that maybe as much as a quarter of his support need was already covered and it helped me to be willing to trust the Lord for the rest.

The immigration procedure began with a long detailed application form to be filled in by the hosting or requesting organization, which was Allow The Children. My experience with immigration issues was zero. I knew as soon as we began the process that if it worked, it would be our next miracle. I read the website instructions. If any mistake was made, any whatsoever, the whole thing would be thrown out and we would need to start again. I fully expected to get bogged down at some point, but I told Govinda we would try. If we were successful, we intended to bring him with his family. A tourist visa would not allow him to work legally. A work visa had too many requirements and was expensive beyond what we could hope to cover. We were applying for a religious worker visa, which we might qualify for as a 501c3 non-profit. Each step of the process was complicated and intimidating. On two occasions, I needed to call the government immigration office for clarification of some issue. I had a case number that identified me. On both telephone calls, someone said, "Oh, *you* are the one who is not represented (by a lawyer)." Evidently, that was an unusual circumstance.

At one point, the next step was for an immigration agent to visit and investigate the agency. We were not allowed to schedule it or make any request about the timing. The lady came to our door only a few days before I left on a mission trip. When we were in the office at the side of our house, we could not hear a knock or door bell at the front door, but I happened to be walking through at the time. Tamara was working that day, but she had left for lunch. Michael and I had frequent meetings and errands out, so no one home was a real possibility. I think the woman came from New Jersey. What would have happened, if she did not find us that day? She sat at my dining room table and asked every question that I had already submitted in writing. I knew the answers well, but Michael and Tamara had never even seen the forms. If they had answered differently, would that have disqualified us? Today we have our own office building, but on that day, I walked her through a bedroom, with the bed propped up on the wall and my desk in the back half of the room. Then I showed her our "main office" which had started life as a two car garage. How big does an organization need to be to qualify to bring in an immigrant worker? She seemed skeptical while looking at my bedroom office, but happier after she saw the garage office. She snapped photos and made notes, then went on her way. Shortly after, we were notified that our application was approved. Now it was up to Govinda. He had to submit a mountain of paperwork to the American Embassy in Nepal and pass the interview.

The day eventually came when Govinda, with his family, stepped through the doors at Washington Dulles airport. I thought their first hours in America would be a profound experience to share with them, but the two children were battling motion sickness and all four of them were exhausted. They spent the drive home asleep.

The entire family adjusted to America remarkably easily, as if they had always been here and this is where they belonged. Govinda took his place with Allow The Children and the office settled into an efficiency and harmony that I could not have imagined. There were still many tasks that only I could do, but all that could were delegated among the two staff members and the volunteers who still faithfully came to help. I was still busy, but it was very manageable. I was able to schedule meetings with donors or potential donors, write letters and make other contacts that began to pay returns.

When we first started sponsorship, we sent the support to Nepal only after we assigned the sponsor and the gifts began coming. This was painful sometimes when I knew that children were in urgent need. Sometimes a new school year was about to start and pastors in our church sponsorship programs were waiting for my list of children with sponsors. Those children who did have a sponsor would be enrolled in school and those still unassigned would need to wait until next year unless the parents could somehow find the money in another way.

For the church programs, where children were in families, one sponsor provided the help that one child received. One sponsor choosing the child would get that child's name on the list and our commitment to send the help. Sometimes sponsors sent the donation for one month (or two or three) and then stopped. The Nepali family was depending on the support and we needed to keep it coming. When this happens, Allow keeps sending the support from our general gifts until another sponsor is assigned, and finding another sponsor becomes a top priority. Our children's homes had set budgets, a minimal level that we must provide, a comfortable level that we hoped to attain and a "wow" level that we did not reach very often. The collective group of sponsors for children in that home made up the budget. Some sponsors (bless them) gave well above the amount we asked and some might drop or miss a month. Whatever came in for that children's home was used to meet their budget and then we added from the general gifts to send at least the minimal level for them.

Blessing for Sponsorship

The Lord sent another angel donor. He was a businessman with a heart for sponsoring children. When he first joined us, he took a large group of children and later on another group and still another. He was happy to help any child. I could assign him to the older ones that no one else chose, or the new ones who had just been added. His support filled in the budgets for our children's homes and rescued situations when an original sponsor had dropped. He made it possible for me to fund new programs and branch into new areas, even new countries. This man was not interested in projects, just sponsorship, and he made himself a blessing for us there. We appreciate every one of our sponsors and we know that many of them sacrifice to be able to help—but when I think of this man and the lives he has touched, the difference that he has made in young lives and continues to make—Wow! is the only word I can write about it.

Church Planting

Church planting has become an emotional term for me. I love it and we do it, but I often find that I need to defend the role we play. When I contact a new pastor or church for Allow The Children, I often hear a speech about church planting which ends with the declaration that "We *only* support church planters!" They generally mean an American man, graduated from one of the Bible colleges that is on that church's "list," who has studied the language and culture and goes to the target people to plant a church. If a woman is involved, she is the wife of the church planter. She supports the effort with hospitality, music, teaching children, *but she does not approach American pastors as I am doing.* After an investment of years, they hope to gather enough people who are or have become believers, to worship and serve together and give enough money to cover the expenses of the church, including a salary for a national pastor. At that point, the missionary attempts to launch the church to continue on without him. If enough of them stay together, accept the new pastor, and money is coming in to pay the bills, the church is considered "planted."

From the beginning, it was a challenge to present our ministry to potential donors. A church that does not know us might assume we are "just a children's ministry" and of course, the name we chose supports the perception. When contacted by a woman, it boosts that view even more. They picture coloring books and such or they look upon the support we raise for children's homes or our medical clinics as a "social ministry," not on the same level as the church planting elite. I usually do not try to convince them otherwise. I just smile and nod because if the Lord is not drawing them towards this ministry, it is not my job to persuade them.

We plant with a different model than this traditional one. I do not see our work as "social," but if it is, our Lord had a thriving social ministry. He cared for the poor and commanded us to do likewise. He held medical clinics along with His teaching/preaching ministry and He made it clear that children were important. We are following His example.

Many of the Maranatha children come from an unreached tribal group. "Unreached" does not mean that there are absolutely no believers. Rather it means that mature, reproducing churches among the people group are few or none, and leadership is not strong enough to meet the task alone. So how could we go about bringing the gospel to this unreached group? The group is located within Nepal and includes true Nepali citizens. The Nepali church is strong, though Christians are a small minority in the Hindu nation. So why not send the Nepali men to evangelize among them? Of course, we do that. Anand was planning and leading teams for village outreach before he ever started working with us. This was one of the areas where our ministries merged. Allow The Children is funding Nepali evangelists who go into the mountains to villages where the people might never have heard the name of Jesus. It is amazing, but true that in our time there are still people who have never heard of the God who created them or the Savior who came to save them. More people who have never heard are born every day. If there is no Word or witness accessible to them, then they grow up without hearing. A new unreached people group might form, especially in isolated places that do not mix with the general population.

The evangelists travel on their own two feet to places where a vehicle or even a pack mule cannot go. They bring medical supplies and they help the sick. They teach on health and hygiene or literacy or agriculture, all topics of great interest to the village people. Then they preach the gospel and they set up the Jesus video, for which someone has carried on his back a generator and petrol. This is front line evangelism and Allow is part of it.

The new believers have come out of Hinduism or Buddhism with no Christian perspective or Bible background whatsoever. How long would it be before these new believers form into a mature church? The answer is—a lifetime. It takes years to disciple a new believer or lead a baby church to maturity. The unreached people group needs trained pastors and we are training them. They need Bibles and we are providing them. They need trained and discipled farmers and shepherds, laborers and mothers, and we are producing them.

A children's home ministry is more than rescuing orphaned and abandoned children. We are rearing children from unreached groups who will return as educated leaders, well-grounded in the Word. Each one of the older Maranatha children, girl or boy, rotates the responsibility of leading the worship in the home. This means that they stand before the group and lead the singing, prayer and reading the Word. They also rotate the musical instruments, learning to accompany worship with the keyboard, guitar and drums. They know the songs of the faith. They work with us when we hold our medical clinics—setting up and translating. They are learning God's Word, but also learning to worship and to serve.

Pastor Training

Church planting means a need for trained pastors. One idea is for Americans trained in the Word to try to gain all the things needed to function in another country such as learning the language and culture, getting a visa, immunizations, and adjusting to the food and climate. Only a rare American can live like the people do, therefore he would also need the funds to maintain his lifestyle, which would include food, housing, and medical care far above his people, and a private school for his children. If there is any political problem or natural disaster, his embassy would evacuate him out of there. Another idea is to provide Bible training for national pastors, men who are already leading and preaching and ministering as best they can. These men already speak the language and they know the culture. They can eat the food. They are adjusted to the climate and they have some natural immunity. If problems come, they will experience them with their people and remain with them to lead.

As soon as the Maranatha Children's Home was completed, we began plans for the church/training center building. We needed it and it was burning within all of us to get it started. I recruited a men's building team, with a contribution towards materials included in each man's trip cost. Several of the men gave well over the requested amount and a few of their churches helped. We were able to start our building.

The Nepali laborers prepared the ground and laid the foundation, leaving the project at the point of raising the walls. I brought eleven American men over for about two weeks of work. There were many tasks--digging, mixing concrete, carrying bricks, and those with the best skills laid the bricks. Since the Lord has not called me to construction work, I decided to do the photography. The plans were for a simple one room, brick and concrete structure with three doors, a few windows, electric lights and ceiling fans. It was not elaborate in any sense, but it would give us plenty of space for pastor training and it would be the center of all kinds of ministry. When we returned to the United States, the men gave reports in several different churches. I had the photos of the construction in progress and the project continued on its way.

Our pastor training was already in progress and had been for years. The church would be a huge asset, but the ministry was not waiting for a building. Michael had been training the pastors since we first started trips to Nepal. Anand was training and discipling before we ever met him and certainly continued in the months between our visits to the country.

There were several different areas of the country where we held training conferences. We moved the teacher about and usually presented the same material to at least two groups per trip. But the plan was to bring all of the men to one place, keep the teacher in one place, and get the maximum advantage of time. Of course, all of this depended on having a building that could accommodate everyone. It was a joyful day when that building was completed. We followed it with a small separate kitchen and another building which provided three toilets and a shower room. We could meet, sleep and feed about one hundred people, perhaps a few more. We also used the building for medical clinics and our child sponsorship program.

Medical Clinics

Our Lord used medical clinics all through His ministry on the earth. Reading through the gospels, He seems to be ministering to the sick as often as He is teaching. People gathered to benefit from His healing touch or perhaps to see something amazing happen to others. They were willing to hear His teaching because He first showed His care for them. People will still come and gather for a chance to get relief from their health problems and they will still listen to the message after we have shown that we care about them.

Anand's brother is a medical doctor practicing in New York. For several weeks each year, he returns to his native Nepal and gives some time to help the people in the villages. Many people in the villages have no access to medical care because of finances or distance—usually both. Taking a doctor to them is incredibly important for their physical needs and the results are an open door for the gospel. Most everyone is able to think of a reason to see the doctor.

We usually set up inside the church. The pastor and a few other area pastors or evangelists are as busy as the doctor. They move among the people, meeting them, giving literature, nurturing a relationship, and praying with those who are willing. We have the Jesus video running and many people sit and watch it over and over. As the people come, it may be the first time they have been inside the church or met the pastor. The next time they come will be easier and many do return to ask for prayer and may also attend a worship service. The church grows after the medical clinics have come to an area. It is also a great way to open a new area. We plan a medical trip every year, moving to a different area each day for about two weeks. Anand plans these clinics each year as part of his ministry strategy. Allow The Children provides the funding for the team expenses and also for the medicines that are given free of charge to the people.

Medical clinics are among my favorite ministry activities. It is completely different from the things I normally do and it is really exciting to see both the short-term and long-term results. We normally start a clinic with the believers from the area. They are the ones who know we are coming and have usually been helping with the set up. As we work through the believers, the Hindu begin to come. The difference is usually obvious—in their dress, their posture, and their apparent comfort level with us. They may or may not be open to listening to any words about our God, but they do want to see the doctor and get some free medicine. Some of the people walk for hours to come to the clinic and then wait in line for hours after they arrive. Sometimes a loved one who cannot walk is carried on a homemade litter, probably very similar to what was used in the first century. The man whose friends opened the roof and lowered their friend down to Jesus was probably on one.

Many of the people have common complaints that can be helped with medicines that are sold over-the-counter in the United States. Even though my professional nursing days were long ago, I am pretty good with aspirin, acetaminophen, antacids, cough syrup, lice shampoo, etc. I see one patient after another, just as the doctor is doing, referring them to him if I find anything out of the ordinary. One boy about eight years old had a miserable infection on his scalp. It looked as if it may have started with bug bites that he probably scratched with dirty fingernails. Now he had a draining, oozing mess that smelled strongly. He was feverish and certainly needed an antibiotic. There are a lot of different antibiotics. Which one is best for this problem and what dosage? I could have simply asked the doctor and I often did that, but I wanted him to look at this boy. He had multiple lesions very near to one eye, but they did not seem to be affecting his eye yet. The doctor immediately pulled his shirt off, which is something that I did not think to do. His left arm pit was worse, if possible, than his head. The infection had turned the flesh "soupy" with pus. I am sure the child would have been hospitalized and treated with IV antibiotics in the United States. The doctor spent some time talking to his mother about how serious the infection was and the importance of keeping the lesions clean and giving him all of the medication on schedule. We injected one dose of antibiotic and gave her oral tablets for him to continue, along with acetaminophen and chewable vitamins. Someone took the two of them off to clean him up and we gave the mother gloves and gauze and antibiotic ointment to take with her.

Medical clinics can result in long and tiring days. It is usually hot, and I am sitting in a straight back, wooden chair. When I get any chance at all, I need to take the pressure off of my aching back. On one occasion, when we were taking a break for a few minutes, I lay down on the floor of the small church and rested my eyes, though I was not asleep. I heard some commotion, but not understanding the words in Nepali, I paid little attention to it. Whatever it was, someone would tend to it and no one would expect me to be the one to deal with it. I probably should have paid more attention. When I opened my eyes, I saw a man's foot and shoe only a few feet away from my face. This was unusual because we certainly did not wear shoes in the church. Out of respect for the church and also to keep the carpet clean, there was a pile of shoes outside and those of us inside were all barefoot. (It is one of my favorite Asian customs.) *Why did this man come in with his shoes on?* As I sat up, I saw that he had only one shoe on and it was planted firmly on the carpet. He was not moving and others were sitting about watching, also not moving. No one was panicked, but there was a definite tension in the air and for several moments. I did not know why. He slowly lifted his foot and I saw a creature underneath that he seemed to have successfully crushed. It was a small snake, pencil thin and slightly more than a foot long. A snake is not my favorite of the animal kingdom, and I prefer not to share close space with them, but I am not terrified when I see one, especially a snake as small as this one. *Why didn't someone just flick it out of the building? Goodness, we have bigger, uglier snakes than that in Virginia,* but the way everyone was acting, it must be poisonous.

"What kind of snake was that?" I asked the Nepali doctor. "Was it poisonous?" He slowly nodded his head.

"Is there an anti-venom for it?" I asked and I was about to ask how one would get the anti-venom. In the United States anti-venom is rarely found in a small hospital and a big city hospital might not have it either. One would call the Poison Control Center and ask them to locate it.

"It was a neuro-toxic viper," the doctor said, "it is one of the most deadly snakes that exist. If it bit someone, they would be dead within minutes before we could even get them to our van."

As I lay resting, someone had seen the snake and announced it. The man had thrust his foot into the first shoe he found outside the door, and he had pinned the snake. I had been about two feet away from my death, if the viper had intended to bite me. We will never know what his plans had been. It is interesting to think about how and when he had come into the church. Had he been there all morning as we were seeing patients, with our bare feet dangling under the tables? Enough drama, we set back up and continued seeing our patients. I wonder how often the Lord intervenes for us and we do not even recognize it?

One of my favorite medical clinics was held in the mountains of Trisuli. Nepal has thousands of remote villages that have no road to reach them and no gospel has ever been brought to them. The place where we set up the clinic was accessible to our four vehicles, but it was central to an area where the people from the remote villages could, and would come. It made my list of favorites because I knew the people are in great need. It was a *long* way to any kind of medical care. These were people who simply survived or died as their ancestors had done for many generations. It was also a place where many had never heard the name of Jesus. It was thrilling to see the Jesus video running and people crowded around to watch it. As they watched, they saw and heard the whole story. Many of them watched it over and over. Members of our team sat with those waiting for the doctor and told the story of salvation with a colorful flip chart of pictures.

I love the spiritual side of our work, but my job was to help the doctor with the patients. I was the only American on the team that year. The women slept in a wooden store house that was literally hanging off the side of a cliff. About nine of us found ourselves a spot on the floor, at the base of a pile of corn about eight feet high and another of potatoes only slightly lower. Bags of rice were piled to one side. The thought of critters sharing the facility with us did occur to me, but there was nothing to be done about it. Since we were high in the mountains, the temperature dropped as soon as the sun set and there was no light except our flashlights. In order to reach the entrance from the lower level, where our vehicles were parked, we had to climb up on loose stones the size of bowling balls to a point that was about twelve feet high.

When packing for medical clinics, it is important to go as lightly as possible. We need to pack people and medicines and all of the audio visual gear into our jeeps. Personal luggage must be minimal. I considered each item in my small bag, deciding whether it was a bare essential. Items which met my bare essential criteria were one change of clothing, toothbrush and toothpaste, hairbrush, water bottle, jacket, bug repellant, and my medical equipment-- stethoscope, BP cuff, etc. I also brought several pairs of glasses, my phone and the charger for it. I had several small flashlights, but since I was on bare essentials and I had a good flashlight app on my iphone, they did not make the cut. On the first day, I used my phone freely. I checked my email with my dandy international data plan. I took some photos, listened to some music and read a book for a while after I went to bed. It did not occur to me that I had no way to charge the phone until the jeeps started their engines once again. No electricity is part of the definition of the word "remote." It was the reason why we carried a generator and petrol for the projector.

At this time in my life, I never make it through a night without at least one toilet trip and more often it is two trips. Our medical clinic was held on the top side of the cliff and the toilets were up there as well. To get to the store house, a man walked with me down a steep, narrow, slippery set of stairs, then across a grassy area to the place where we would have to climb up the rocks to the door. There was no chance at all that I could survive the stairs alone and it was just too far away for me to be wandering in the dark. It was also dangerous to try to go down the moving bowling ball rocks which would be necessary before making my way to the stairs. The only other route was up the face of the rock just outside the door of the storage building. Women were going that way all day, and I had watched them. Someone had cleverly cut four tiny little ledges into the rock which could, theoretically, be used as toe holds. The problem was that the rock was smooth and almost vertical. There were no hand holds. None of this bothered any of the Nepalis who were going up and down the rock as if it were a set of proper stairs.

On the first night, I used my phone light on the rock and then tried to remember the positions of the toe holds as I climbed with one hand, while the other hand held the phone. There were only four toe holds to the top. How hard could it be? There was still a hike to the toilets upon arrival at the top, and the return down the rock was no easier than the climb up. A slip would have meant tumbling to the bottom and becoming a patient instead of a nurse. What if I became hurt badly enough to need to go down the mountain to a hospital? Well, that just was not one of the options in the middle of the night.

The climb of the second night was similar, but there was a treat at the top. A group of Hindu had arrived late to see the doctor. The men from our team were there and some of the local Nepali believers who were helping. It was a large group of about seventy-five people. They slept in the community building where we would set up the clinic again the next day. Meanwhile, our evangelists were doing their job. It was late. The women team members (in the store house) had been asleep for hours. Our men were teaching and preaching and singing with the full attention of Hindu villagers who had never seen anything like this before. I took a place in the back and watched for a while. I should have anticipated that they would call me up, but I just did not think about it. It happened. As one man came to the end of his comments, I was called up next. I could have declined, citing lack of preparation or fatigue, both of which would have been very true. I had before me a chance to speak to a group of Hindu people *who probably had never heard the Name of Jesus before this night.* They were seated and were willing to listen because of the medical help that we had brought. The others could handle it and certainly do a better job than I could, *but this was my opportunity which I could take or let pass.* How many other opportunities had I lost in my life time? Opportunities to witness, to help, to learn, to encourage, to be a blessing, to serve? I did not want to lose this one. The only copy of God's Word in English was on my phone. I quickly scrolled to a certain passage. I borrowed a Nepali Bible and laid the phone inside it. It was not really deceptive. It was a communication that they would understand more easily than if they saw me reading from the phone. I read the Scripture and then I spoke with Anand translating beside me as we had done so many, many times before. Only a few minutes earlier I was lying in a storehouse, thinking about my full bladder and fretting about climbing a rock wall. Now I was sharing Words of Life to people from a remote mountain village who had never heard. If I was afraid to be the only American on a team, I would have missed this. If I had insisted on always sleeping in a nice hotel, I would have missed this. If my bladder was able to make it through the night, I would have missed it.

On the third night, it was cold and raining. My phone was almost out of charge and I did not want to get it wet. I had to climb the wet rock in the pitch dark in the rain and survive the remaining hours of the night wet and chilled, but I loved it. I felt like a real missionary.

Medical clinics are as close as we can come to ministering in the way that the Lord worked. They take a lot of planning and preparation. Unlike the Lord, we need to carry medicines, which require funding, yet medical clinics are one of the best investments I have seen. The people come and they appreciate the help they receive. They watch the Jesus video. They meet pastors and evangelists who speak their language. Some of them do return and attend worship service in the church. Sometimes this return happens soon. Some even declare their intention to "follow Jesus" on the day of the clinic. More often, the fruit of the clinic might not be seen for months. The results are in His hands. We do not try to measure it or "count decisions." We simply do our part and trust Him to use it as He chooses in the hearts of the people.

Jannah

Jannah Cooter first joined a trip with us in the summer of 2010. Although she was still in high school, she was a good team participant, and she was interested in missions. Just as I had known Tamara, I had known Jannah since before she was born. Her parents were active members of our church and good friends. Just as with Tamara, I had visited within a few hours of her birth with no idea that I held another missionary for our ministry, that I had no idea yet would even exist. Jannah was part of the tapestry the Lord was creating. Through her college years, Jannah joined us for several more trips and she began volunteering in our office. By the time she applied to Allow The Children as a full time missionary, she had already worked closely with Tamara for some time and it just seemed natural to include her with us.

Shortly after Jannah came to us, Tamara married and moved two hours away. Through the miracle of technology, Tamara could and did continue most of her tasks remotely by laptop, but some things just required feet and hands. Those feet and hands were Jannah's. Her work assignments came from me or Tamara, occasionally from Michael. She carved out a role for herself. How could we have kept the office manned (or womaned) with Govinda alone after Tamara relocated? The Lord knew we needed Jannah and He was already preparing us for the day that He would move Tamara. This was one more encouragement we had that the Lord was watching over this ministry and drawing the people we need in amazing ways.

Mission Trips

Mission trips are the best way I know to grow a ministry. Most of our mission team members become child sponsors when they return, if they were not already. Taking a group to see a project draws funding not only from them, but from others as they share about their experiences. Both Tamara and Jannah joined Allow The Children after making trips with us, and I suppose the same could be said of Govinda as well, after he made a mission trip to America. Taking people to another country is a huge responsibility. Each person makes a major investment of finances and time, often giving up vacation days with their families to go. Each person has different goals, and part of my job is to discover and help fulfill them. Some want *to see*. Some want *to do*. Some pastors are not happy if they are not speaking almost daily. Some people are sick with worry that they will be expected to speak. Some men want to hammer and nail for the maximum time possible. Some women want to pick up children or do some activity with them. There are the possibilities of injury, illness, political events and natural disasters or an emergency back home to consider. The travel can be strenuous, the food is different, the time changes can be difficult and the weather is unpredictable. Trips require careful planning for tickets, lots of communication, arrangements in the country, and a project with all of its necessary preparation.

Helping Americans to be a part of missions is one of the tasks I love. Even if they never travel, they can "touch" the mission field simply by sponsoring a child. They can make a difference in the life of one child, watch him grow up and see what he does with his life. We take groups for construction projects, teaching seminars (pastors, women, and children), and helping with our administrative work for the sponsorship program. The Lord uses these to bless the people of the destination country and also works in the hearts of the team members. It is an important part of our ministry and one of my joys.

Children's Home from the Slum

Our construction trips to Nepal were huge in getting the Maranatha Home and the church built. It was an encouragement to the Nepalis that Americans were willing to come and do the labor, and it moved people and churches back in the United States to help fund the projects. On one such trip, we brought the work team back to the capital city on the day before their departure to the states. We were walking through the slum ministry in the city, the poorest of the poor. Allow The Children was helping a small church plant that had started with a Bible club for children. A Nepali pastor had the heart to work among these people. Slum dwellers are people of a variety of circumstances. New arrivals into the city who are looking for a job, often "camp" in the slum area because they have nowhere else to go. If they get the job or find a relative to take them in, they leave soon. But the slum is the main residence of beggars and petty thieves, alcoholics and drug addicts. Homes are made of construction scraps, tarps, bamboo. The filthy river is the place to bathe and dinner is scavenged from the trash thrown out by nearby shops. In the middle of the depravity is a simple, one-room concrete church which we had helped with funding to build. Nearly one hundred people gather there now for services. Poor people, transitory people, and beggars who would not be able to support a pastor anytime soon attend, they are hearing the gospel and responding to it. It is a profound thing to see, and the plan was to walk the men through the narrow passageways among the homes and then to the little church.

Unknown to me, the pastor had an agenda to present. We stopped at the church and stood in a circle. The men asked a few questions about the slum ministry, and then the pastor took out some papers that had been folded in his pocket. Each page was a photo and story of a child. I had heard most of the same stories before—mother left and unheard from, mother left with another man, father dying of tuberculosis, mother widowed with five children to support and has no skills. What I had not heard before was orphaned and living under the bridge alone at age seven, arrested and jailed twice for stealing food at age eight. One child lived with and was regularly beaten by a drunken father. He had witnessed his father murder his mother in a drunken rage. One child had been put out of the family home (such as it was) because of attendance at the Christian Bible club. He was nine years old, with nowhere to go and vulnerable to all kinds of abuse.

The pastor wanted to start a children's home for eight boys. He had been working with them since the start of the Bible club. As far as he could tell, these boys had come to faith in the Lord, but they were returning to terrible situations. I had to agree with him. When a nine-year-old Hindu becomes a believer and is rejected from his home because of it, it is the responsibility of the church to take care of him. The pastor wanted to step up and accept the responsibility, but did not have the means to do so. There were others.... What about the orphan living under the bridge at seven years old? What about the boy whose father went into rages and had already killed his mother? What about the boy who was stealing food because he was hungry? I did not know it at the time, but the pastor and his wife, who had one toddler son of their own, had already taken one boy from the streets into their family and another boy who was his nephew. If he took anymore that would be a children's home and the expenses involved would be too much for him without a donor.

I get requests like this almost every week. People come to meet me when

I am in the country, looking for a donor for their project. When I am in the United States, the requests come by email from many different countries. Some of them know someone who knows me and some are website surfing. I usually zap the emails and explain to those who come in person that Allow is not accepting new ministries right now. Something about this request "dinged" in my mind and heart. I wanted to do it. Everything about it was a fit for us. I already knew and trusted the partner. It was connected with one of our existing ministries. It was exactly the kind of ministry that we do, and I loved the idea of being part of changing the lives of beggar children from the slum. A new children's home would need about two thousand five hundred dollars start up to rent a flat and for one-time expenses like furniture. We could cover that, but the on-going support would need to be found. A children's home needed a minimum of three sponsors per child and four each to bring them to a stable, comfortable level. I smiled at the pastor and told him that I would pray. It was too important a responsibility to make a decision quickly and he would not expect that. The men of the building team stood without comment. I did not know that this request would come and the pastor did not know that this group of men would be with me, but it was all part of God's plan.

By the next day, I was confident that this new children's home should be born into Allow The Children. Anand was positive about the plan. My pastor was part of the building team. I shared with him that I wanted to move forward with the new home. With no hesitation, he immediately pledged *nine hundred dollars per month* for the project. When I told the rest of the team at breakfast, four of the men pledged to sponsor a boy. I sat back in awe. We had all of the support needed for ten boys and I did not even have the photos and histories on the children yet. The Lord was funding this project. He only needed my obedience.

The Nepali pastor contacted the eight boys he had originally chosen to help. We would go to the slum the next morning at which time we would fill in the history sheets and I would take the photos. American children would not be happy to be going into a children's home. I wondered how street hardened Nepali children would feel about it. When we arrived, fifteen excited boys were waiting for us with huge smiles. The eight boys had invited some friends. A children's home meant regular food. No more scavenging. No more begging. No more petty crime. They would go to school and have a clean, safe place to sleep. Fifteen boys wanted to come. We could not take that many. I could not support them all and the pastor could not parent all of them. The whole project could collapse and then we would be helping zero boys. It was an incredible ache that some of these boys would need to be turned down. If I let myself think about it, it might be more than I could bear and I could see the agony in the pastor's eyes. Though it was painful, the choice of who would come had to be his decision. We took histories and photos on all fifteen. I told him that we could support ten. He nodded with gratitude and misery combined, if that makes any sense. Ten boys would have a chance for a different life. If they studied and made the grades, they could complete basic education. They would see a doctor when they needed one and a dentist regularly. They would hear and study God's Word daily. Like all of us, they would choose for themselves how they would walk their faith, but they would know the way. They would know it well. Five boys would return to their lives in the slum. Of course, there were many other children in the slums, but these fifteen were asking for our help and we were going to say no to five of them. I kept my face dry and my stomach contents down. We made copies of the history forms. I handed the copies to the pastor and tucked the originals into my own bag. I would not even look at them until he told me which ten would be Allow children. I spoke my prayer of thanks that the decision was not mine and I prayed for wisdom and direction for him.

Within two months, the children's home was launched. It was the fastest, most trouble free children's home plant in the history of our ministry. Ten boys were living in a basic, but very decent flat within walking distance of the slums. Actually, there were twelve boys, counting the two already in the pastor's home and not counting his own baby son. They had all received medical exams. They were enrolled in a private school. They each had a bed. It was an incredible satisfaction to see these boys clean and dressed in smart school uniforms with a tie and a good pair of shoes. They were already living different lives. This is what we do. This is how we serve the Lord. We make disciples—strong, grounded and educated witnesses for the Lord.

Joy and Sorrow

Most of the time, I had the joyful sense and assurance that what I was doing was pure and good and promoting the Kingdom of the Lord. Sometimes, the terms pure and good did not apply. Not everything in our ministry flowed smoothly all of the time. Sometimes the problems could be attributed to misunderstanding and differences in expectations. On other occasions the problem was sin. We were badly cheated a few times. We had some painful disappointments in relationships that were dear to us. We worked with children's homes, in some cases for many years, but then had to withdraw for a variety of painful reasons.

The experiences were very, very difficult, but the ministry that remained was worth bearing the heartache and risking it again. Just like my emergency department days, some of the treatments worked. Some of the patients got better and some died. Just like my apartment management days, some prospective tenants screened well, but they did not work out in the long run and some evictions became necessary. Just like parenting, there is both joy and sorrow.

The Home Office

Allow The Children was born on our dining room table. It was not long before we moved into a downstairs bedroom. There was a small desk and a file cabinet. Soon Allow supplies filled the walk in closet. We gave up our two car garage and had it remodeled into an office. Then there was space for desks, computers and printers and two work tables in the middle of the room. We began ordering paper and envelopes by bulk, but there was no place to store the boxes. By the time Tamara joined us full time, I moved back into the bedroom to use as my office. This left a work space for Govinda when he came. When we did the garage remodel to make an office, we thought it would be sufficient forever, but we never expected the ministry to grow as it did. Jannah was not with us then, but volunteers regularly blessed us with their time. With me out of the main room, the space was on the edge of manageable, but we were growing and there was nowhere else to expand. We often talked about buying a storage building for Allow and it would have helped a lot, but was not the final answer to the problem.

My bedroom office was furnished with my desk and cabinets in the back and a bed stood up on its end against the book case in the front part of the room. It had been that way for so long that I no longer saw it. Donated items took up too much space. They were stacked in the main office, and my office, and in the storage room in between, in which we needed to keep a walk way clear. We had nowhere to put our office supplies except under the work tables. It was impossible to keep the room uncluttered. This did not matter much in every day operations, but when a potential donor stopped by, who did not know us, it seemed uncomfortable and unprofessional. I felt it hurt our credibility, especially when high dollar amounts were under discussion.

We needed more space, but that was not the only issue. Allow The Children needed a home of its own, a headquarters where it could function smoothly, and survive past the life times of the parents. We needed a place that offered better *accessibility* for our donors. As we continued to grow, *visibility* was important and, yes, *credibility* too. As long as Allow was in our home, it seemed to be a hobby ministry, a "Mom and Pop" operation. We were way past that, but when a potential donor stopped by our office, he was shown into a room with a bed propped up against the wall and had to step over boxes to get there. My dog may have left a bone chewed up in the middle of the floor. Our personal lives were all mixed up with our ministry. In most ways I loved that, but one of the goals was to enable Allow to grow up and live independently of us.

We needed a real office, but of course that required real money. We had some funds set aside, mostly the accumulation of our own donations. This was undesignated money that could be used for an office, but could also be for expansion of the ministry or some emergency need. We should not spend the cushion down to nothing. *What did God want?* That was the only question that really mattered.

In 2011, Michael and I agreed that we should search out office space for Allow The Children. Several amazing free options came to us, but each one slipped away. We waited for over a year for one building to become available, but at the last minute, it just didn't work. So in 2013, I began the earnest search for a building to purchase. We could make a good down payment that should enable us to get a monthly payment on a loan down to less than a rent payment, which seemed to be the best stewardship plan to us. I looked into everything available within the location areas we considered acceptable. My default activity for months was to look for new commercial listings on the internet. We were not interested in renting, so my eyes skimmed over anything listed for lease.

We considered and decided not to buy a unit in a professional park. We looked at houses that were in foreclosure. We were very close to making an offer on a dentist office that was cheap, but needed extensive renovations. The search was hard work and I was constantly at it. We found a big building that had been a machine shop, now in foreclosure. The inside was a mess, but it offered lots of storage space and some offices in the front. It would need some work, but the low price offset some of those costs. We offered on it and my dreams soared. I was already moved in mentally and emotionally. I was thinking about how to hurry up the closing, not landing the deal. Someone else jumped us on it and we lost the contract.

In my discouragement, I decided that I was finished looking. We would rent something for two years and within that time, we would buy a lot and build what we wanted. That approach would meet our need and relieve a lot of pressure. We had been discussing that plan all along and I knew that Michael would agree. Office space for rent was everywhere. It was just a matter of picking one and, since it was not a long-term plan, it should not be a difficult choice.

The very first one I arranged to see was a nice free-standing building in a very convenient location. It was not as big as I wanted for storage, but the work space was very good. It had a simple, circular flow to the floor plan. There was an open area for desks, a small kitchen, one bathroom and plumbed for a second, beautiful big windows, and best of all it was on a main road. When the agent walked me through it, I casually asked if the owner might sell it. He thought not and even asked her. She seemed settled on renting it. However, when I looked it up on the internet, I saw that the building had been for sale in the recent past, though it was now off the market. We made an offer to buy, not rent, and after a few back and forth negotiations, we came to a wonderful agreement. The good location meant that the price was high, but the seller *would donate a significant portion back to us for the tax credit.* We had a contract on a building within only a few days of deciding not to buy a building. I had been driving past it for months, but I ignored it because of the "For Lease" sign on it. The Lord showed it to me, as soon as I was willing to go, and then the Lord negotiated a price within our means.

When the sale contract became fact, a few kind donors came along side. When the day came for the closing, *we had all of the money.* We bought the building without a loan. I am still not sure how all of that happened. It was simply a work of God.

Two more donors stepped up and offered to fund a matching gift campaign for the furnishings and remodeling we needed. The building seemed to be in good condition, but there were some things we wanted to do, such as completing the second bathroom, adding internet lines, removing some non-functioning plumbing, and painting. We needed to buy some things such as desks, storage cabinets, a good conference table, special order blinds for the big windows, a refrigerator and microwave. I had no idea how much all of it would cost. The amount the donors suggested to raise seemed like far more than would be needed, but what a blessing! Small and large gifts began flowing in and they matched each one until we successfully came to the maximum amount. Alongside the financial donors were those who gave generously of their time. Men and women donated their time and special skills to help us make the building ready and to save costs. We were so grateful for each one. I wrote dozens of thank you notes, experiencing the amazement over and over of how the Lord brought it all together—everything we needed within the funds He provided. We were able to buy everything and fix everything we needed. The money held out to the end, nothing lacking and nothing left. Amazing.

The home base was solid and secure and there was no doubt that the Lord had provided it with His own hand.

Section III

TO THE UTTERMOST PARTS

Allow The Children was born out of our ministry in Nepal. It was Nepal where we laid down the relationships that we needed to launch and it was Nepal that came to feel like home. After we were firmly established and growing, opportunities came to spread the same kind of ministry to other countries. The Lord called all of us to be witnesses for Him, even to the uttermost parts of the earth. These are our efforts to reach some of the uttermost parts. Just as we love each new child who comes into a family, we cherish each one of these unique ministry works that He has placed into our hands. *(Some names and identifying details have been changed for privacy.)*

Pakistan

After the September 11 attacks, Muslim bashing became acceptable among believers in America. It was almost patriotic to discuss them negatively and to hold the opinion that every last one of them was a terrorist who would kill us all, if given the chance, and we should keep them out of America. As we visited churches for the ministry, words of hate and fear came even from pulpits. I remember one time in particular that a song leader in a small country church spewed out a stream of Muslim vomit to responding AMENS and then saw no conflict as he led the people in singing a hymn about love. In the course of his sermon, the pastor asked the congregation what they would do if a family of Muslims moved into a house next door to them. The answer that came to my mind was *take a cake to them.* God's people sitting around me seemed to be thinking differently. Of course they were afraid, but where was love? *Were these people concerned about mission work in closed Muslim countries? Did they know how difficult and dangerous that is? Did they think that the Lord loves Muslims and wants them to come to Himself? If He was sending you to evangelize among Muslims in their country, would you go? What about if they came to you? The Lord was drawing and allowing Muslims to come to America where the gospel can be freely shared with them. Win them to Christ and the fear of attack can be resolved. Yes, it is an awesome, seemingly impossible task to reach them all, but how about just one? How about the one who moves in next door to you?* These were my thoughts, not notes from the sermon, and the reason why I started thinking of adding Muslim children somehow into the Allow program.

Through this and some other experiences, I longed for some fruit among Muslim people. I tried to fight it off. "I am already doing my part," I said to myself. We had some good ministries going that were reaching Hindu and Buddhist people, including some unreached tribal groups. We had not completed the evangelism of Nepal quite yet, and there were some good reasons to stay on that task and keep our resources going to them, but I could not shake the thoughts from my mind. I began looking for a contact within the Muslim world.

I was the only westerner and the only woman unveiled on the flight into Lahore. The immigration lines were long at the airport, but I was pleased to see one of them with a much shorter line, marked for "unaccompanied women." A female immigration officer had me cleared within a few minutes and I stepped outside into a hot and dusty atmosphere, thick with the followers of Mohammed. It would have been a good idea to arrange a schedule that would have allowed me to arrive in the morning, but I had not thought of that. It was already late and the airport was poorly lit.

Brother Azad stepped up and identified himself to me. Had he not been there, it would not have been the first time that a contact failed to meet me at the airport. It has actually happened several times, but I am glad that it did not happen in Pakistan.

Azad wanted me to sit in the middle of the back seat with his wife and son at the two windows. He did not want anyone to see that an American was in the car. I was not especially happy with the plan. Everything outside the windows was very interesting, and I would have liked to have been next to one, but there were plenty of interesting things to come. Azad's neighborhood was about two hours away from the airport and had not been planned for vehicular access. The hired car stopped a couple blocks away and we walked through some narrow corridors to reach his home. Azad explained to me that I was the first foreigner he had ever had in his home and he did not know how the neighbors would respond. Anti-American sentiment ran high. He had filled in the forms required by the police and he had honestly told them that I was an American. This was a good thing because we were going to need to submit my passport to the police on the following day. Registering with the police is common in the countries where we work and not out of the ordinary for me.

"So the police and the pastors all know that you are an American," he said. "But I told the neighbors that you are from U.K. So if someone asks, please tell them you are from U.K."

I have a faith-based aversion to deliberate lying, but no particular problem in simply withholding the truth. I actually deal with this issue of nationality regularly in Nepal. It usually comes up with a shop keeper who is going to adjust his price if he learns that I am American rather than European or Australian. I normally smile and answer that I am from "out of town" so that was my plan for this situation.

Azad, our contact and potential partner in Pakistan, was a mature believer and a businessman. He was raised by Christian parents and was well-involved in ministry, though he was not a pastor. His late mother founded the nearby Christian School. He was a leader and lifetime member of his church. His wife spoke English, but was quiet and timid around me. Though I knew him only through a few months of email correspondence, the contact with him came from a trusted resource who knew him well. I was very comfortable with him and his family.

Their home was a basic concrete structure of two bedrooms, a center sitting room, an eat-in kitchen, and an unusually large toilet room. The toilet room was entered through two large double-doors off the kitchen. Each of the other walls had a large window with no glass or screen and wooden shutters. Judging by the time they spent in the room, no one but me closed all of the shutters every time. Using the Asian toilet in the squat position, one was not visible through the eye level windows, unless someone walked right up to the window, but I just could not handle it. I closed them every time. The only bathing facility was a bucket, also common in Nepal, and familiar to me.

One of the bedrooms was filled with perfumes which were part of Azad's business pursuits. There was a bed in the room, but it would take some work to gain access to it and it seemed clear that it had not been used for some time. I was given the other bedroom and the family slept in the sitting room. The door to my room would not fully close and the house was small, so we were all sleeping within a few feet of one another. As we were preparing for sleep, Azad came in and sat on the end of my bed. He was holding two hand guns.

As he handed one of the weapons to me, he asked, "Sister, do you know how to shoot the gun?"

I was surprised at the question. "Yes! I can shoot the gun. But I do not know *who* to shoot. Maybe you should do the shooting." I examined the gun briefly. It was fully loaded. I laid it on the table beside my bed. He nodded and left the room.

As the house quieted, I could hear critter feet scurrying about and crossing the bottom of my bed several times. I only caught quick glimpses, but enough to see that they were rats, four to five inches long. The thought of rabies and getting bitten came to my mind, but there was absolutely nothing that could be done. The creatures lived here and I had to sleep here. There was nowhere else to sleep.

Throughout the week of my visit, my host seemed anxious and worried for my safety and perhaps his own and that of his family as well. Yet I did not feel unwelcome. Quite the opposite, the family seemed honored and delighted to have me with them. We spent some time calling several relatives who wanted a few moments to talk with the American. I repeated to each one of them that I was happy to be here, the flight was good, yes, the food was good.....

I am not certain what problems Azad anticipated, but he seemed to relax as each day passed without incident. Some may question that I traveled to Pakistan alone. It might seem more secure and wise if, for example, four men went in together instead of one woman. My thought is that the four American men would draw both attention and provocation. In contrast, one woman is no threat and not much of a curiosity. Women do not do anything important or government-related. We bake cookies and sew pretty things and make trips to visit friends. A simple explanation of my presence, that I came to help poor children, might have been easily accepted. A group of four men would draw more questions than that. Going in alone, with a low profile, seemed the safest course to me. I had no intention of being reckless, endangering myself or the partner.

The next morning, we walked the short distance to visit the school where Azad was well-known as the son of the founder. A large sign was displayed identifying it as a Christian school. It was Christian because the founder and leaders were Christians and because it offered a Bible class, but the class was only attended by the Christian students. All students, regardless of religious identification, were required by the government to study the Koran, taught by a Muslim. About seventy-five per cent of both teachers and students were Muslim. At the beginning of the school day, all students and faculty gathered in the yard for pledges to the flag, followed by both a Christian and a Muslim prayer. The morning prayer was the only Christian influence allowed for the Muslim students, and it was tolerated only because of the equal time given to the Muslim devotion. If I became a donor for the school, I would be allowed to gather and teach only the Christian students. One could speak to the Muslim students one-on-one, but at great risk if they went home and shared anything with a parent that could be considered influence towards converting to Christianity. Since it was a Christian school, this was a very sensitive issue and the Muslims on staff were watching carefully. I never understood why Muslims would want to send their children to a Christian school, but evidently some did.

Pakistani women in this area usually wear loose clothing that covers well. Only a few wear the traditional burka. All women, both Muslim and Christians, cover their hair with a veil, but not usually their faces. Little girls, from the time they can walk have a veil. To go without one seems to indicate a woman of loose moral character. Older women tend to tie them tightly to cover any wisp of hair, although it is common to see them worn loosely and swept over the shoulder. They are actually quite beautiful and functional, protecting the head from both the hot sun and the flying dust. Azad's wife removed her veil as soon as she entered the house. Women guests coming into the home usually left their veil on, unless a relative. That I removed mine seemed to show a level of familiarity that pleased them.

If a Muslim converts to Christian faith, there are harsh government penalties for him, but his own relatives might kill him before the government had time to act. Death is the penalty for anyone else involved as well. Proselytizing, especially among children, is at the top of the list of infractions that could find one separated from his head.

Friday is the day that Muslims worship. Businesses, schools and offices are all closed on Fridays, and open for normal business on Sundays. For that reason, Christians meet and worship on Fridays. Azad's church was only a short walk from his home. The church might seat one hundred fifty people if it was full. About half that many were gathered on the day I attended. Women were carefully veiled. Children were few. The worship was quietly emotional and powerful as always for believers living in an environment hostile to their faith. Every person present greeted me and made me feel welcome.

One man, perhaps in his early thirties was alone, without family members with him. He participated in the service like everyone else and spoke pleasantries to me. Azad stepped in and engaged him in conversation before he could ask me any questions. Nothing about him would have alerted me, but Azad said he was a government plant. Every church had one. He presented himself as a Christian and behaved as one of the group, but he was a spy. His job was to watch and report if any Muslims attended, and also anything else unusual, such as a visiting American. Azad said he would probably come to his house as if for a friendly visit, but with the hidden purpose of finding out what I was doing.

My answers could literally cost us all our heads if I did not speak carefully, and if he suspected I was speaking carefully, that could also bring problems. I understood and I thought I could handle it, but the stakes were high. The man came as predicted. Azad met him in the yard as I sat in the house. Azad's wife came over and sat, taking my hand, and we prayed together. I was not really afraid of the meeting, though perhaps I should have been. We could see a lot of smiling and waving of the hands between the two men, both of them keeping the conversation light. After a few minutes he left. Azad had told him that I was napping. According to Azad, everyone knew that this man was a Muslim and a spy, but pretended that they did not know. He knew that they knew, but pretended that he did not know.

The church had a sad history. They had a good pastor for twenty-two years. He was said to be a strong man of God and preached deep Biblical truths not staying on superficial topics as many preachers did for fear of offending the government agents. Less than a year earlier, suddenly and without any warning at all, the pastor and his family converted to Islam. He was still living in the area and as best anyone knew, he was a faithful and sincerely practicing Muslim. The assumption was that his family was threatened if he did not convert, although no one knew that for certain. If church members tried to talk to him about it, he encouraged them towards Islam. The event devastated the church. Attendance dropped by more than half. The people who remained were confused and discouraged. The children's Sunday School had stopped. Everything other than the one weekly service had stopped. They did not have a new pastor. The few men in the congregation rotated giving the message each week. I asked Azad if he thought the pastor had been a true believer.

"Yes, he was," Azad answered with so much grief that I did not ask anything more.

Several neighborhood children did small chores in Azad's home for pay. They were obviously very poor. None was enrolled in school. None was older than nine. All of them were afraid of me. Azad told me that their families were Christians, but did not attend church. Two children were working in the kitchen one morning cutting vegetables. The little girl stiffened up, but tolerated my gentle hug as I pulled her against me.

"Watch out for the lice," Azad said from the sitting room. The girl was wearing a veil, but as I looked closer, her head was alive with moving white specks and likewise, the boys.

"Cooking oil will kill that out," I told them. They listened carefully as I explained and Azad translated how to treat the lice. I never saw so much lice anywhere that I have traveled as in Pakistan. Azad's young son was an exception, but every other child I looked at seemed infested with them.

Next morning we set out to visit some orphans. I was considering bringing our Allow The Children program to Pakistan and Azad was trying to show me some areas of possible ministry. I tried to explain to him that I did not question that children in need were readily available. The struggle I was having was finding a ministry connection. Azad would certainly make a good partner, but he was not enough alone. We often sponsored children who were all under one church or living together in a children's home. In either case, there was a committee to receive the funds and supervise their use. The children were all attending a church and being taught from Scripture. Azad was hoping I would take his little household workers into sponsorship. If so, he wanted to enroll them in the Christian school. But it did not quite fit for me. The school was not enough discipleship. The children did not attend the church and even if they committed to begin now, there was no children's program and no accountability for the sponsorship. Without a pastor and "ownership" of the program, it could not work. Azad suggested that he gather them weekly in his home for Bible training. We would be, in effect, paying the families to send their children to Azad's class, and at the same time it would expose them to God's Word. If we had another "anchor" ministry, I might give this idea a try as well, but it could not stand alone.

Azad had the "orphan visit" day planned in advance. We were going to visit families in the general area who had taken in an orphan. Prior to my arrival this is what Azad thought I would want to do. People were expecting me, probably hoping I would give them money. The situation was somewhat uncomfortable, but Azad wanted to follow through on it. We had walked to the school and to the church, and now we were going out through the streets of the city and he was worried about it. Three pastors arrived on motor bikes. I learned later that these men were the source of the contacts for orphans. Azad brought a "closed" motor rickshaw. Open basket seats attached to a bicycle were ubiquitous, but this one was different. It was a metal seat with sides attached to a motor bike. In most countries of Asia, I had no hope of "blending in," but in Pakistan, women of my size and coloring were not unusual. If I was seated in the rickshaw, veiled and not speaking, there was a chance of transporting me without drawing attention. Azad put several children in the rickshaw with me, both in the front seat beside me and in a small back facing seat. Two pastors on motorbikes took their places slightly ahead of the rickshaw. Azad on his motor bike, and the third pastor flanked the rear.

"Don't be afraid," he said, "we are here with you."

I was not at all afraid. I did not even know what I should be afraid of. Would people throw rocks at me if they knew I was an American? Should we risk the children? We moved out slowly. The traffic was busy and my "guards" merged with it, disguising the fact that we were traveling together.

It worked. We traveled all about the city that day and no one took any notice of me at all, but when we stopped at a home, it was a different story. Most homes had a gated courtyard and a covered place to sit that may or may not be attached to the house. As we entered a yard, a surprising number of people seemed to be waiting. The pastors and more people followed in behind us. The neighbors were sitting or standing on the walls or on their roof tops. Everyone wanted to see the foreigner and to see what was going on. Many children were running about. It was not clear to me which one was the orphan and Azad did not know either. When I asked the pastors, none acknowledged the family as their members. Azad asked the family if they were followers of Jesus or Mohammed. I cringed. The answer was always non-committal, which meant that they might be Christians keeping a low profile with the neighbors or they might have been Muslims not wanting to lose a chance to get some money. Either way, this is not how I wanted to do this. I did not take photos or histories on any children. We went to the next house and repeated the whole scene again. Then a third house, before I could convince Azad that this was not productive.

Azad knew of two Christian-run orphanages that might need help. We scheduled to visit them the following day with the same transportation and protection. If they were in need and like-minded spiritually, this might be how we could get started in Pakistan. If I felt confident with the children's home leadership and Azad had a reference or two on their integrity, if they were active in a good church, if I found nothing to disqualify and they did need a donor, this might work. No matter what they told me, I would need a pastor or some similar witness to verify it. Then I could leave Pakistan with perhaps three good men—the housefather, his pastor and Azad—all involved in the launch of the partnership.

This plan did not work either. Both children's homes had good donor partners. The church did not work. There was no internal structure to connect our ministries together. The church was hurt and needed help, but I could not stay in the country long enough to nurture it. The school did not work. Some believers were there, but they were under guard. They were providing education, but not discipleship. I could not see that more money would make any spiritual difference. Sadly, Azad alone did not work either. He was willing to do anything I asked and he truly wanted to help the children. He was a good leader with no one to lead. I felt discouraged and maybe shell-shocked as I left Pakistan. It seemed like a battlefield with bleeding everywhere, and no way for me to help. I thought Pakistan would be a new birth into our ministry family, but it was a miscarriage. I felt the way women do after a miscarriage. Why did the Lord allow the life to begin, but not sustain? Did I do something wrong?

I still longed for fruit among Muslims. Had I misunderstood the direction from the Lord? I did not want the trip to be a failure, but I could not see how to make it a success. Was the Lord speaking and I had not listened? All of these thoughts were tumbling in my mind as the time came to leave Pakistan.

My schedule was a flight from Pakistan to Delhi, India, with a short layover and then a one-hour flight *home* to Kathmandu. I was tired and emotionally drained and thinking about resting for a day or so in familiar surroundings. Arriving at my gate in Delhi there was a sign announcing that the flight to Kathmandu was cancelled. It was a small Asian airline. It was late afternoon and they had no more flights for that day. Their office was closed. I was stranded in Delhi.

Spending the night in the airport was not an option that I considered. I spend too much time in airports as it is and I do not like them. My plan was to find the airline office of any carrier that was departing for Nepal. I would buy another ticket and work on the refund later. I am glad that I thought to exchange some currency at this point, otherwise, a few minutes later, I would have been out on the street with no money.

There was a desk near the door under a sign: *Tourist Help Desk.* That is where I went next. I explained the problem and showed the woman my ticket. I think she looked only at the name of the airline—an airline that had no more flights for today. Like most Asian airports, Delhi did not allow anyone inside unless that person had a valid ticket for that day. The reason I was inside the airport was because I disembarked from one flight and my connection was cancelled, but she thought I had somehow slipped in past the well-guarded doors. She called a guard and told him I did not have a ticket for today. (She spoke in Hindi, but I caught a few of the words which were similar to Nepali.) The guard did not touch me, but clearly indicated I must come with him. He walked me to the doors and exited me from the airport.

My goal changed from finding another flight to surviving the night. Taxis were driving by, dropping passengers and offering service to me. The problem with a taxi is that they are always outrageously expensive at any airport. I could not negotiate a price with them because... I did not have a specific destination. In Nepal, taxi drivers at the airport quote a price that is twice a reasonable rate. I knew nothing about the prices in Delhi, and they would discover that very quickly. I tried to hail a Tuk Tuk, a little one passenger moto-vehicle, which are incredibly cheap. After two or three empty Tuk Tuks refused to stop for me, I came to understand that they were allowed to drop but not pick up passengers. It is a practice, common in many countries, meant to protect the airport taxis and to prevent the small motos from congesting the airport. I needed to get off the airport property and then I could get one.

I have been to Delhi many times. I did not remember that it was very far to the road and there was a nice sidewalk, but all of the other times that I was on this road I was in a vehicle. It was a lot longer than I remembered. I set off pulling my carry-on bag, and was so thankful that it was my only luggage. As I expected, a cheap little Tuk Tuk picked me up as soon as I reached the main road. The driver wanted an address. I did not want to tell him that I did not have one. We did some back and forth about it for a few moments, but he finally drove in the direction I randomly pointed. My plan was to find a reasonably safe hotel, but not one of the "palaces" that was close to the airport. I directed the moto driver with gestures and successfully found an area with hotels. As we stopped at the first one, I struggled to pull my carry-on bag out of the small space. Generally, the passenger can count on the driver not to leave until he is paid, but he might gamble that the contents of the bag are worth his fare and take off with it, so the bag went with me. There was no vacancy at the hotel and that was the same story for the next several stops. Darkness had fallen by then and I needed to find a place to sleep. I was not afraid at all, though I probably should have been. I paused for a few minutes of prayer and moved on to the next hotel. No vacancy. I had money in my bag and a few credit cards. I could pay for a hotel, if only I could find one, but we had tried all that were in sight. I would have to set off in search once again. I really, really wanted to take care of myself and I felt no sense of danger at all. My driver had been very helpful. I could keep trying for a little longer. I also knew that the streets of Delhi were not the place for a woman alone at night.

I pursued another option. I knew an Indian family in Delhi, missionaries supported by our church. The man had stayed in our home many times, but it had been years since I had any contact with them. They were very busy people and they were not expecting me. Delhi is a big city with heavy traffic and I had no idea how far away they were. Coming to get me might be a lot of hassle for them. It was before the days when I carried a phone. I did not have the means to call them. I asked the desk clerk of the hotel that had just given me the latest "no vacancy" news if I could make a phone call. I expected a "no," but she pushed her desk phone towards me. I carefully dialed the number that I had from so long ago and heard Annie's voice. I explained that I was in Delhi and my flight had been cancelled....

"Do you want to come here?" she interrupted me.

"Yes Ma'am," I answered the older woman. I was surprised at the relief I felt.

"Well, where are you? I will send a car for you." I did not know where I was, but I handed the phone to the desk clerk to answer that question. I stepped outside to pay my Tuk Tuk driver and then sank down into one of the chairs in the hotel lobby to wait.

My friends were busy as I expected. They had a prayer meeting in progress in their home, but they sent a hired driver across town to get me. When I arrived, they quickly showed me to a bedroom, then returned to their meeting. I enjoyed a wonderful shower and when I emerged from it, a young girl came bringing me a bowl of delicious pasta and some fresh fruit. I did not realize how hungry I was or how tired I was. I crawled into a fresh, clean bed and lay thinking about how the Lord had met my needs. I felt a sense of comfort, not only in my present circumstances, but also in the whole Pakistan ministry issue. It was a miracle of His hand that I was now sleeping safely in this house. It was a miracle of His hand that I was safe in Pakistan. If I had come out of Pakistan with a new ministry, it would have been by His hand, not mine. That there was no new ministry was also His hand.

Bangladesh

Shortly after my disappointing trip to Pakistan, the invitation and opportunity came to go to Bangladesh and consider ministry there. The potential partner was well-recommended and actively engaged in ministry of several kinds. He had contacts with churches all over the country. I began an email relationship with him and prepared to make a trip into the country.

Bangladesh is a Muslim country and was once a part of Pakistan. The similarity ends there. The people of Bangladesh speak a different language. They look more like Indians and Nepalis than like Pakistanis. The country is larger than Nepal and has some significant advantages, like the ocean access. The cities of Bangladesh are choked with overpopulation. Heavy traffic makes road transportation stressful and inefficient. With a reported population of 160 million, Bangladesh is among the most densely populated countries in the world. Poverty and its accompanying way of life abounds. The great majority of the people are Muslim and the government rules from that perspective. Most of the Christians seem to be of Hindu background, and the Muslim background believers are often "underground" and cannot be accurately accounted. Churches are free to meet and worship, but "proselytizing " or anything at all that seems to be an attempt to influence a Muslim to convert to Christianity is rigorously forbidden. Bangladesh is an easier country to travel and work in than Pakistan. Foreigners are not common, although not so rare that they seem suspicious. Americans are tolerated, and the programs and aid are seriously needed. There was no need for us to fear walking openly on the street. Head gear for women is optional and usually not worn by Christian women. When it is possible to look beyond the poverty, Bangladesh is a beautiful country. It has mountains and many bodies of water including the breathtaking *Bay of Bengal*.

Michael was with me on our first trip into the country. The incredible heat hit us as we stepped out of the airport. The exit was crowded with people waiting for passengers, but we managed to find our contact quickly. The man already had a pattern and testimony of faithfulness, both in spiritual matters and handling of finances. He was a good leader. He immediately set about to tell us and show us what he was already doing and had good suggestions to fit with our work. Within the first few hours, we both had high hopes that this would work for Allow.

The guest house arranged for us was simple and very comfortable. We had air conditioning, but the electricity failed several times during each night. When it happened, the room heated up unbearably within minutes. We needed to open the windows, which was not easy. It hurt my hands to do it. For a man, who has big strong hands, it was no issue at all, but it did require getting up from chair or bed to do it. I happened to have such a man in my room. When the electricity popped back on again, we needed to close the windows, to maximize the cool. Michael and I argued during the night about who should do these tasks. I thought we should take turns. Michael did not want a turn, although he did want to be cool. His idea was for Sue to do it. I wondered if other missionaries had arguments about things like this and I concluded that they did. My exalted assumptions about the spiritual strength and maturity of missionaries were more realistic by this time, making it easier for me to identify as one.

On a day when we drove to a different place to see a ministry, we arrived at a hotel at about ten pm. We had been passing along the shoreline for a time before we arrived, and I could not wait to make acquaintance with it. After we checked into the hotel, Michael headed up to the room. He was not at all surprised that I headed for the water—the Bay of Bengal. We would be starting out again early in the morning. This might be my only chance to see it, and touch it, and tell it how much I loved it. The partner saw me leave the hotel and he was close behind following me. We were about a block from the water. The streets were still busy with people, even people wading through the water. Some were purposely moving on towards some goal. Others were slowing down from a hot, busy day and just enjoying the night and the waves gently lapping the beach. No one was actually in the deeper water swimming, except one

American. I was hot and clammy with my hair full of dust from the windows down drive. I headed south as hard as I could, past the breakers, going into the cool salt water with all the joy and pleasure I have always had. My new partner was a bit surprised I think. He set up pacing along the beach and shouting at me not to go out farther. He did not know that though this was my first time in the Bay of Bengal, the Atlantic Ocean was a good friend and night swimming was not new to me either. When I emerged from the sea, he talked worriedly about undercurrents pulling out and waves dragging under. *Yes—love all of that.*

This partner seemed to intuitively know what we needed to connect in ministry. We spent enough time with him to start a good relational foundation and with the strong references we had for him, we trusted him. By the time we left Bangladesh, we had plans in place, and we were moving forward. Pakistan was like trying to find a place to plant. Bangladesh was like harvesting. It seemed that possibilities were everywhere and it was simply up to us to decide which one and how many to pick.

Michael and I discussed it and we both felt confident enough to begin ministry with this partner and to follow his confident leadership. Over the next few months, we started a children's home for orphaned and abandoned children who would from this time on be under the discipleship of the Word of God. This good partner put the pieces together, rented a house and assigned house parents. The Lord drew children in need and very soon, remarkably soon, we were making a difference in their lives.

Titu was the son of a pastor who had died in an accident. The people of the church were caring for the widow and two sons as best they could, but the church members were poor themselves. We went out to visit his home in the village. They lived in a thatch house with only a small patch of land that could be farmed. They had one goat and a few chickens. The home had the telling look of bare survival. We could not solve all of the problems, but by taking Titu, the available food could be shared among the remaining two, rather than three. We would be sending Titu to school, an opportunity that was not otherwise available to him, and one that his younger brother would probably never have. It was sad that we were not including both brothers, but even if we could, the mother should not be left alone. This idea—taking the older son and leaving the younger one with the mother—was the partner's plan and we would not interfere with it. The mother spoke no English, but I knew the Bangla word for "thank-you." The woman fell on my shoulder sobbing and repeating that word over and over. I can only guess what it meant to her to have one son under care and education. I hoped that the two of them left would be alright.

We were taking a boy of a Christian father, but Muslim step-mother, who was under continual abuse. Another boy had been abandoned at birth in a hospital and raised by a Christian couple, but now he was ready for school and they had other children of their own. Their family resources were being stretched and they were looking for a place to "rehome" this child. One girl had a father who was an alcoholic and frequently abused the family. One girl was of illegitimate birth and the family had been looking for a placement for her so that their daughter (her mother) could have a chance to marry. One girl was the daughter of a widow living with extended family, which included a male who had tried to molest her. The mother could never leave her alone and was constantly in fear for her. Two children were from a poor Muslim village. We had a total of thirteen children to start the home and I needed to find sponsors quickly. Each precious child who came to us was a treasure to be cared for and discipled as a light and a witness back to the people from whence s/he came. The potential of this investment just cannot be measured.

The children's home was sheltered with a rented building. An exterior door opened to a stairway with two flats on each level. Each flat held two tiny rooms and a toilet room. On the ground level was the "gathering" room on one side and a room rented by a Christian (Bangla) family on the other side. That they were there was a blessing for us. They often joined in the devotions, so the children knew them and their two children. They provided two more adults in the home, even though they were not really officially part of it. The flats on the next floor up were for the house parents on one side and the girls on the other side. The top floor flats were for the boys on one side and the other side was not completely finished and not often used.

Another ministry program we started was sponsorship for children of pastors. Our new partner had contacts throughout the country. He knew which pastors were serving faithfully and which had deep needs. He gathered a group of pastors and we processed one child of each family for sponsorship. Helping these pastors is a way to lift a little bit from their shoulders, and to join in and encourage their ministries. Creating this partnership drew the men together as a group. It was an encouragement that a believer in America would know their names, would pray for them specifically and simply care. One pastor had six children and was rejected by his extended family because of his Christian faith. Another pastor had a son in a long-term hospital stay following a rickshaw injury. We visited his rented home, which was two tiny concrete rooms with no window and certainly no air-conditioning. They kept the door open and cooked outside on a little brick wall. Another child lived with a grandfather who had been a respected pastor, but now suffered from dementia. The girl's father had died and the family struggled for survival. We took about fifteen children of pastors when we started the program, each with a difficult story.

After the beginning work in Bangladesh was stable and healthy, we went "up the mountain" to see a ministry area that was close to the heart of our partner. I went to Bangladesh to establish a ministry among the Muslim people, and we were doing that. What we were going to see on this day was completely different. The tribal mountain people are protected by the government. Great efforts are made to prevent outside influences from coming in and changing their way of life. They are a people left behind as the world has changed. They still live as the generations before them have lived—working the land, raising animals, making the things they use. An educated man is rare, an educated woman even more so. Medical care is not easily available, but centuries of the strong surviving and the weak dying off have produced a hardy people. Bringing the gospel to restricted areas is not easy and cannot be done in the usual ways.

To reach the place, it is necessary to drive for hours up the mountain. It is a hard drive, a rough and narrow road with winding curves. The posted advice is to hire a jeep and a driver who is familiar with the road, and we always do that. The partner must get a special permit to take a foreigner into the restricted area, one that is not easy to obtain. We stop at three police checks along the way where my permit and passport are examined, and I must sign a log book. If I am not out by dark, I am not certain what would happen, and whenever I ask, the men just shake their heads at the horror of the thought.

When we arrive at the place where we must leave the jeep, I am usually tired from the drive and the early hour awakening, but there is more to come. We park the vehicle at the edge of a river bank. At one time in history there was a concrete stair leading down to the water, but was now rough and crumbling. The descent is quite steep and it would be easy to lose balance and fall. I try to keep my eyes on the next step, not the destination far below. Thus far, I have successfully made it down each time.

Either wet or dry weather brings completely different experiences. If dry, the top soil is deep and loose covering my feet as they sink down and making movement difficult. If wet, moving along is much easier—too easy. Moving might occur at a time before I am ready—all the way down a hillside. We must make our way to the narrow, hand-carved boat to cross the river. In rainy season the river might be running very strong. The boat is powered and guided by pushing sticks along the bottom. I am not at all afraid of being personally dumped into the water, but the thought of my camera and phone soaking and floating is a little bit exciting. When we arrive at the opposite side, there is another vertical cliff, this one with no crumbling stairs or any natural help at all. Whether wet or dry, the effort of the climb is challenging for me, but there is no choice. Then there is a jungle walk to reach our children's home. It is not really a long walk, but when I am already exhausted from the climb, the hike seems longer.

The first time I visited the place it was an open field for sale. The partner had done the advance work and had begun the negotiation process even before we confirmed our participation. He saw a place to make a center for ministry outreach in the mountains where there was no Light at all. The plan was to start with a children's home as the first step to planting a church. There were no believers here so we would have to grow our own. We could raise children grounded in the Word who would form the first members of the church. The partner would choose the house parents, supervise the construction, screen the children, and so many more tasks. It was a huge project. All of the materials would need to be brought up the mountain by jeep and shoulder-carried across the river the same way we had come. The plans would need to be carefully made. If the building was found to be one concrete bag short, it would be a very long haul to obtain another one. Of course, the whole project hung on the integrity and godly leadership of the house parents. Because of the distance and the difficulty in reaching the area, the partner would not be able to supervise as closely as we would prefer. The house parents would make the difference between housing and feeding children and raising faithful Christ-followers.

Allow The Children's job was to find the funding. The money seemed to be a small issue as we discussed many plans, even though nothing would happen without it. I did not know where to find it, but as I looked out over that meadow with its mud, grass and weeds, I somehow knew that it was our assignment. I looked at the men and told them "we will pray." There was nothing more to say. I could not promise them the needed funds, but I desperately wanted to do this project, and I urgently prayed for the privilege of being part of it.

The money came. One donor gave a gift large enough to make hope turn to reality. The Lord drew others and we sent enough into Bangladesh to lay the foundation. We wanted a building that provided enough space and kept everyone dry during the rainy season, but the partner wisely did not seek to build something that looked like a mansion among the stick and thatch homes that surrounded it. It was a simple concrete building with three rooms—one for boys, one for girls, and one for house parents. We built a separate toilet building in the back and another building for the kitchen. We needed a deep well and several thatch structures for goats, etc. As each stage of construction neared completion, we had the funds in hand for the next stage. When the time came that we needed it, the money continued to come. Some donors were responding to the need in Bangladesh and some were giving to the general fund, but somehow it came.

The next time I visited, the buildings were full of beautiful children who came from some of the most remote mountain villages that there are, from an area that is government protected from "outside influences," from a country where only the very smallest percentage of the people are identified as Christians. The children came from families that were poor and uneducated and isolated. For all of these reasons, and as far as we can know, these children had *never heard the Name of Jesus before they came to live at the home*. If we can raise them up and disciple them in God's Word, the result could be strong witnesses for the Lord—ready and able to carry the gospel to their own people. This home generally has thirty to thirty-six children. Most of them are orphans or half-orphans. They came from rejection or tragedies in their lives. They came to a place in the remote mountains of Bangladesh where they could hear about the living Savior. *Think about that.*

The children performed the proof of what they had learned by singing and reciting verses. As a foreigner, I was forbidden to teach them, and I did not—but the Bangla believers could, and they did. I pondered the great truth once again that the Bangla believers could work this important ministry. It was an unspeakable privilege to be a part of it along with everyone who sponsors children or donates for this work. The Lord draws the tapestry together to bring the gospel to these people.

On one occasion, when we were visiting the children's home, we had a burst of drenching rain. As we waited it out, the soft, dry soil became a slick, muddy mess. I barely made it to the river bank without falling. There was no chance at all that I could get down to the river upright and with all bones intact. Even the Bangla men were struggling with their footing. With humility, I sat down in the mud and did a slide. When I arrived safely at the bottom, I was covered in slimy mud, not only on my back side, but seemingly all over. I could not get back in the jeep like that and I could not tolerate the mud for the hours it would take to get down the mountain. The river was flowing strong, but it was the only remedy for the mud. Someone took custody of my shoulder bag as I stepped into the water, and it was no real surprise that the current took me. One of the men grabbed for me, but I just waved him off. Truth was that I was hot and filthy and a swim was just what I needed. It was really more of a ride than a swim. I simply kept my head up and slowly worked my way across as the current pulled me downstream. The partner knew that I loved the water and was not too worried. When I touched land on the other side, I was alone in the mountains of Bangladesh for a few minutes as I walked back along the shoreline. For this hike, I was rested and refreshed and I really loved it.

When I went into the water, I briefly considered the likely contamination of giardia or the possibilities of reptiles swimming along with me. I did not think about leeches. I had no experience with leeches before this day and wish I could still say that. It was a bit discomforting to pull them off and watch the blood flow from the place they had been attached. I detached three from visible, accessible places and became aware of another that had gone under my clothing—which made me wonder whether I had found them all. Someone once asked me if it was difficult to pull leeches off of myself. *Noooo!* It was not difficult at all, considering the other choice was leaving them on. On the positive side, my problem with the mud was completely resolved. The heat of the day was no longer bothering me and my bag made it safely across in the hands of one who chose boating instead of swimming.

When booking the flight schedule to the city in Bangladesh where we worked, a stop in Dhaka was unavoidable. Sometimes I could get the connecting flight with only a few hours layover, but it was often necessary to stay overnight in Dhaka. I have taxied alone in many Asian cities and fancy myself capable of survival. The partner would schedule a guest house and try to include an airport pick up. That was the easiest and safest plan, especially after dark, but it did not always happen. I knew that he fretted about it, and sometimes he made the six-hour trip by bus just to be there with me during the layover. I thought this was unnecessary, but truly, Dhaka was often an adventure. Vehicles charge into intersections with traffic continuing in all directions. Rickshaws and motor bikes cram into any open space, including the sidewalks, and the wonder is that there are not more accidents. When there is an accident, the drivers exit their vehicles and stand shouting and waving their arms in the street. The assignment of blame is important both financially and for continuing employment if either is a hired driver. Sometimes the pressure is too much and fights break out using fists or any available weapon. When violence erupts, the rest of us just keep our seats in our vehicles and watch. If a police officer is about, I have seen them also wait for it all to settle. One time I saw a man with a sledge hammer bash the windshield of a fellow motorist evidently in retaliation for some aggravating offense. As he moved to the side window, the driver scooted out the opposite side and ran. This was probably a good personal decision, but he left two lanes of traffic blocked and even more people unhappy with him.

An opportunity came to meet a potential partner, based in Dhaka, who had a ministry in a jungle village. I was interested for several reasons. It would be good to have some productive purpose in Dhaka to use the time and it would also be helpful to have a second ministry partner in the country. A side benefit would be to have someone who would help me with the transportation and accommodations in Dhaka. I began the email correspondence to start the relationship.

With arrangements made, I landed at five thirty one morning in Dhaka.

My normal route is to go to Nepal first and find a round trip flight from Kathmandu to Dhaka, but this time the itinerary was from the United States direct to Bangladesh. Since I never sleep well on a plane, my favorite schedule is to arrive in the destination country in the evening and have a good night's rest. Then I am usually adjusted and ready the following morning. The most difficult schedule is the one I had this time—an early morning arrival with the whole day ahead. It was a very full day at that. I had never met this partner, however he had no problem finding me. In the thick of passengers flowing from the immigration desks there were very few white westerners and only one woman traveling alone.

The next step when arriving in Bangladesh is to wait on a crowded platform, eyes always on the luggage, for a specific car to arrive—the one the partner had hired. It had been waiting with meter running ever since he arrived at the airport. Once he knew I had arrived, the partner called the driver, and he began the process of entering the long line snaking around the airport parking lot and slowly working his way to the platform. As cars pull up, their passengers load with no hurry at all. Some vans send a man running inside to call their passengers. Some sit and wait, convinced that more people will come. The police presence on the platform accounts for whatever level of efficiency there is, but the constant shrill whistles and shouting jars my sensibilities and strains my aggravation tolerance. Leaving the airport brings no relaxation as the driver maneuvers through the traffic. To the newcomer in Asia, it seems that every turn brings a close encounter with death. Horns are constantly blaring. Brakes jerk the vehicle. Huge trucks stop or veer off at the last possible moment, seeming to barely avoid a collision. We always have an air-conditioned vehicle, but the system cannot keep up with the soaring temperatures in Bangladesh.

We dropped my luggage at the partner's home and proceeded to the village which was several hours outside of Dhaka. The travel time was not wasted. I needed this interlude to talk and build a relationship with the man who would be a field partner with Allow, if I accepted the ministry. So we talked, and I remained turned to "high intensity" level as I worked through issue after issue, each being important both for the partnership decision and development.

We drove as far as we could and then began the walking trek to the village. The walking trek ended at a waters' edge, where we boarded a small village boat with a cover, like the old-time covered wagons, but had no seats. We crowded into the hollowed out floor and floated all the way to the border of our village. The village was built of thatch homes and (surprisingly) sheet metal. Now we were walking through people's yards, which seemed to be the normal practice. Most families had several buildings within their "compound." Most had a cow or a goat tied up. Chickens and ducks roamed freely. There were dogs, pigs, and occasionally a water buffalo. One family had beehives and there were some little ponds of fish farming.

The people looked up when I passed by. Foreigners did not visit every day; in fact, I believe that I was the first one. The reaction was not positive or negative or even curiosity. We had arranged in advance for the children to meet with me, therefore, the whole village knew why I was coming.

I was quite tired when we came to the home of our host, but the work was just starting. We were at the home of the man who was the pastor for this village. He also farmed like everyone else. He had several sheet metal buildings and one was for the use of the church. It was mostly empty, but had a wooden desk and cabinet in one end. The children were gathering. Some of them had an adult along with them, but many were alone, obviously wondering what was about to happen.

I met Apon that day, whose family was shunned by most of the village because they were Christians. Srabonti's mother was a widow. They lived with her grandfather, but he was not able to provide much and certainly no chance for school. Swajib's mother was also a widow and worked as a house servant, which meant bare survival wages. Pijus was the son of a widow and had a handicapped brother. Shadhin was an orphan living with his grandmother who needed help herself and could not provide enough for him. Bristi's mother died and her father remarried. Other children in the family attended school, but not Bristi, so her days were spent in household work. So the stories went for a total of thirty new children to come into our program.

As we completed the photos and histories, the children and adults packed into the small building, sitting…. and waiting. After many times in villages much like this one, I knew why they were waiting. I should have planned some message, but my time in the United States was so packed full in the days before leaving for a trip, that I just had not thought about it, and my exhausted brain was not up to speaking without preparation. Yet as I looked at them and they looked at me, I knew it was going to happen. The partner and the pastor were busy talking (in Bangla) and working out some details, but I knew it was coming and I had better gather some thoughts. My Bible was somewhere down inside my tablet, so I took out the device and started the process of bringing it to life. I do not like to speak from an electronic tablet in Asia. I think it is still important that they see the authority of a Bible in the hand of the speaker, but in this case, it was the only English language option and my Bangla is just not very good. Sometimes in this situation, I bring the Scripture up on my phone and lay the phone inside of a Bible in *any* language. That works better when standing and using a podium, but on this day I was going to stay right behind the desk where I had been sitting, comforted by the knowledge that the Lord often taught from a seated position. The room was not large enough to stand and I did not have the oomph to do it.

"Sister, can you speak God's Word?" came the request I was expecting. My heart was not in the best condition for what I was about to do. I had no study preparation and no prayer preparation—both my own fault. This is the most important thing we do in this ministry, and I should have given it the priority it deserved.

I nodded acknowledgement to the partner, who would translate, and paused for a few moments attempting to get my spiritual bearings. I had a passage open that I had taught many times in the past. I knew the material well and if imparting factual knowledge to these people was the goal, I was on solid ground, but my heart was not ready to try to reach theirs. God's Word is a precious living thing not to be handled or delivered lightly. "No preparation!" kept sounding in my mind, and I was ashamed of the memory that it was not the first time. I stepped off the plane in Bangladesh. I went through the luggage and immigration procedures found the partner and drove for hours out to this village. My mind was on the administrative issues and I had done it well. I had thoroughly interviewed this man today during the drive and I had good references on him before I came. I had good photos of the children and completed history reports already in my bag, but none of those tasks compared to the importance of this moment.

I was struggling even to keep myself awake. I was in a jungle village of Bangladesh with people waiting to hear anything I wanted to say. I could give a word of greeting. I could tell them how nice it was to be in their village today. I could talk to them about how important it was for the children to go to school, and now that we were sponsoring, they should be enrolled as soon as possible, but those logistics were the partner's responsibility. Our thirty children and an assembly of adults were packed inside, and people gathered at all of the windows. They were just as important as a stadium of thousands. As I took my pause, I let the thought wash over me again as it had so many times before: *I had an awesome privilege.* Many others would love to have the assignment that I had today. I looked down at the Scripture that came from God Himself. I began to read to the people, feeding one line at a time for the translator. As I spoke to them, the Scripture spoke to me. I felt a surge of alertness and energy, and He did what He had done many times in the past. The Lord took over and started giving me words which I spoke as they came to me. As the translator repeated them, I waited to hear what I would say next. It was an indescribable experience. I remember feeling a great confidence about what to say and when to stop. I was able to forget about me, about how I felt physically and emotionally, and focus on Him and the Word. *His strength was made perfect in my weakness.*

The meeting came to an end, and the people began filing out. Many of them wanted to speak directly to me and I tried to respond with the translator, but I was starting to crash again. A woman brought some soup and a banana and I ate some of both. Some men carried in a bamboo platform that is used for everything in the village—beds, chairs, tables, and work benches. I had no way of knowing whether the platform was for me, but I could not stay upright any longer. I was barely conscious as I slipped over to it and lay down. People were still walking about, and the men were still talking at the desk, but I was asleep almost immediately.

When I woke, I had a few moments of disorientation. It was dark, but I could see that I was inside a cage with bamboo rods underneath me. It was a cloth cage… and then I realized that it was a mosquito net hanging from a hook in the ceiling and falling down on all sides of me. I was in an Asian village. I have been in a lot of villages. *Which one was this? What country was this?* And then it all came flooding back. It was Bangladesh. I did not know the name of the village, which was why I could not remember it. I was hours into the jungle, and I had less than twenty-four hour acquaintance with anyone here. Moonlight was coming through the open windows. I saw the desk and remembered that the men were still sitting there talking when I ended my day on this bed. My shoulder bag was somewhere over there—containing my passport, tickets, money, everything. I felt a few moments of anxiety about that, then I saw that someone had put it in the bed with me. My bladder insisted on a trip outside. I had no idea where a toilet was. I would have to wander about until I found one. The thought occurred to me that I should be careful to remember my way back. As I swam my way out of the net and stepped down to the floor, I saw a woman lying on a pallet. I tried to avoid waking her, but it was not going to happen. I knew she was there, for just this purpose—if I needed something during the night, and so that I would not be wandering about the village in the night. We had no common language between us, but she put two and two together and led me to the toilets, which were not especially close by. I would have been a while finding them and successfully returning to the correct house would have been even more of a question. Thankfully, the girl guided me safely back and lifted the net for me to get back inside.

Still affected by the time change, I was wide awake now and I had the prayer time that I had missed earlier. I prayed for the village and the children I had met. I prayed for the girl on the floor. I prayed for the ministry and what part we should take in it. The Lord gave me an overwhelming sense that we should add this village group into our sponsorship. The thirty children from yesterday had very sad situations. I knew that if I had agreed to take forty children there

97

would have been ten more with difficult stories. If I could take fifty children, there would have been fifty there. We were not solving all of the problems. There were still children in terrible need, suffering in poverty and not able to get the education that might make their situation better. We could not help them all, but I felt very settled that we would help thirty. Thirty children could grow up educated and discipled by this village pastor. The building where I slept was a meeting place for just a few families of Christians, but one day there would be a true church and a people called out for His Name in this village. Allow The Children will have a part in His plan. That is all I wanted—a part in the kingdom work that my Savior is doing.

Cambodia

I made my first trip to Asia in October 1994. Michael and I had made a previous mission trip to Europe which gave me some international travel exposure, but this was my first experience in Asia. Thailand and Cambodia quickly had my heart. Bangkok is an international city with a special Asian flavor. The farther we went into the rural villages, the more sense of belonging I felt. In Cambodia, we worked in a village of believers displaced from their homes and saved during evangelistic services in a refugee camp. When they were able to leave the refugee camp, the new believers chose to stay together and so they formed into a Christian village. They built stick houses, which had almost nothing in them except the people themselves and a few cooking implements. A small wooden church in the center of the village was a modest structure by any measure, but none of the bamboo thatch roof homes was built of any better quality than their church. People who had nothing materially and very little hope for a future of anything but raw survival praised their God with a fervor I had never seen in America. As they sang and worshipped in the little church, their voices rang out through all the Cambodian countryside around us, and I dissolved in tears. I am not sure whether my love for Asia was actually born on that day, or if I simply recognized it for the first time. God was preparing me for the ministry to come.

Cambodia almost does not belong with these stories of the other countries and how Allow The Children began work in each one. My three trips to Cambodia predated the founding of Allow, actually before we even thought of being in missions full-time. Cambodia is included because the experiences had a profound effect on my life towards missions. I still gulp a little bit when I think about it. We often say that our work started in Nepal, but in many ways, the beginning of the things we do now all started in Cambodia. I hope I can adequately share the story...

My first ever stop in Asia was in Japan, an airport layover on the way to Thailand. I was traveling with two women, both meeting their husbands in Bangkok, who had traveled over earlier. The Japanese airport looked disappointingly like most other international airports, and it was difficult to taste any true flavor of Japan.

My second ever stop in Asia was only a few hours later in Thailand. Stepping off the plane in Bangkok was my first experience of being slapped in the face with heat at oven level. Bangkok is a large international city with modern high rise buildings, good roads, late model vehicles, and most of the comforts of the United States, yet it is not unusual to see a village-dressed woman walking with a bamboo pole over her shoulder and a basket dangling at each end holding her wares for sale. Bangkok was the first place that I was surrounded by Asian culture with so many new life skills to learn. Some of the easiest ones were being careful not to drink water from the faucet, a shower with no hot water, using a "squat" toilet, removing shoes before entering a building and adjusting to the time change. All of these issues would become normal to me in the years to come.

We had a "down" day, so we took a canal boat (for tourists) and enjoyed the ride through the waterways about the city. The people provided fascinating sights along the canal. They lived their lives in front of us as we floated past. The stick houses were built in water and the floor level of most rested just above the water. We could see inside as a family squatted around their morning meal. One man leaned out of a window to brush his teeth. People were half or fully submerged, bathing in the canal. Breakfast dishes were dipped into it and wiped a bit. Clothing was being washed in the canal and then hung along the rail. The toilet? Yes, that too. It was all part of life on the canal. Each home had a little boat tied to it—the only way to travel. It was a village within the city.

On a street corner was a rather elaborate Buddhist shrine. People, created by the living God, were kneeling and bowing intensely in worship at this shrine. It was circled by a rod iron fence about four feet high and was covered with fresh flowers. This separated the worship area from the busy street around it. As we watched, some people seemed to stay for a long time, while others just stopped by quickly for only a moment or two. The face of a little boy, about three years old, will be forever in my memory. His mother had brought some offering to the Buddha and was kneeling and bowing up and down as others were also doing. This little guy looked up at me and we had a moment of eye contact. Then he knelt and bowed as his mother was doing, but kept glancing up at me and we locked eye contact. His mind was not on the Buddha, but he was learning to worship the idol as he watched his mother. Unless he had some chance to hear the Word of God, there was a lifetime of Buddha worship ahead of him and eternity lost. I did not have any tools in my hand to share the gospel with him. If I did have a way, he might respond and he might not, but would he ever even have a chance? It was a pivotal moment for me. It was a spark that burned in me and influenced the ministry that came later. I can still see the boy's eyes and I see him when I do have an opportunity to teach children in our countries.

We have so much Light and there is so much darkness in Asia. Little children, like him, are growing up without ever hearing the Bible stories that permeated my childhood. Perhaps I had never stopped to ponder what a privilege it is to teach children. Just like this precious little boy, they are going to learn what we teach them. They will worship as the adults in their lives worship. How incredibly important it is to lead them in the way that they should go. At that moment, I wanted more than anything to have a group of Buddhist Thai children (or maybe just the one little boy), a translator, and a prepared gospel story in my head. Yet the little boy I was watching was out of my reach. *How could I reach them? What could I do?* I ached with the thoughts, and I could not imagine any of the answers. The little boy bowing to the Buddha is still a picture in my mind today. I could not reach him, but by the grace of God, many others have come under our care and teaching. I do not want to miss an opportunity to help any precious one of them.

That night, we had dinner with a wonderful missionary family who had gone to great lengths to make a delicious and authentic Thai dinner for us. A large table was full of amazing, colorful dishes, all waiting for us to taste. Along with the exotic choices was one innocent looking bowl of white potatoes. I love potatoes any way that they are cooked, so I took a generous bite. One bite was enough. My mouth and throat burned all the way down. My stomach and my whole digestive system raged. Most of the food was not spicy and I spent the rest of the meal spooning rice and soft fruits into myself trying to neutralize the effect of the potatoes. That one bite of potatoes also stole most of my sleep. I was up and down, tossing and making toilet trips for most of the night. This was my first experience with Asian spices, and it made a lifelong impression on me.

It was about four am and I was awake when the light suddenly switched on in the home just across the street. There were big windows and no curtains. It was like a giant television screen only a few feet away and it was right in front of me, even when I lay back down in my bed. I was not really peeping. Their home was open to whoever happened to glance in the direction, and of course they knew it. It was almost like being in the home with them. I watched the early morning routine of the large family. A load of fish was dropped in the street and they sat cleaning it, preparing it (I suppose) to sell in the morning daybreak. Just upstairs, other family members were making themselves ready for the day. They sat in a circle on the floor and ate something from small bowls. Some would move downstairs to work on the fish and others would return to the upper level to eat. Children were still asleep on their pallets. It was all very ordinary in many ways, but it was an experience the Lord wanted me to have, and He may even have kept me awake with the digestive issues so I would not miss it. Watching them helped me see the Thai people in a way that was different than seeing them on the streets or on their jobs and I have never forgotten that night. When traveling to another country, we all tend to stick with our American family or friends. We visit tourist sites (or even ministry projects), sample some local food and think we have experienced the country. It is a far different experience to be in the homes of the people of the land, to come to know them and the way they live. That night, the Lord gave me my first experience of being in an Asian home even though I was not really in their home. It started my longing for a relationship with the people, not just doing something for them, but doing it *with* them.

I love Thailand. It is called the land of smiles, and so it is. I had never visited a country where I was made to feel so welcome and most people projected happiness in their dealings with others. Most customer service of any kind was excellent and it was just a consistently pleasant experience. The surrounding Asian culture was fascinating with just the right amount of challenge, yet it also felt secure and manageable. But it was time to go to Cambodia.

The flight from Bangkok to Phnom Penh was about thirty-five minutes. The serving cart aboard Royal Air Cambodia was held together with duct tape. I was going to learn that the entire country of Cambodia needed duct tape.

We expected Cambodia to be a bit tense. As I understood it, the government did not object to westerners visiting. It was the Khmer Rouge, a rebel group that could possibly cause us problems. Pol Pot, the infamous leader during the war was still alive at that time and in hiding somewhere in the jungle. Everything I had heard about him was the definition of depravity. The Khmer Rouge overthrew the Cambodian government in 1975 and ruled for about four horrible years. Communication, trade and travel with the outside world stopped. Many of the leaders and the educated among the Cambodian people fled the country, but Pol Pot's regime executed any who remained. They executed doctors, teachers, Buddhist monks, Muslims and Christians, ethnicities other than their own, and disabled people. They wanted a dependent, agrarian people who would be easy to rule. They even executed people simply because they wore glasses, which indicated that they were able to read. Over three million people died, about twenty-five per cent of the population. When his government was overthrown in 1979, Pol Pot escaped with his faction into the jungle and they held on to their identity and some measure of power. The fact that he had never been captured, and was still active, was a very understandable source of fear. I was in the country again, a few years later in 1998, when he was confirmed to have died. It seemed as if the whole country sighed with relief.

During the flight, we learned from a newspaper that the Khmer Rouge was offering two thousand dollars for any westerner turned over to them. This was the equivalent of eight years salary for a professional. The military was supposed to be controlled by the government and therefore not a threat to us. Yet three hostages, recently executed, had been taken off of a train by soldiers and handed over to the Khmer Rouge. Cambodia is considered one of the poorest countries in the world. They often cannot pay their military for months at a time and two thousand dollars must look very tempting. Khmer Rouge was also warning westerners to keep their women and children out of Cambodia.

It was dark when we landed and there were no lights on the tarmac. My first thought was that we certainly were not in Thailand anymore. It was incredibly hot. The air was stale and smelled of fuel. Small guards with huge weapons were all around.

Traffic was busy, and the few private cars, were almost all in poor condition. The unpaved roads were about six lanes wide, with no lanes marked. Most of the vehicles were bicycles or motor bikes. There seemed to be no traffic regulations at all. Drivers moved in whatever open space could be found.

Our hotel looked very fine from the outside, but the inside was less so. Our desk clerk had a big gun leaning against the wall behind him, so we could feel secure. My room was tiny with a variety of identifiable smells and a few I did not recognize. The odor seemed to improve when the air conditioning creaked on. The bathroom had three towels. All were old, badly stained, and damp. They may have been permanently stained, washed, but just not completely dry, or they may have been left from the previous occupant. One faucet on the sink worked. Both faucets in the tub worked, but both delivered cold water only. This was not a problem, but the ceiling in the bathroom was missing enough tiles that two men could have come down through them from the adjoining room. No need for them to do that though, because they could just as easily come through the door. The doorknob was loose and the lock did not hold. Just jarring the door would usually open it. It took me about five minutes to learn this. The men who worked in the hotel certainly knew it as well. There was no piece of furniture that could be moved to block the door. My traveling companions were in other parts of the hotel, not nearby, not even on the same floor. I was very much alone.

I seldom struggle with fear for personal safety. I expected to be alone on this trip and I did not expect the room to be up to American standards. I did not expect to feel completely safe and secure, and I did not expect that to be a problem. I knew that Cambodia would be an adventure. What was the problem, anyway? No one had been threatening or discourteous to us in any way, but about the time my door shut and I was alone, an overwhelming fear settled over me that must have come from Satan. I was so puzzled with myself. I was near to tears—not the trickle down the face kind, but a major irrational sobbing with vocal noise—something well beyond what the circumstances justified. It was not like me to get so ruffled, and I certainly did not want anyone else in the group to know how I felt.

It did not help my composure that one of the men in our group was knocking on my door about every fifteen minutes and asking if I was alright. He seemed to be even more anxious than I was. I was calmly writing the events of the day in my journal as he came by. My plan was to hold on and wait until it was late enough that he would stop coming. Then I would let the sobbing come and get it over with. I was aghast at the thought of him coming and catching me in tears. That just could not happen. I held in the tears, for one hour and then through another hour, but my control was shaky.

Finally, I decided to pray. It had to be a short prayer or I would risk losing my emotional control. I said something like, "Lord, could you do something? I just do not think I can stay in here alone tonight." It was more of a cry than a question. I did not ask the Lord for anything more specific, because I could not think of any solution. The other two women were with their husbands. I wanted Michael, but he was on the other side of the planet. This was another new experience for me. Usually when I pray, I know exactly what I would like for the Lord to do. I have the plan all ready for Him. All He has to do is use His power to make it happen. But I did not have any idea this time.

Within moments of my prayer, there was another knock on my door. When I opened the door this time, the man's wife was with him. She came rushing into my room, obviously very upset.

"There's a BIG RAT in my room!" she cried out. "Can I sleep in here with you?"

I was surprised, but very calm. "Well, if you are afraid, I guess it would be alright," I very generously answered.

As it worked out, her husband did not want to sleep in the room with the rat either. In a few minutes, the second woman joined us, and the two men slept in the other room. As I lay down to sleep, I pondered my secret knowledge of why a rat had come into that room. A loving Father had responded immediately when I cried out for His help. He allowed my friends some stress and inconvenience, but He did it to meet my need. Sometimes bad things happen in our lives—like rats—because the Lord is using us for some purpose of His.

Neither of the women, now sharing my room, were fighters. They would not provide much protection, but my fear was gone as we lay down to sleep. It was as if the Lord was a parent giving a child a Teddy Bear. He reminded me that He knew my situation, and He was watching. I confessed my lack of trust, which would have been a good idea a couple of hours earlier, and I slept soundly. I was alone in the room the next night and for the rest of the trip. It was not a problem—not any problem at all.

The next morning, the streets were alive with activity as we left the hotel to attend a church. Our vehicle had to compete for a place on the road. Sights that are familiar now were brand new then and listed in my journal—a woman on the back of a motorbike nursing a baby, individuals with all kinds of things on their heads, naked children, people toileting themselves on the street, a Buddhist funeral procession and men with huge guns.

Almost every man walking along the road, whether in uniform or not, carried a gun. In most cases, the gun seemed as long as he was tall. I was told that they were all in the army. If not in uniform, it may be because he did not have one, or because it was his day off. Even if he was off duty, he must keep his gun with him. If he lost it, he faced jail for years. He also carried it because skirmishes with the rebels were not uncommon in the city, even coming to gunfire.

To reach the church meeting, we walked through a little neighborhood of bamboo huts. Most were small thatch structures, not likely to survive in any climate except this one. The home we entered was larger than most. It had a solid wood floor with mats that provided seating. The service was in progress as we approached and we recognized the tune (but not the words) of an old familiar hymn. There was a pile of shoes outside the door, which was a clue about what we should do with ours. About thirty Cambodian adults sat on the floor with open hymn books. Children leaned against mothers. A chicken walked through the room. Someone hammered nearby. An airplane roared overhead, and the meeting had to stop for a few moments. It was a curious mix of old and new to be sitting in a bamboo hut with all sound drowned out by an airplane.

As I scanned the room, and especially the children, a small boy caught my attention. He was sitting on his knees beside his mother and he turned to look at me. I remembered the little boy at the Buddhist shrine in Bangkok and for a crazy minute, this seemed to be the same child. He was about the same age and size and he was sitting on his knees. This boy was watching his mother and learning just as the Bangkok boy had done. His mother was singing heartfelt praise, worshiping as the other boy's mother had done, but this worship was different. I could not hold back the tears. *This is what I wanted to do. I wanted to bring people, both adults and children, in Cambodia and other places, any place—to the point of worshiping the true God.* At that moment, there was nowhere else that I would rather have been.

We had read security advice that westerners should remain in the capital city and even then to be out only in the daytime. That evening and for the rest of the week, we drove several hours out of the city and held services in a village of Christian Cambodians. We returned to the hotel late each night.

As we arrived, the worship was already in progress. These people had lost everything in a mudslide, been displaced from their village, survived in a refugee camp and come to the Lord under the ministry of an evangelist who went there to work. Now they had formed a new village of bamboo stick homes. Research has shown that people have lived in stick homes like these since at least one thousand years before the time of Christ. Life in the villages must be much the same as it has been for centuries: working the fields by hand, laying thatch for homes, weaving cloth for clothing, cooking over an open fire, sleeping together on bamboo mats in a single room, no medical care, little education, the stifling dust of dry season, the flooding of wet season and the open ditches behind the huts for body waste (without toilets or enclosures of any kind). The people had gathered together praying together and worshipping with a fervor I had never seen. The church was packed with about two hundred adults and an abundance of children. They loved a contemporary praise song that was familiar to me, but I did not know it well enough to place it. They usually opened and closed every gathering with it. The emotion in their voices carried me with them in worship, but I did not know the words. Several months later, when I was back in the United States, the song came on the radio when I was driving my car. I remembered it as the oft repeated song in Cambodia. It was a moving praise and evangelistic song, with words (now in English) about filling the world with His glory and setting hearts on fire. Their hearts *were* on fire and it spread to mine. I had to pull the car over to the side of the highway and I sobbed. I was shaking and broken in emotional pieces for about an hour before I could drive again. I did not know what the Lord was doing in my heart and my life, but something was happening.

It is difficult to describe the feeling of connection with God's people in a culture where almost nothing else can be found in common. I felt welcomed and comfortable. The services went long, but it mattered not. It was just a joy to be with them. The blessing was more than I can express. It was also humbling to see these people, with so much spiritual joyfulness, who had nothing materially.

I met Jenla that night, a pretty twelve-year-old girl, who liked to be near me. Every night she came to me and helped in small ways. She did not speak any English, however she taught me some words in her own language, and we were communicating a little bit. I walked around the village some, visiting in the homes and Jenla stayed beside me, making introductions without language, helping me find the way back to the church. I never met her family or knew where she lived or what her circumstances were. I do not know if she went to school. Those are all things that I would know about a girl like her if I went into a village today and met her. Now I would have a way to help her, but at that time, I suffered in my helplessness. I dreaded the last day that we were in the village. It seemed likely that I would never see her again, and I have not. I had no way to maintain the contact. She is out of my reach. But she did know the gospel, and she was hearing God's Word regularly. Years later, I would remember Jenla as I set up sponsorship for other children like her. As a young girl stood before me in Nepal or any of our countries, and we processed her information, I sometimes remembered the gentle girl from Cambodia. I wonder if she is safe and whether she has been able to finish some education. I would love to know how the Lord is using her life. If I could, I would have sponsored Jenla. I could not have solved all of her problems, and even today, I cannot do that with our children. If a sponsorship program was available for her, I could have almost guaranteed her education. I could have kept in contact with her and been a part of her life. I would have a contact in her country and her area who would know if some major event affected her. I longed for all of these things that were not possible.

More than half of Cambodia's population was under fifteen years old. Their leaders had fled the country or been executed. The new generation coming up was forming their own culture. Cambodia was traditionally Buddhist, but the leadership was gone and the devastation left the remaining people with little hope from their religion. The young Cambodians were very open and willing to listen to the gospel, although a troubling reality was that they were open to anything fed to them by others as well.

Michael and I made another trip to Cambodia a few years later. We met Cipho (pronounced: see-poe). Cipho was a tiny woman, small even for Cambodia. She stood less than five feet tall, with a slight bone structure and delicate features. Her hair was jet black, coarse and wavy, typical of her people. She wore loose slacks and a long sleeved blouse. Her English was quite good, but the natural high pitch to her voice, almost a little girl squeak, made it difficult for me to understand her speech. She looked at least a decade younger than the thirty-five years that she claimed. As a teen, she had seen her mother and brother murdered by the Khmer Rouge soldiers. She lived in a refugee camp for a period of time. Somehow she had received a good education, including the study of English, and she had come to the Lord.

We stopped by the bamboo home of a family that was caring for Cipho's very tiny eighteen-month-old daughter, Elizabeth, during these few days while Cipho was working with us. The baby had been born prematurely and was probably nutritionally deprived, then orphaned when her mother died from the complications of the birth. Cipho had adopted her. Elizabeth had been recently hospitalized and still did not look well. As we arrived, she was standing naked by a bucket of water, receiving a bath. Cipho immediately took over her care and cuddled her for a few minutes.

Our next stop was to see the church in Cipho's village. As part of her support for her ministry work, Cipho is allowed to live in the church. The building was more solidly constructed than most of the others in the village. It was two stories of sturdy cinder block and wood. The main level was a large open room with a tile floor and folding chairs leaning against one wall. It was a simple room, with only a few pieces of furniture, but it was clean and obviously a place of worship. A small room in the back was a kitchen, better equipped than most others we had seen. A steep, narrow staircase in one corner led to the upper level. This floor was built of sturdy planks with every room opening to a central porch. Cipho's room had an American type bed with a mattress and pillow. She had a small table and lamp. There was a shelf with a few books. Her lifestyle was not comfortable, but she was a step above the desperate poverty that was so common, and her home was secure.

Cipho's husband and oldest son lived in Phnom Penh. I never learned an explanation for her family circumstances. Cipho referred to the man as her husband, but she said he now had another wife. One natural son, thirteen years old, lived with Cipho and she had two adopted children—the baby, Elizabeth, and a little boy, three years old who had been orphaned. Cipho's father was elderly, crippled and in extremely poor health. Her young stepmother had at least a half dozen small children, Cipho's half siblings. Though they lived elsewhere, Cipho provided for them as well as her own three children from her one hundred dollars monthly ministry support.

Even after the war, the Khmer Rouge continued to terrorize the people. The purpose was to keep its presence known and to try to rebuild power, I suppose. A rail line existed, but foreigners were not allowed to ride it because of fear of being kidnapped by Khmer Rouge. The rule existed not only to protect the foreigners, but to cut down on vandalism and hijacking of the train system, which terrorized the citizens and disrupted travel. The Kymer Rouge blew up bridges, and tyrannized city leaders and educators, and spread thousands of land mines in rice fields. If an aid group came along and cleared out the land mines, Khmer Rouge might return in the night and plant them once again or maybe they would wait two or three nights before they planted again. Workers could never really know if their fields were safe. A common practice was to send a small girl through the fields before the men entered to test the safety. The little girl was the most expendable, the least risk for the common good.

An entry in a travel book about the city of Sisophon was rather short. It warned that Sisophon was off limits to visit. Khmer Rouge presence in the area made it too dangerous to go there. Sisophon is where we were headed the next morning.

Knowing that I am a nurse, Cipho offered to take me to visit a Cambodian Hospital. It was a surprisingly large facility, with many simple concrete buildings, all centered with an open courtyard. A group of young men were playing volleyball in the yard. They all looked very healthy. Cipho said they were probably staff. We toured a few similar buildings—the admission building, the outpatient rooms, a lab with very little equipment. All of the buildings had tile floors that were the norm in Asia, and large open windows without glass or screens. A wide overhang protected from rain. The open windows were necessary for air flow in the heat. A family member *must* remain with each patient to give personal care, help with toileting, providing food and cooking it. If a doctor prescribes medicine, the family member must go to the pharmacy in the town, purchase it and bring it to the hospital. The walls and floor were filthy with years of grime. The beds were large wooden platforms, with a headboard, footboard and wood slats in between. There were no mattresses, pillows or linens unless brought in by the patient. Most patients lay directly on the wood frame. None had any covering over them. None was needed in the heat. I did not see any trash receptacles. Trash was littered on the floor—old bandages, remains of meals, even needles—and most of the people were barefoot.

The children's building had six beds to a room. Cipho stepped to each bedside and asked the reason for the hospitalization, then turned to translate it for me. Most were babies or very small children less than three years old. They lay naked on the wooden slats. All had an intravenous line in and most had a plastic bag of ice cubes on their chest to treat fever. Malaria was a common answer to Cipho's question. One child had dengue fever. One child had meningitis and suffered blindness and paralysis—brain damage from the high sustained fever. Another child had tetanus with limbs horribly contracted as is characteristic of that disease.

The next wards were occupied by adults with about twelve beds in each.

Sometimes it was difficult to identify the patient. No accommodations were made for families. Most were sprawled on the bed, sometimes three or four family members with one patient. A bag of rice and rice cooker leaned against many of the bedposts.

Cipho continued speaking to each patient and sometimes asked me to pray for one. She stopped by one man, obviously close to eternity. He was passed consciousness, blood dried around his mouth, and the "death rattle" in his breathing. I hoped my prayer gave some comfort to his family, who sat stoically waiting for the end.

The next ward was filled with recent amputees. Most were young men in their twenties missing a leg just below the knee and usually a vicious wound on the other leg. The stumps were bandaged, but the other wounds, some more than a foot long were left open. All of these were victims of land mine explosions, and of course, these were only the ones who survived. Small girls, the most common victims, did not survive.

The next ward was men's medical. We walked through, stopping for a moment by each bed as Cipho asked about the medical problem. We came to a man who looked miserable. He was taking short gasps of breath, certainly in pain. His face was set in hopelessness and resignation. Cipho told him that we would pray for him which triggered a Khmer conversation.

Cipho turned to me and said, "He asks who we will pray to." It was a good question. I grinned at Cipho and she chattered on with the man. A woman, who seemed to be his wife, listened intently and there were several other family members listening as well.

Cipho turned to me and calmly said, "He has heard of Jesus Christ and wants to receive Him as Savior." Then she waited for me to answer.

"Cipho... is he a Buddhist? " I asked. I guessed that there was not much chance that he had been brought up in Sunday School and had some basic grounding in Scripture.

"Yes, he is Buddhist," Cipho was saying, "but he has heard of Jesus Christ and wants to receive Him as Savior."

I tried to encourage Cipho to share the gospel with him, but she only stood waiting for me. The man was waiting for me too. It is certainly possible that he was being manipulative and hoped to receive some financial benefit from the American, but it was also possible that eternity hung in the balance. Evaluating the authenticity of his desire was not my job. For the next few minutes, I shared the gospel with him. Cipho translated smoothly beside me. I spoke for about thirty minutes, aware that he did not need a theology degree, but he did need to know *Who* Jesus was and that we were praying to Him.

Family members and some of the patients from the other beds in the ward gathered around us. People from outside the building were hanging in the open windows. More people happened by and joined the group. A crowd was forming, and I was preaching the gospel in Cambodia to an audience of Buddhists.

When I finished all that I had to say, I asked the man if he understood what I had said. "Understand some," was the response Cipho translated. I would have to say the same thing myself. Regarding God's Word and the way He saves us, I also only understand some.

"Do you believe the things that I have said?" I asked him.

His answer came in Cipho's soprano chirp. "Yes, I believe!" I felt my heart thrill at the words and my control threatened to break. It was a precious, sacred moment and one that I will always remember.

"Do you want to give your life to Jesus Christ and follow Him?" I asked and he acknowledged that he did. I asked Cipho to take the lead now. I did not want the translation to detract from this new birth. A gentle smile replaced the hopelessness in the man's expression.

The crowd of people had not moved. I asked if anyone else here wanted to follow Jesus Christ. Several women indicated that they did. Cipho and I moved from one of them to another, speaking for a few minutes and praying with each one. The man's wife told us that she had prayed along with him. A patient across the room, attached to an intravenous line, waved to get our attention. He also wanted to follow Jesus Christ. As we spoke and prayed with each one of these, Cipho gave each one the contact information for her church. She promised them that she would return tomorrow to visit each one and bring them a Bible.

Night had fallen when we left the hospital and our van was a long way away. Cambodia did not have streetlights. As Cipho and I walked through the dark streets, I do not know whether I have ever felt more fully secure and aware of the presence of the Lord beside me.

Next morning as we prepared to go to Sisophon, I dumped some bugs out of my glass before pouring my drink into it. At the beginning of the trip, the incident would have been noteworthy, but at this point, it just did not matter. The important thing was that I saw them before I swallowed them.

The drive was among the worst in my life. The dirt road was a series of potholes and ruts. We were jostled about, bumped and thrown against the side of the vehicle. My head hit the ceiling several times. I was holding on, but my arms were jerked until they ached. The dust outside made a thick cloud. Even with the windows tightly up, my sunglasses kept clouding over with dust. We passed walkers and bicyclists, all with cloth wrapped around their faces, trying to manage the dust. Cambodia was nearing the end of hot season. Things had been dry for a long time.

Our room in Sisophon was just inside the hotel entrance. The only window opened to the indoor hallway and had curtains on the outside (in the hallway) enabling anyone interested to check on the occupants of the room. We had an air conditioner, but it was almost useless. It blew air, but did not get cool.

The plan for the day was a medical clinic in a nearby village. I was the only medical person in the group. I am not a doctor, however I would simply do the best I could to be of some help. In a place like this, even over-the-counter medicines could not be had because of cost or knowledge. Cipho and I unpacked and organized the medicines. I had brought a lot of them from the United States. Some had been bought in Cambodia.

The church was the same stick construction as most of the buildings. This one was on ground level rather than raised up as the others. It was about ten by twenty feet with two small windows and a thatch roof. We sat on wooden benches without backs.

The people were gathering quickly and soon began crowding into the little church building, blocking the air flow on a day that probably approached 105 degrees. We worked for five hours without a break. Cipho translated as each person described his ailment. I distributed aspirin, acetaminophen, vitamins, antacids, anti-diarrheals, antibiotic eye drops, antibiotic and antifungal ointments, lice shampoo, worm medicine, cough syrup, and some broad spectrum antibiotics.

Most of the patients were children with their mothers. A common complaint was fever, made even more miserable in the hot, dry climate. I could not know the source of the fever and it worried me that it could be a simple, self-limiting virus, or a life-threatening disease that needed a proper diagnosis and specific treatment. I gave aspirin and acetaminophen, but over and over I told a mother that her child was very sick. He needs to go to the hospital. When a family is struggling for food and survival, medical care might be out of reach, even if the condition is serious. As I recommended the hospital again, a mother's eyes seemed to be saying, "Can't you help? "

One little girl, about nine years old had advanced jaundice and her skin was hot with fever and she could barely stand. I gave her mother "the talk" about going to the hospital; however I knew that it was unlikely that she would take her. If she was the only one, I would have taken her myself, but I had seen a dozen children already who needed to be hospitalized.

Several children had hacking coughs. I listened to the chest of each one with my stethoscope. If anything unusual moved around in there, I gave them a course of antibiotics. If the chest sounded clear, I gave them cough syrup and vitamins. One child had scabies. I had no medication specifically for that, but the lice shampoo would help. If a mother said her child had worms, I gave her the pills for that without trying to confirm the diagnosis. They knew more about worms than I knew. An older man came complaining of an upset stomach and cough. I gave him antacids and cough syrup. "He is a very important man," Cipho whispered to me, "a general in the Army." I wondered which army?

A woman, about thirty-five and obviously very sick, entered the little church and struggled to a place where she could sit. We had no organizational support for the clinic. There was no way to see the people in any kind of sequence. When I finished with one person, another moved into her place. It was not really a push and shove situation; people were concentrating on advancing forward as those ahead of them were seen. I knew that she would have difficulty claiming ground and she had probably been outside for a while already. I stopped the next person from coming and gestured for her. She painfully made her way to me and my heart was heavy with the knowledge that I probably could not help her very much. She had chest pain, abdominal pain, difficulty breathing and weakness. Her palms were sickly pale. Her heart rate was fast and erratic. Her abdomen was tender everywhere that I touched. Her symptoms could have been surgical, but my judgment was medical. Her illness was acute now, but she had the "look" of someone with a longstanding disease, possibly cancer in the later stages. I could not know for certain that it was cancer, but I did know that she was dying. As I looked into her eyes, I saw that she knew it too. I did not give her my talk about going to the hospital. This woman was so sick, that if she could have gone, she would have already, and maybe she had. Now Americans were in the village, giving out medicine and she had come for help.

I gave her some ibuprofen and vitamins. "I am sorry. These will not make you well, but I hope they will help you feel better." She nodded, gestured her thanks and slowly rose to leave. I watched her all the way out the door way, even with the crowd pressing around me. I was not ready for another patient yet. I stopped and took a drink from my water bottle. *Where was her family? What would it be like to be so sick and so very alone? How far would she need to walk to get home?*

Cambodia cannot care for her sick as America does. I knew that. On the day this woman dies, hundreds of Cambodian people will also die. With the high infant mortality rate, many of them will be younger than she. But this woman was a little too familiar, too close to my own age. If I have a twinge of pain, I can ride in my comfortable car and wait in an air-conditioned office to see a qualified physician, who will help me or send me to another one who can. God may hear me complain silently, if not aloud, about how long I have to wait or how much I need to pay. If I need a medical test, I may fret about the physical discomfort of the procedure or the emotional anxiety of awaiting the results. I probably will not fill my heart with gratitude to the Lord that I can have the test, that the equipment used is sterile and works properly, that the results are accurate, that the medication or further treatment needed is available, that He has already provided the means to pay for it, and that my future is secure no matter the results. I remembered that my days are in His hands just as those of the Cambodian people are—and their eternal home can be just as secure as mine.

A woman and her child patiently waited and I turned my attention back to the clinic. None of the babies were diapered and I was caught in a urine stream at least twice. Hours passed and the crowd seemed to grow no smaller. One of the men in our group stepped in to say, "Sue, there is a sick baby coming." I barely acknowledged him. *What did he think these were all around me?* I had been seeing sick babies all day, but there was something urgent about the tiny naked person coming through the door. I stopped the random progression of people to reach for her. She was flaccid and unmoving and my first thought was that she was dead. I quickly put my stethoscope on her back. She was not dead, but definitely not well. Her heartbeat was fast, as it should be for a newborn, but it did not sound normal to me, though I claim no expertise in pediatric cardiology. She did not have a fever, but newborns can be very ill without one. Her mother said she was five days old and the umbilicus seemed to be at the expected point of healing for that age. She was very small, but might not have been premature. Cambodians are genetically small people and it was common practice in the village for a pregnant woman to severely restrict her food intake in the last months. The hope was to have a small baby that delivers easily. It seems incredulous, but these people have seen women die horribly after days of writhing in labor with a baby that could not pass through the birth canal and this is their solution. Newborns have a rough start after such maternal nutritional deprivation.

As I was doing my exam of the baby, Cipho was talking to the young mother. "She cannot make milk," Cipho said.

"What?" I pinched the baby's skin and it stayed exactly in place. *Dehydration.* That was the problem. The nutritional deprivation during the pregnancy certainly contributed to the problem of her milk production. This baby needed fluids and quickly. I told the mother that she needed to drink lots of clean, boiled water, eat good food and get rest. Hopefully, her milk would come. For now, we needed to get one of the other nursing mothers to feed this baby.

Cipho did not translate that. "No, they will not." She said.

"What?" I said again. *The baby would die!* This was probably a perfectly healthy baby, starving before our eyes. We had seen dozens of nursing mothers from this village today. Was it possible that not one of these women was a friend of this mother and might help her, at least now in this emergency situation? I decided that I would fix this situation. I would find a woman and pay her, if necessary. This baby needed milk. Even as it was, we would have to drip the milk into her mouth. She was too weak to suck.

"No one will do it," Cipho said again, though she was not aware of my thoughts of paying one of them. "She would be afraid of not having enough milk for her own baby." This baby would need milk from a surrogate for at least two years, if her own mother's milk did not come. That was a lot of money to leave with her. She would probably find something urgent to spend it on or her husband might take it from her. If we had sponsorship in place, we could divide it into smaller parts, but we had no structure to manage such a plan.

"Can we buy some bottles and powdered milk?" I asked Cipho.

"Yes, in the market," she said.

So it was possible, but how could I make it happen? There were still many people waiting to see me and more sick babies. I could not give her money in front of all the others and I wanted to be sure she was able to buy the milk. This girl had just given birth. How far would she have to walk in the heat to get to the market? Would the baby survive through all of the necessary steps? How could I get a ride for her? Then the answer occurred to me. I do not know why it took me so long to think of it. We had a hired car and a driver. Michael was waiting outside for me.

About that time, another man from our group stepped into the church. I handed him the baby and told him to take her to Michael. The mother did not know what was going on, but she would follow her baby. "Ask Michael to take this girl to the market, buy bottles and powdered milk and then take her home," I said to him. "And give the girl a bottle of our water as soon as you are out of sight." We needed to hydrate the mother as well as the baby. I knew that there was a Cambodian man with Michael who could translate. They could do the market trip and I would continue in the clinic. I did not have much hope for the baby's survival. I suffered from regret for not finding some breast milk immediately to drip into the baby's mouth. Her need was urgent, but as our car pulled out of the church yard, the opportunity to do anything more ended. Other sick babies were waiting.

As we returned to our hotel that night, bouncing roughly along, I succumbed to a satisfying and overwhelming fatigue. I did not care that my hair was askew or that my clothes were soaked in sweat. I knew that I looked awful and smelled terrible and that my body defenses were probably fighting off some bugs they had never encountered before….and none of that mattered.

Years later, I happened to meet with our contact for this village once again. He told me that the baby lived! She was strong and healthy. I questioned him carefully to determine that she was the same child. He knew the mother and family well. He was certain that she was the one they took to the market that day to buy bottles and milk.

I cried a lot in Cambodia. The Lord was preparing me for many things to come. I learned a lot of lessons and gained a lot of experience. My love for the work in Asia began in Cambodia. Years later, when we founded Allow The Children, these experiences were a part of our history that molded the structure of the ministry. Cambodia is certainly a part of the story of Allow The Children.

Burundi

Burundi is a land-locked African country suffering from both poverty and the aftermath of years of war. Most of the people are poor farmers. It has all of the problems of a developing country including illiteracy, underemployment, political instability, poor transportation, inadequate medical care and overwhelmed utilities. More than half of the population is under fifteen years of age and less than half of those receive any education at all.

Allow The Children Ministry began in Burundi through Jim and Vicki Brooks, who made their first trip in 2004. They found an existing ministry operating a school for the blind and a school for the deaf that needed all kinds of help. Sponsorship for these precious children was set up and begun. We soon had a ministry list of blind African children who could go to school and eat and receive needed care with sponsorship help. They learned music and crafts which could help them to earn income as adults, and they learned about the Lord. Likewise, a list of deaf children was added and as we helped them, another deaf child and then another was able to come to the school. Most of these children had no language before they arrived. Learning sign was the first step to the rest of their education and it opened the way for them to "hear" the gospel. Families might be ashamed of handicapped children, keeping them hidden away with little food and never letting them go outside or have any life experiences except what they had in a small room. Many of the children had histories like this before coming to the school. The school was not only providing education, but literally their lives.

Allow also connected with a ministry that operated a clinic and received abandoned babies. Many of the babies were born to mothers who had AIDS. Chances were high that the babies were also infected and finding someone to care for them was difficult. They formed a plan of recruiting Christian widows as foster mothers. These women were usually in need themselves, but sponsorship met the needs of the babies as well as providing significant help for the widows.

I wanted to personally sponsor one child from Burundi. I chose a child the same way most sponsors do—a small child with a cute photo. The one I settled on was a beautiful little girl, an orphan, about five years old. She was wearing a blue denim jumper and pulling one sleeve of it up as she stared directly into the camera. I taped her photo on the spot near my computer where I would see it often. I deposited three months sponsorship and began a pattern of daily prayer for her. As my eye caught her photo several times a day, I often wondered what she was doing and what her life was like. She lived in a very needy, overcrowded orphanage and I knew they were regularly short of food. We were trying to build up their operating support with sponsorship, but it was just getting started and the need was still urgent. I wondered if she was hungry and ached to think of the likely answer. At least we were doing something to help and every sponsor added on for her program helped. About a year after we started, some serious problems developed among the leaders of the home. We had no choice but to end the partnership and withdraw our support. I fully agreed with the decision. It had to be done, although it meant dropping the sponsorship for my child. I was surprised at how much emotion I felt about it. Praying specifically for someone truly does form a special bond and I still think of the little girl often. My new child, a boy, was in our Rainbow program. His mother died from AIDS and he was HIV positive. His foster mother was also his aunt, his mother's sister, and she had a child of her own.

Rainbow is a delightful African ministry that might have become a children's home for orphaned and abandoned babies. Instead, it developed into a foster care program, matching babies in need of families with Christian families willing to help. In many cases, it was a widow, herself in need, who accepted care of a baby. We assigned sponsors, which provided a flow of funds meeting needs of the widows and the children. The Rainbow ministry supervises the use of the funds, the care and well-being of the children and provides medical care.

It was November 2008 when I first visited Burundi. I came in after a ministry trip to Nepal and landed a day before Michael arrived. He was coming from the United States and would continue on to Nepal after our overlap in Burundi. I would return to the United States. We actually traveled like this a lot back in those years. We would schedule so that we could meet somewhere to do something together or just to be together for a few days.

Jim and Vicki Brooks were fully managing the Burundi ministry and raising all of the funding for it. We did not intend any active role during this trip. We wanted to see it and meet the partners, just because it was part of Allow The Children. We had been looking forward to it for a long time. Because of the schedule to include Burundi, I traveled through the busy London airport as a hub. I was changing from a major airline to a small African Airline and sure enough, my luggage did not make it onto the flight. I had one change of clothes and some necessities of life in my carry on piece, and that is all that I would have for the week in Burundi.

My first impression of Burundi (and Africa) was that it did not look so very different than the other places in the world where we had traveled. Though it was my first time on the African continent, I had been to India, Thailand, Cambodia, Laos, Vietnam, and of course, Nepal. There were many similarities, but every country has its own special flavor.

The body of the Christ is the same all over the world. I was greeted by dear believers and we experienced the sweet fellowship that comes with those who are bound together in the Lord. Home base was a ministry compound with a large church appropriately in the middle. It was the mother church of many others.

The deaf school was in the compound, now educating over one hundred students, the only school for the deaf in the country. It offered education only through the sixth grade level, which is huge in the lives of these children. After graduating, the stronger students tested for secondary school. If they were successful, they attended with hearing students, having to find a way to pay for it on their own. The other option is a two-year sewing course that provided a good income-potential skill for a deaf student.

Another important ministry was the Timothy Bible School. Allow had done some projects to help with the construction of the building. It now stood as a nice classroom, a sleeping room full of bunks and a small office/library. On the opposite side of the bunk room was a kitchen and dining tables. About thirty village church leaders gathered for training for a month several times each year. It is a structured training, with teachers coming in regularly; the missionaries on the ground taking their turns as well. As these men receive training it is multiplied over and over throughout the country. It is exciting to think of the spiritual impact.

The last of our ministries was the school for the blind, which was about forty minutes away. Three very simple buildings stood in a semi-circle, facing a grassy center ground. One was a dorm for about sixty blind and visually impaired students. Another was divided into three classrooms, and the third was an office on one end, a multi-purpose gathering room in the middle, and a kitchen/dining room on the opposite end. The blind students had a craft teacher who filled the important role of training them to do something that could bring income. Beautiful baskets and trays were stacked all about the room ready for any opportunity to be sold.

Michael arrived in Burundi the next morning. I was sick with fever, dizziness, weakness, and nausea. Besides feeling miserable, there was also the question of whether I could be a danger of contagion to those around me. These factors needed to be considered when deciding my participation in the plans of each day.

I missed the morning worship service, though I could hear the singing from the flat. It was uniquely beautiful. I expected the rhythm and the beat. The melody was familiar and different at the same time. The source of the volume was enthusiasm as much as numbers. I was greatly disappointed at missing the fellowship with them.

We spent a day with the Rainbow Center, surrounded by the children and their foster families. The children were remarkably normal, considering their traumatic histories. Many of them were running about and happily enjoying the time together with others who they obviously knew well. The children were growing up in families with love. We were distributing bags of staples today. The little boy I sponsored was part of this program and I enjoyed meeting him that day. I thought again of the little girl who was in an orphanage somewhere nearby. I wished that I could visit her, but there was no reason to go and I knew it would not be a good idea. Like so many others, she was out of my reach, but I *could help* the ones in the Rainbow ministry. This was our assignment from the Lord and we needed to serve it faithfully, giving our best to Him.

As the gathering time with Rainbow moved toward the end, we had a wonderful treat. A band of Burundian drummers marched into the yard and presented a performance that would have been tragic to miss. They were tall men, who seemed to be jumping at least their height while marching in neat formations and keeping their steady drum cadence. It was a piece of traditional Burundian culture and I loved it.

On another day, we drove up into the mountains to see a people and a ministry planted in a very poor rural area. I missed most of the experience because of my health issues. I was lying down in the back of the van for most of the trip. When we stopped, I tried to rise up and join the group, but I could barely walk because of dizziness. I remember beautiful mountain ranges and little village churches made of the local materials. At one stop, the people filled the church and we had a time of worship together. I was there, but struggling physically and was not able to be fully involved.

Thankfully, we were able to meet the objectives of the trip. We met the leaders. We saw the work. We spent some time with the children's ministries and we visited some churches that had been built or at least roofed through Allow The Children. Despite my illness, the trip was a blessing and I had obtained a good overview of the ministry, which was an important goal. I had breathed the air of Africa and felt the dirt on my feet. The faces of the people were stored in my memory and I knew that I could find my way back.

Over the next few years, we watched the development of the ministry through the frequent photos and reports that came back to us from the field. The church planting and the pastor training seemed to explode and flourish. As quickly as little churches were built, others were waiting. The Word was going forth in Burundi. Timothy Bible School grew in numbers and structure. The students were men who were already leading churches, who came in for short periods of intense study. Allow The Children was actively recruiting and sending teachers for two sessions a year and funding the costs of those sessions. The schools for the deaf and blind were also growing and serving the needs of children who literally had nowhere else to go. They were making lives for themselves on earth and making ready for eternity as well. It was a very good ministry, very good—and very used of God.

Jim and Vicki committed their full attention and investment in Burundi and they did a good job. For that reason, Michael and I gave our time to the other countries. We did not intend to allow six years to pass before visiting Burundi again, but somehow it happened. The Brooks were both struggling with long-term medical issues that prevented them from travel. They managed the United States side of the work for a while, but the time came when they reluctantly needed to step down. Our office was already managing the finances. We easily integrated the Burundi sponsorship data with all of our other country records. The difficult step was to transfer the decision making and leadership role.

We needed to make a trip to Burundi and so it was booked for September in 2014. Four of us made the trip, each with an individual agenda. Mine was to meet with every ministry leader, form a strong line of communication, move the relationships forward and ultimately make a smooth transition. Michael shared all of these goals and also had plans to do some teaching in a village.

I remembered the Burundi leaders from the earlier trip and it was incredibly valuable that we had made at least that one trip. I had a few questions and a few changes to make in the management of the sponsorship programs. I processed some new children and I committed to some small projects that the ministry needed. The programs depended heavily on the sponsorship and they were probably worried about it. I made a deliberate effort to set them at ease. We all needed to move forward with confidence and we did.

The trip could not have gone better. The Burundian leaders welcomed us graciously and facilitated everything we needed to do. We had good conversations that helped us all understand the various roles and responsibilities of each of us and how the organization would look as we moved forward. There were some administrative issues to clarify, but no conflicts at all. We enjoyed good quality time with each ministry group and felt their gratitude that we were willing to continue the partnership with them. We came to understand the relationships and the structure of the national leadership in ways that just cannot happen except in person. A highlight was a night when the whole group went out to a restaurant for dinner. It was an outdoor seating area under a thatch roof. We were on the shoreline of the beautiful lake that forms part of Burundi's border. The waves gently lapped the beach and a cool breeze blew. All of the leaders were fellowshipping and interacting together as the family of Christ should do. A good translator sat beside me, which enabled me to interact with the others. We talked and laughed and ate. During that evening, we came to feel affirmed and accepted as a part of the group—and it was very, very sweet.

Ghana

The Allow Ministry in Ghana began in January 2014. Michael and I made a trip to visit a contact pastor, connected with us through one of our board members. Allow The Children was already working on the African continent, in Burundi. So while it was not our first step into Africa, Ghana was distinctively different. Ghana is a west coast country. Accra is a well-developed international city with good roads and modern buildings. The educated people speak English. White western tourists were not unusual. We stayed in a comfortable guest house with air conditioning and internet. Familiar food was not too hard to find. The weather was comfortably warm and the air felt clean.

The Ghanaian pastor led a large church in Accra that ministered to the children in their area. Schools were available in the capital city, but they cost money. Many of the poor children were not able to attend and therefore were growing up with no education at all. If the church could provide some education at any level at all, the children would come and they could be taught spiritual things as well.

They began with a few of the poor children, and those numbers quickly grew. The parents were street vendors, fruit sellers, or laborers. Fathers might be dead or deserters, crippled or unknown; intact functioning families were few. The various rooms in the church building were used for classrooms and some remodeling was done to define space for the different classes. The teachers were church members, mostly people who knew how to read and were willing to teach others. Qualified teachers taught in the government schools and received a paycheck. Teachers for this ministry school were paid little, if anything at all. There were very few books or materials. Only some of the children had uniforms and many of those were in poor condition. Walking about the classrooms, it seemed that the teachers were doing an excellent job with next to nothing in materials or equipment. The children could not write, but they could recite, and they could learn many things.

Especially impressive was the report that there was a small group of Muslim students at the school and a few of them had come to the Lord. For their own safety, their faith was walked in secret, but it was exciting to hear that these students were growing and learning and that they remained fully assimilated in the Muslim community. When they were mature and grounded, they would be in prime positions to influence others among their own people.

When we spent a few days in the village, we saw the conditions that we know well—poverty, bamboo huts, field laborers, bicycles as transportation. Naked children played in the dirt and babies were usually tied to a mother's back.

We saw an "open air" church. It was a building made of bamboo with a good tin roof, but walls were not built solidly. Vertical bamboo shoots were placed about four inches apart, creating a defined space and support for the roof, while leaving unrestricted air flow. It was a good idea. Non-attenders could see what was going on inside and perhaps be drawn to join in worship. The cost was virtually nothing, except for the tin.

We asked to use a toilet in one village and someone showed us the path across the road from the stick homes. I have used a variety of toilet facilities in my travels. I expected a hand built "squat" toilet perhaps with walls of mudbricks, textile or even plastic tarp. Nope. As I followed the "women's path" through heavy vegetation, I came to a dirt pit, wide and deep enough to be a basement if in the United States. Loose wooden planks, about three inches wide, spanned the pit. I had no benefit of a demonstration, but evidently one would take a walk out over the pit and squat somehow between the planks. Multiple planks provided for accommodating several simultaneous users. There was no hand hold of any kind, but stability would be a major goal. Falling in the pit was just unthinkable. It took me less than seconds to determine that I did not have the life skills for this and I chose an alternative. When we returned to the car, Michael shared a description of a similar experience on the "men's path."

We arrived at the destination village, where the people were already gathered and singing. The church was packed. We could feel the emotion as we approached. The crowd opened places for us and we were soon joining in with the beautiful African worship. Michael spoke that night. We slept soundly with our hearts already knitting together with the brethren in Ghana.

When we returned to the city, I spent a day taking the photos of the school children and writing the history report forms. The school enrollment was over one hundred, more than I could reasonably expect to cover with sponsors any time soon, but I wanted to have the materials for sponsorship in hand. We started a small sponsorship program for children of pastors as we have in our other countries.

On the project list was remodeling and equipment restocking for the kitchen, uniforms, and consumable work books. As we joined in partnership, we would fund the school's efforts in educating the children and sharing the gospel.

All of our other ministries were a fit for Ghana—pastor training, church planting, medical clinics, more sponsorship. We looked forward to the future and what the Lord would give us to do in Ghana.

Haiti

Haiti was called the poorest country in the western hemisphere, even before the earthquake of 2010. Recovery was still very evident when we first went to the island in 2013. Tent cities were common. Rubble was still piled about the streets. Poverty is the way of life.

The source of my contact with ministry in Haiti is a little amazing, except for the Hand of God which is most certainly the explanation for it all. Let me see if I can remember all of the deliberate and unlikely steps: (1) My childhood pastor left the church and went on to another ministry when I was still very young. I remember him and his wife, but there is really no reason why he would have remembered me. They moved several states away and we had no mutual friends or continued contact. (2) Somehow they connected with our ministry and were on our newsletter list for years. How did they ever find me under my married name? (3) They had no child when I knew them, but later on had a daughter. This daughter was a full-time special education teacher in the United States and also very involved with a mission group in Haiti, eventually forming a small ministry organization of her own. (4) I never even met their daughter, but she contacted me a few times inviting me to travel to Haiti with her. I usually answered with an invitation to Nepal.

I had no particular interest in Haiti and no personal desire to go there. I knew it was a poor country, but whenever I thought of it, especially after the earthquake, my impression was that plenty of aid work and evangelistic work was already going on there. I wanted to go to places that were less served. This attitude prevailed for quite a while, but Haiti kept returning to my thoughts until the time came when I simply knew that I needed to go to Haiti. I did not have any sense about a specific place or ministry, but just a willingness to go and to see what the Lord put in front of my eyes. My Haiti ministry friend was not able to go when I needed to travel, but she set up the necessary appointments and introductions for me—interestingly not with her own ministry. She was not looking for more funding for her own work, only more help for the people she loved.

I have heard that there are numerous organizations already working in Haiti both for humanitarian and evangelistic purposes and I agree. It is true. I heard that there is widespread corruption at every level and I agree. It is true. I have heard that Haiti has high levels of dirt and crime and disease and I think that is true as well. Haiti also has children who fall through the cracks of all of that international aid; children who are victims of the corruption. They need committed believers of the family of Christ to stand with them in very difficult circumstances. I like to work in the hard places and for very different reasons than some of our other ministries—Haiti is certainly a hard place. In the end, the issue is not where a missionary wants to go or would find most pleasant to go, but where the Lord sends. Against my own preferences, I felt the impression from the Lord to serve Him in Haiti.

Michael and I landed in Port-au-Prince and settled into a nice guest house for Americans. We had driven through some rough, grimy streets to get there, but inside the walls, it was fresh and clean, colorful and safe. We were shown to a comfortable room, and a delicious dinner was shortly served. This was our home base. We must stay in, locked in, we were told, especially after dark. Venturing from the guest house seemed to be a flirt with danger. The vehicle, the escort, and the timing of any outing must be carefully planned. Our hosts were an American couple serving in Haiti as missionaries. The guest house was only one of their responsibilities. Several potential partners and ministries were scheduled for us to visit, beginning the following morning.

One of the places we visited was a children's home about three hours from the capital city. We had learned that over one hundred children were living there. The donors for the work had pulled out for reasons not completely clear. American donors drop for all kinds of reasons, both good reasons and sometimes not good reasons. One hundred children were too many for us to try to take in the beginning, but we agreed to make the visit. We found some simple but solid concrete structures built as a project of a church or ministry group that had no on-going involvement in the ministry. Scrap wood buildings trashed the compound. A huge tent, faded and torn, was the only place to gather a group. Most of the children were inside the tent when we arrived, singing under the leadership of a boy who could have been twelve. Some food was being cooked over an open fire off to one side. Finding shade in the hot sun was challenging, and any bit that I happened to see, such as a tree with branches, was already occupied by as many bodies as possible. Over all, it was a miserable, impoverished place that certainly needed help, but way beyond what we could support. The only possible reason to keep children in a place like this was that they had no other place to go, and that was the reason these were here.

We made another visit to a different orphanage, one of less than twenty children, who were also living in appalling conditions. The story was that they had lost their building in the earthquake, and were still trying to survive and recover. I took the photos and histories that we needed and hoped that we would be able to raise the living condition of these children before very long. I did not want to decline help to them because of their need, but I also cringed to call them an Allow The Children home. We had children's homes in other countries that were at a very minimal standard. What was the difference? I am not sure I can define it. I had come to Haiti to help. These were some children who needed help. The one hundred (plus) children's home was too much for us, but there was no rational reason to refuse the one of twenty children.

We also agreed to start a small children's home in a city about six hours away from the capital. It was the ministry desire of a single woman who came very strongly recommended by two pastors. She was working as a child evangelism leader for a group of several Baptist churches. She was very motivated and appropriately enthusiastic about the prospect of a partnership with us. She had a small rented house and the means to care for a few little girls. We would partner with her for the funding support and see what the Lord would do with it. With these two ministry projects, we had a toehold in this new country.

On my next trip into Haiti, I came alone and I stayed in a different guest house. The place we stayed in before was closed for one month while the house hosts made a trip back to the United States. This home was built into the city street with a gate at the front, but no side or back yard. It had three levels, accessed by a wonderful curved wooden staircase. I had a private room, but a shared bathroom at the end of the hallway. A happy American group was laughing and talking on the porch when I arrived, but when I returned that night, they had gone to return to the United States. As I ate dinner, a very thin, half grown cat joined me hoping for some scraps. The workers in the house chased it away, but when I had a chance, I shared a few morsels with it and I quickly became its favorite person. This guest house was managed by a Haitian man who lived nearby, off of the property with his wife and several children. He greeted me warmly and assigned my room, then he left for his home. The cook and one house worker also finished their work and left. It was a large house and I was fully alone. Fortunately, I enjoy solitude. I also enjoy thunderstorms. Some rain and thunderclaps were coming as darkness fell, and the storm escalated through the night. The electricity blinked a few times and then it was gone, but lightening brought nearly daylight that lasted for several seconds at a time. Just to complete the picture, the cat made a skin tingling *yeowl* at intervals. He must have been terrified by the storm. I walked about the dark house a few times trying to find him and call him to me, but he did not show himself. Though I was essentially alone, I knew that there was a guard at the front of the house. He must have been there, *because there is always a guard*, but I never saw him. It seems likely that I would have been afraid, but I was not—not at all. I had a wonderful night's sleep, listening to the storm.

The next day, I was scheduled to go out to the big orphanage. In between trips, I had received some pressure from some of the missionaries living in Haiti, to try to help the children there, and of course, I felt badly for them too. I still felt that it was too much for us, but perhaps I could start small and build. Any help was better than none. I was going to visit them again and reconsider what we could do. I had arranged a ride to the village which was several hours away. The plan was that I would stay in the orphanage for two nights and then the driver would return to pick me up. I would give them some money for my expenses. It would not be a comfortable stay, but I would survive it.

It was incredibly hot and the storm during the night had left the air heavy with humidity. Bugs of all kinds were everywhere. The children's home received me and showed me to a big plywood box "room" which would be my accommodation for the next couple of days. It was furnished with a simple wood framed bed and a table. My box house did not have a window, but the boards were not placed too closely together, which allowed for air flow. I did have a door that would latch from the inside and a clasp that effectively locked. The toilet was a short walk away, down the side of the property and around behind a building. I would need to make that walk at least once during the night. Under other circumstances, that might have been intimidating, but I was certain that I was very safe. No one wanted the potential donor to have an unpleasant experience.

In addition to the house father/potential partner, there were at least a half dozen Haitian men who seemed to have some role in the ministry. One was the always present guard and one was a gardener. The others did not seem to have a specific title, but one of them spoke minimal English and allowed me at least a little communication. Some women were there, going about different tasks, paying little attention to me. The children milled about on the grounds. There were more young children than I remembered from the last visit and fewer older ones.

I gave the men some money for my expenses and several of them immediately left the property. In an hour or so, they returned with a bag of ice poured into a chest. They brought orange juice, soft drinks, cheese, bread and peanut butter, a bag of cookies, potato chips and a case of about a dozen bottles of water. I could survive on these things for a couple of days.

It rained again during the night, although not quite as violently as the previous night. I did need to make the hike to the toilet, but my mind was on slippery puddles more than the distance and the dark.

In the morning, I spread thick and delicious peanut butter onto a slice of fresh loaf bread and drank directly from the orange juice container. I watched more than one hundred children line up for a cup of mushy porridge and a piece of flat bread. Various aid organizations were still providing staple supplies such as rice and beans, for orphanages. I had seen some bags of (presumably) food stuffs in the storage building—but not many bags for such a large group and nothing in addition to it.

We spent the day organizing children name lists, photos, and histories, which was time-consuming because of the language barrier. One of the men was translating for me, but it was a struggle. The whole group gathered under their tent and I enjoyed the singing, but the translator was not good enough for me to speak to them. I passed a second night with them, fretful and unable to relax, but with no clear reason why. My wooden box room was not dirty or unpleasant in any way. Everyone had been very hospitable to me and made me as comfortable as they could within their means. I was not even mildly anxious for my own safety. That was not the problem. I was not responding to the poverty. I have spent a lot of time among people who have nothing, both those who have lost all of their possessions and those who never had anything in the first place. That was not the problem. But something did not fit. I was not settled in my spirit about the partnership with this ministry. Of course, I did not need to feel happy or comfortable or excited about a new ministry. *What did the Lord want?* That was the only question.

My hired driver picked me up in the morning as scheduled. The ministry leaders were hoping for some assurance that I would become a regular donor for them but I was not ready to offer them, any   long-term commitment yet. I prayed about it on the way back to Port-au-Prince. I could not really define the problem; therefore it was difficult to discern an answer.

As I entered the guest house, the Haitian host called a greeting and then stepped out of his office to make some small talk about my ministry and activities in Haiti. He had no acquaintance with the other contacts who had originally asked me to consider partnership with the orphanage. As we talked, his tone and his expression changed from light to serious. This man had some totally unrelated experience with the same orphanage. He asked me questions and then I asked him some until we were both satisfied that we were discussing the same place. He told me about a recent guest who was the American donor for the home and who had separated from them for some of the best reasons there are. My host only knew part of the issues, but I heard enough to give him my email and asked him to pass it on to the previous guest. The man did contact me and the story he told me was confirmed by a pastor and another man who was near the end of the process to adopt a child from the orphanage. The orphanage was a fraud. Only a few stayed on the grounds full time. The others were brought in from their families in the surrounding neighborhoods to make a "performance" for a prospective donor and hopefully get some money. It is a known practice in Haiti. Allow The Children was spared from what would have been a painful episode. There are thousands of orphanages in Haiti and this one was three hours away. There are thousands of guest houses in Haiti. What are the random chances that this donor and I would have booked exactly the same guest house? Of course, it was not random. The Lord had planned the meeting, perhaps not intervening earlier so that I would have the learning experience.

The smaller home of twenty children that we took during the previous trip, also did not work out. That situation was different, but fraud was also involved.

The girls' home did successfully plant, though not without some problems. The housemother and I had some different expectations that needed to be worked through, but she did take good care of the girls. All evidence was that they were growing up in a healthy, God honoring-environment.

One Haitian pastor was starting to develop as our primary partner. He offered his help to drive me to other places I needed to go. He worked a schedule for me among others who wanted my time. He was a good translator and he made himself available or found another translator for me when I needed one. He wanted me to see a ministry that was important to him, and I agreed to go.

To say that the ministry was on the top of a mountain is not descriptive enough. It was a vertical, hand-built road with rocks and ruts, sharp curves and drop offs. The truck groaned all the way up. We created choking dust that completely covered people who were making the arduous climb by foot. At the top was a one-room church building that badly sagged to one side as if it would fall any moment. In the foreyard, was a new church building under construction—the project of another American group. Inside the church, we found over one hundred children being taught educational lessons. This was not an official government school. There was no school on the mountain. This was a pastor and a few of his people who were trying to impart some knowledge to children who would otherwise grow up with nothing. They were teaching the gospel, as well. They were giving the precious gift of education or at least reading and arithmetic and they were grounding their future church members.

The children were packed onto backless wooden benches and sat facing different directions according to their class. One class might touch backs and sides with another. Some of them had uniforms, but a great many did not. They had no materials, no tablets, no writing utensils, and no desks. But they could listen and recite and they were certainly doing that. Sponsorship would mean that they could get uniforms, materials and possibly some food. I began to take the photos and histories we would need to partner with this ministry. This was a good plan for God's people. The Haitian leaders on the ground were already doing what they could to assist the children. I felt very willing to join with them and bring our assistance. We called it the mountain school. It hung on the edge of the mountain top. We could walk right up to the cliff and see far and wide in all directions. It was an incredibly poor and breathtakingly beautiful place. If we are called to take the gospel to the *"ends of the earth,"* this is certainly one of the ends. It is a poor village, on a very difficult to access mountain, and aid groups are not likely to find it or want to go even if they knew of it. These are children who need a chance to hear the gospel and a chance for education to make this life better for themselves. It was a place that God had shown to Allow The Children.

The daughter of my childhood pastor had a friend who lived in Haiti and was trying to do what she could to help a little orphanage. She was an American girl, actually not a girl, but a mature woman in her thirties, with mission experience in two other countries in addition to her present term in Haiti. She visited the home almost daily. She knew the pastor/housefather well, and she had learned Creole. Her close work over a length of time is what compelled me to consider another orphanage after negative experiences with two others. The description of poverty and lifestyle in this home was the same as the others. The children were living in very minimal economic conditions. They did not have enough food. They needed help and their American guardian would work with me to get some sponsorship support. I set up the sponsorship and she made the opportunity known among her contact list. Sponsors started coming and we had some good support for them in an amazingly short time. A few came from our general resources, but the great majority was the work of this new contact. It was a good partnership and a good ministry. I felt confident in it from the beginning.

How does a small nation surrounded by the ocean on three sides have a desert quality dry season? Haiti was right at the end of such a season on one of my trips in for managing the sponsorship programs. It was hot and the ground was cracking. The rains were expected any day and all of the people were waiting eagerly for it. I was in Haiti for less than twenty-four hours before I joined them, watching the sky, thinking constantly of water and plumbing and being wet and clean once again. The water system in Haiti is to keep a reservoir on the roof. The rain filled the tank and supplied the water to the house for such things as washing and toilet flushing. Drinking water must be purchased separately by those who were able to pay for it. Also, for those who were able, wash water could be bought by truck. They would come by and fill up the roof reservoir and it would work the same as the rain.

My primary partner had graciously invited me to stay in his home this time. I loved being in the village community in any of our countries, which provides a completely different experience than staying in a tourist facility. Staying in the home with the partner is also the best way to build the relationship. He had bought water during the dry season and was now trying hard to make the last truck load last until the rains come, which could be any day, even today. What a waste to buy the water if the rains started today. His family consisted of his wife, three children, his brother's son, who lived with them and an American guest. I was given two bottles of water to drink each day and I could get more, if needed. For washing, I was given a small bowl of water only if I asked for it. I think they would have given me all I wanted, but the rest of the family needed it too. The toilet could not be flushed. One simply added to whatever was there and when absolutely needed, someone brought a bucket of water to dump into it. This is what was done in homes and in a service station along the highway or in a nice restaurant. Water did not run from any sink faucet. If desperate for hand washing, the only solution was to use your bottle of drinking water. It is the way of life during the dry season. Heavy dust blew constantly through the air. Haitian women keep their hair cut close to their heads or they wear a scarf about their heads. It is a good plan and I know why they do it. After a few days, my hair was full of dirt. Any attempt to rinse it made mud. Wearing a scarf is my plan for the future.

Over the next few days, we made the horizontal trip to visit the two children's homes and the vertical trip to the mountain school. This man with his truck and his translation skills and his church contacts had grown into the partner that I needed. We started a sponsorship program for pastors' children, as we have in our other countries. It is a help and encouragement to some faithful pastors as they minister to their people, and it also creates a group for pastor training and many ways for us to have an impact for the Lord in Haiti. It took more than two years before I felt that we were "planted" in Haiti. It was more difficult a task than of the other countries and I would hesitate at the thought of starting once again from the beginning. Haiti is a difficult country. It is an "uttermost part" of the earth in a completely different sense than geographical. With all of its many problems, it is also the home of dear, committed believers who are marching forward for the kingdom like all of the rest of us. We are so grateful that we can join with them and labor beside them.

Guatemala

Allow ministry in Nepal, Bangladesh and Burundi was growing well and very satisfying. We were traveling several times a year and often taking groups of others along. More and more people were showing interest and wanting to go along on our trips, but finding issues like the travel distance, time away from work and the costs irresolvable. I occasionally pondered the thought of establishing some work in a country closer by. If I heard of some possibility in Central America (for example) I perked up and listened. A Spanish speaking ministry would be a nice balance for the other things we did and we could fit a few short trips in between the longer ones to the other side of the earth. I never felt "called" to one specific country or even to one type of ministry. I was a missionary and part of what I loved to do was to provide a way for others to participate in a mission project.

One of our sponsors gave me a contact with a ministry in Guatemala. I pursued it only a little before I knew that I wanted to make a visit and see the whole organization. I began the arrangements. The potential partner was an American citizen of Guatemalan heritage. He was poor when he came to America, but built a successful business. His ministry was to help the people in Guatemala who still live in the terrible poverty he came from and take the gospel to them at the same time. The compound in Guatemala provides housing and meals for teams and facilitates projects and ministries of all kinds.

When Michael and I visited the ministry, we were impressed with everything we saw. A structure was in place to manage several teams of Americans, each with a project and agenda of their own. A trip could be planned to include construction or a work project of some kind along with preaching in churches, children's ministry, really whatever the team wanted. This was very different from our ministry in the other countries, but it accomplished a few important things. It allowed people to get a taste of a culture different from their own. It gave them the means to do something to help. Construction? A need would be matched with the size and the funding of the group. Guatemalan workers who knew what they were doing would work alongside the Americans. The host ministry would have the materials ready and arrange the transportation, all huge issues if trying to manage them from the United States. Preaching? They would contact and schedule churches, have the transportation ready and plan a place for lunch if it was far away. Children? They had a large orphanage on the grounds and it was also possible to go into villages, collect children and have games, crafts, music and Bible stories. They would send a translator with you. Medical? If you brought the medical people and provided the funding, they would buy the medicines, prearrange a village in need, and transport the group.

We began forming mission teams and going to Guatemala to do some projects as service to the Lord and as a way to spread the gospel just a little wider than what we had been doing. Our first project was to build a house for a widow and her six children. The woman's husband had worked for the mission compound. He had been killed by a member of the extended family during a dispute. After his death, her husband's brothers were trying to take the little house away from the widow, which they felt belonged to them. It was not safe for her to stay there. She was also unable to leave the home for fear that her few belongings would be taken and the men would not allow her back inside when she returned. Her security issues were solved when the ministry decided to allow her to move onto the property compound.

The Allow The Children team would build her house. When we arrived, the concrete block foundation was already in place. Our group was to mix the concrete by hand, carry over the blocks, and set them according to the instructions given. Our new construction would join a growing row of homes occupied by ministry workers. The house would be two small rooms with an outdoor extension on one side that would become the kitchen. There would be no electricity or plumbing, but we did hope to hook up some running water for the kitchen sink later on and add a toilet too. We worked two full days and part of most of the other days on the project. The Guatemalan laborers stayed at it every day, which is how it came to completion by the end of our trip.

Almost all of our teams went "to the dump" to participate in the feeding center. The ministry compound prepared food three days a week and the people of the village came to receive it. The project was on-going and a pavilion had been built to facilitate it. We had a nice concrete floor and tin roof—very nice indeed in the pouring down rain, which was the case during the rainy season. Tables were carried and set up. The people were ready with their own containers and we had a few to give out if anyone needed one. Team members served the food into each container as the person came to the table, followed by a drink of lemonade or something similar. It sounds simple, but it was often a very humbling and moving experience and having team members in tears was not unusual. Logically the dump is the place where trucks come in and dump waste from the surrounding area. The feeding center was set up here because the very poor people who lived around it were coming and digging through the garbage to find any morsel that they could to eat. Adults and children and elderly were scavenging regularly and it was heartbreaking to watch. So now, at least three days a week, they can come and receive a simple meal. As our bus takes us in, we see the people walking along, hurrying as they see us coming. Some come from great distances carrying little ones and assisting elderly ones. It is easy to see how important the meal is to them. Our team members take their container and pour hot, delicious food into it—usually a blend of rice and pasta—from our cooler. They are feeding hungry children who get very little else and it is very gratifying.

The ministry leaders helped us mix in some other activities such distributing some supplies in a village, preaching and teaching the children in a village church on Sunday, and hiking to a water fall. It was a good ministry week for a group of Americans. They did some hard work, but not so much that it caused anyone any strain or heatstroke. On the last day, we brought the family in to meet them. We dedicated the house and gave it over to them, watching as they began the process of moving in. The widow had a small baby in arms and an older child about six who had both mental and physical handicaps. She was unable to work a job because of the care needed by these two children and her situation was quite desperate. It was a really good feeling to know that at least her housing issue was resolved. She had a teen aged son who would now have a job with the ministry as a builder. We did not know it, but he had been working with us all week on his own house. In addition to these, she had three more school-aged children. These three would have the blessing of attending a very good school that was on the compound, also attended by the children from the orphanage and children from the nearby town as well. The family had suffered a terrible tragedy in the loss of their father and their home in the village, but the body of Christ came around them as it should and each of us—the ministry compound and the Allow team—did what we could to help. This is a worthy investment of ministry time and funding. Coming to the aid of poor widows and orphans is a command from our God. It is not a secondary ministry to the elite church planting and evangelism work. It is part of the responsibility of any believer and certainly needs to be part of the work of a mission agency. Along with the benefit to the widow, I could see some of the impact the trip had on the American team. It was a unique and amazing experience for us all and I was ready to invest Allow in more and more of this important work.

Our next project was to build a house for a pastor. The church was in the village of Chiquimula, Guatemala. It was a simple, concrete structure of one room, built on the side of a hill. It had a deep foundation that footed a whole story below. There was plenty of space inside to make a house. So for the next team, our funding and our activities were applied to making that happen. Step one was to move a huge pile of blocks from the topside to the ground level below. This involved negotiating a steep pathway that wrapped around the side of the building. Fortunately, we had a whole class of high school seniors with us. Several of the teens found some good solid footing on the path, continuing the line both before it and after. They passed the blocks from hand-to-hand until all of them were restacked at the bottom. For the next week, the building/remodeling continued on, resulting in three nice bedrooms, a small kitchen around a corner and an open space in the middle for sitting. It was basement cool down there, so it worked to have windows only on one side. The home provided a place for the pastor and his family to live in the same village they served. Previously, they lived in a different, rented place some distance away and only came in on Sundays. So this project was a blessing to the family as well as enabling them to be near their church and their people. As we worked on the house, we also came to know some of the people. Allow The Children set up sponsorship with the children of the village as well as the orphanage on the main compound. This gave our team members a way of continuing helping and being a part of the life of one child that they met while on their trip.

Our next team built a greenhouse, which is a bigger project than one might think. Clearing and leveling the ground was the first challenge and it kept everyone busy for the first couple days. Then sides were built up a few feet, very much as would be done for a house and that took two days to complete. It was a good project for a smaller group and we enjoyed knowing that we had provided something that was needed and productive. Ours was one greenhouse in a row of perhaps twenty of them. Each one was assigned to a family who lived on the compound to work and care for it. The widow, for whom we built a house during an earlier trip would get one. The family would receive a part of the vegetables grown and part of them would go to the ministry to help feed the orphans and the elders and the team members, too. Greenhouses are often built to protect plants from cold weather. Ours was built to protect from bugs and birds and the scorch of heat, since the interior could be kept humidified.

The Guatemalan ministry was building a little hospital on the grounds. We gave several trips to that project, just picking up work at whatever point they happened to be and often combining with other groups. It was an important project for taking care of the issues, especially the sick babies who were constantly being brought from the surrounding mountains. They were often shockingly emaciated and barely alive. If the family had abandoned them, they would go into the orphanage, if they survived. But many times, the mother came along as well, living in a building next to the "baby house" designated for them, while the child was under treatment. We did not provide the hospital, but we had a part in it. Many hands and dollars, from many different places, came together to make it happen. It was very satisfying to be on the grounds on the day that the babies were moved to their new facility where they could receive the very best care possible.

The elder home was a U-shaped building at the entrance of the ministry compound. Rooms were built around the three sides with a dining room in one corner and flowers planted in the center. It provided simple living for some homeless elder people and it was clean and very beautiful. The elders were free to walk about the village and the compound. Many of them held small jobs on the grounds or even in the village. Some others were at "nursing home" level of care and needed significant help. Two of our teams took the project of replacing the roof for the elder home.

The Guatemalan laborers would not let our men go up on the roof, but there was plenty to do as they passed down the old nearly worn out sheets of metal and received a new one to attach. The work proceeded slowly, but it was very satisfying to see the new roof shining up one side of the building and slowly progressing over all of the building. It was too long a task (and too much money) for only one team. That year, we had two teams back to back, so where the first one left off, the next team picked up and completed the project. While boys were working on the roof, the girls painted. We completed all of the exterior building and the surrounding fence and several of the interior rooms.

In the late afternoon, when the work day is finished, we often take the teams to the top of the mountain to spend some time with the children in the orphanage. Different things happen there. Sometimes the team members just play with the children, throwing balls or climbing on the equipment. If the stories are known, there are some very special children to meet. One of them is Andrea, who was the mother to three children when she was only ten years old. Actually, she was the oldest sister. The parents disappeared, leaving the four young children alone. No one knew why they left or how long the children had been alone before the situation became known. Andrea, completely on her own, kept her infant sister safe and alive and the other two siblings as well. Evidently, the children foraged for food and somehow managed for an indefinite period of time. When they were brought to the orphanage, the older three were together, but the baby was taken to the baby house and needed to stay there until she was eating independently. The separation was excruciating for Andrea, who was not even allowed to visit. One of the ministry workers made a video of the baby every single day and took it up the mountain for her to see.

Our largest Guatemalan project happened in a year when we had three teams scheduled for Guatemala. Building a church was usually beyond what we were able to fund, but combining the three groups enabled us to do it. The first group, in March, cleared and leveled the land and built the foundation. By the end of their week, we had a floor and walls about two feet high, posts at each corner and a tin roof. It was already functional as a worship "shelter." It defined the space for the people and provided the visible testimony as a place of worship, and it was covered in the event of rain. It was a great blessing for the village as it was, but our goal was to complete it.

The village for our church construction project was in a jungle, about an hour away. Transportation to the village was an adventure in itself. Our team traveled each morning in the back of a pickup to the river's edge. There was a small boat to take them across, a few at a time, then a walk to the point where another truck could pick them up and take them on to the village.

Our second and third groups came in June. They picked up where the last team stopped and continued building up the walls, then applied the stucco and then painted. When the last group finished their week, a beautiful little church stood in a place where before there was none. A Guatemalan evangelist was already working in the village and would continue working towards planting a church. Seeing that little church completed was a ministry highlight for me.

All of our ministry countries are different. Guatemala is unique because we are partnering with another ministry for projects. It is a good plan, an amazing benefit, to have some trusted people on the ground to make the arrangements and to help in all kinds of ways. Working together helps everyone and we accomplish so much more than could be done alone.

Nicaragua

When we were preparing to go to Guatemala for the first time, I was alert to any possible contacts in any of the other Central American countries. I was considering several different ones for a time, but one-by-one most of them disqualified in one way or another. One of the issues I felt important for the main partner in any new place was English language skills. I work with a lot of ministries without English, but I need one main partner in each country who can speak and write English and help with communication with others who do not. Nicaragua had all of the pieces that I needed, except this one. I decided to go anyway, knowing that we would need to hire a translator for major discussion meetings and we would struggle along at other times when one was not available.

Michael and I landed and met a man who was already full-time in ministry. His family was a wife and three beautiful little girls. We spent some time with them and came to the point of loving and trusting them very much. They wanted to start a children's home with children they knew who were in serious need. On my next trip in, the partner took me from home to home, visiting the children and showing me the life situation of each one. Most of them lived with a grandmother who was struggling to meet their needs. One grandmother was caring for six grandchildren. She had raised three children of her own and all three had left their children with her to go on to other pursuits. The stories of the parents were similar. None of them had an active father. Some of the mothers had left with a new romantic interest. Some of them had gone to another place, usually one of the nearby countries, to seek out a new job. One child that we visited was living with her mother and the extended family, but substance abuse problems made it an unsafe environment for her. We decided to launch the children's home with nine children. With the partner's own three girls, we had a total of twelve. Two among these were "day care" for two mothers who needed the help in order to keep their jobs. They would pick up their children in the evenings. We had not had the day care situation in previous children's homes, but to the extent possible, I wanted to allow the partner to define his own ministry. They do not all have to be cookie cutters of one another. This partner's vision was to use the home as a means of ministry outreach to all of the families and it was a good thing that they would have daily contact with these two mothers. We agreed with the plan and provided the funding as they began the new home.

This little home was one of our favorites over the years. Every one of the children was cute and affectionate and seemed very happy to be together with the family. When we visited, we often stayed in the home and it was a special event. The children were well-behaved overall, but the boys, especially, performed some mischief which either parent handled well. There was no sense of regulation or tight discipline. The daily routine happened in the casual, unhurried atmosphere typical of hispanic culture. The children knew songs and Bible verses, which they were eager to recite to us, and they prayed with the confidence of children who do so regularly. Everything seemed in order. Dealing with large and small conflicts with our children's homes is part of my job, but this one always seemed to be humming along well and for many years, I think that was true.

When we returned to the United States, I was able to communicate with the partner through email with translation software. As the years quickly brought more advances in technology, it became easy (when I was in Nicaragua) to sit in a restaurant or anywhere with strong wifi and type and translate back and forth. His wife was studying English and was progressing well. His daughter spoke very good English, so in the home discussing casual topics we usually managed without problems.

The same partner asked us to start a program for children of pastors on the Island of Ometepe. The island is in the middle of Lake Nicaragua, taking over an hour of travel by boat to reach it. There are two choices of boats for the trip. The big boat is a ferry and our vehicle could go along. A vehicle is very nice to have on the island, because the public transportation is an adventure. This boat has nice seats in an air-conditioned cabin, good rest rooms and it would certainly seem to qualify for approval by whatever agency might be inspecting boats. The other choice is the small boat and it is also an adventure. It sits low in the water. The hull fills quickly with all kinds of personal belongings being carried home from the mainland. One must step over sacks of food stuffs and whatever in order to gain a hard wooden seat. A seat in the middle can be crowded and stuffy. On the outside, next to the open windows, the lake splashes in regularly. There is no air conditioning and this boat might not have passed the inspection for boats. If we had the car, of course, we must take the ferry. If we did not have the car, we were usually in the small boat bouncing along.

The Island of Ometepe was formed by two volcanoes that tower up and provide landmarks. One of them is still active. It has a cloud of ash around it constantly and regularly spews more out. The trees and all of the vegetation in the area around it were completely covered with the ash. I do not know why it was not considered a dangerous volcano. It certainly had some fire burning within it, but for some reason they did not expect it to blow up any more than what it was doing daily. People on the island lived from farming and fishing. There was a small tourist trade with a few expensive tourist hotels, but no industry, or anything that would provide jobs as far as I could see.

We gathered the pastors together and formed a plan for pastor training two times a year. We started sponsorship for one child from each pastor's family. All of the pastors had some other job. The churches were not large enough to support them through the ministry alone. The sponsorship would be a significant blessing, covering the costs of one child for school. It took some of the load from each pastor's shoulders and gave some encouragement that believers in the United States cared about a family on an island in Nicaragua.

Over the years, we visited most of the little churches led by our pastors. They were made of sticks and thatch, like village churches anywhere. Most of them were only one room. They were beautiful places of worship for God's people in very special places.

When we first started in Nicaragua, we worked with another ministry which we called the "prostitute rescue." It was led by an American woman who had a heart to reach women who had been caught up in prostitution—both to help them leave that life and to show them the way to a new life of faith. On Tuesdays, the ministry hosted prostitutes from the area who came into the compound for the morning. They even sent a bus out to transport them and one of the challenges they faced regularly was women fighting on the bus to get a seat. On the compound, they had a time of worship and a gospel message. Those who came to Christ gave testimonies. Different helps for leaving the "life" (of prostitution) were discussed and offered. Then at a planned time, the meeting ended and the women transformed the room in a flash. The rows of chairs parted and work tables set up. Craft materials were spread out over the tables and the women set to work making sets of handmade greeting cards. These were packaged and sold in America. We took quite a lot and sold some of them. We had some regular customers for a while, but when we came to the point where we had to generate and keep customers, it was just more than I wanted to do. Yet it was important to keep money coming. The pay the girls received for making the cards is the reason they attended on Tuesdays, and they were hearing the gospel.

Prostitute work is tough from any perspective. A common history is that a girl grew up in this kind of life and had skills for nothing else. Her mother and often even her grandmother were prostitutes. I was surprised more than once to meet older women with very rough appearances who apparently still made their living that way. Fathers are completely unknown. They have no education—only survival. Sons born to the women move into labor jobs or crime and usually drift away from the family group, but the women stick together. Daughters are drawn into prostitution before they are old enough to make any other choice. As the mother ages and the daughter is sought for, it is her duty to do her part in making money.

The prostitute rescue compound has some buildings where women can live for a period of time during their transition out of the lifestyle. Young girls, who do not have a baby, live in a common bunk room and are enrolled in school. Mothers are given a private room to live in with their children. Boys, eleven years old and older, are not allowed to live on the compound. One goal of the ministry is to train the women in something that could bring them at least a menial job. They are trying to give them some training in sewing and cleaning and, of course, there are Bible studies. The women were Tuesday participants who responded to the invitation to live on the compound for a time and change their lives.

The stories were heartbreaking. One little girl, about ten, never knew until she came to the compound that most people slept at night and waked during the day time. For her entire life, her mother had been working all night and they slept during the day. One woman was eighteen years old and had an eight-year-old child and a toddler. She had given birth to the first child at the age of ten and then continued in prostitution to support her children. A fourteen-year-old girl had recently come, but she had been wanting and begging to come since she was twelve. Her mother had a debt and would not allow the girl to come until it was paid. Another young girl was Josefina, thirteen years old. She was pretty and sweet, loved school and professed her faith in Jesus. Her mother developed an interest in the manager of the rescue ministry, the only man on the staff. He lived on the property with his wife and children and served as the manager and a very able guard. He had been in the military police and was a good man. He successfully resisted the woman's advances, but she threatened to leave the compound and take Josefina with her—back to prostitution—if he did not pay attention to her. The situation was tragic. Josefina had been in the program for several years and was doing well in school. She was horrified at the idea of leaving, but that is what happened. There was so much heartbreak in the prostitute rescue work, but the fruit, when it did come, was very, very sweet. Some of the women did break out of the lifestyle and changed their lives.

We set up sponsorship for this ministry for the children who were less than eighteen years old, whether they were prostitutes or children of prostitutes. The money was going to the ministry, not the individual. We presented the work in some newsletters and the website and drew some sponsors. The problem in this ministry was that the women came and went so often. They might live on the compound for four months and I processed them into our program. The next time I came for updates, as many as a third of them might have left. I could not continue receiving sponsorship money for a child who was no longer under our care, so I set about the work of explaining each situation to a sponsor and trying to move them to another child. For some sponsors, this was an emotional event and they worried much about their child who evidently returned to prostitution. Sometimes, they would take another child and if they did, the same thing might happen again soon. Most sponsors did not wish to change over to a third prostitute rescue child. They might agree to go to some other kind of child at this point, but more often, we lost the sponsor. If we had sponsors constantly calling and requesting children, maybe we could have kept up with the constant changes. Sponsor finding is intense, challenging work and it is stressful to lose them within months of signing them. I really wanted to help this ministry, but sponsorship did not seem to be the way to do it. I came to the point where I did not assign a sponsor to one of these children unless the individual child was specifically requested. When a child left and a sponsor was willing to move to another, I looked for one from a different program. It was not long before the sponsors were all reassigned. I did work on project funds for them for a while, but when a large church moved in and began funding for them, I quietly ended our involvement.

Our main partner, who was also house father of the children's home asked our blessing to take the pastorate of a church. He had several years of Bible college training and had been a pastor in the past. We were very happy to agree in writing and to also write the recommendation that he requested. The two responsibilities—the church and the children's home—seemed very compatible and complementary of each other.

For over a year, all seemed to be going well. *Then something happened.* I received an email from the partner, awkwardly translated by software as usual, but this one was different in several ways. Parts of it seemed more formal than the way he usually wrote and some parts made no sense, but one line was very clear: *"Please forgive me, I have done a very great wrong."* Over the next few weeks, I came to know that our partner had been unfaithful to his marriage. Someone in the church had come to know of it. When his board of elders questioned him, he admitted the wrong immediately—and while he did not name the sin, he admitted wrong to me as well, so there really was no question of the guilt. He lost the church. Our children's home dissolved. There were some legal issues involved as well and the police began investigating. The police seized their bank account—the one we used to send their support, their lap top computer and their cell phones. The next day, he fled the country, abandoning his wife and children. His girls had scholarships to a Christian School, but now lost them. His wife quickly placed the children (not their own) back with their relatives. For some, the placement seemed okay, but several of them were going into very unfortunate situations. For all of them, the example of failure of a pastor and the man who had been father to them for many years, was devastating. For his own children, to go from a respected pastor's family to shame in the community and joining those struggling to survive was devastating.

It was six months later before I could make a trip to Nicaragua. This mother

140

and her three girls came to my hotel room. She sent the two younger ones out, keeping the oldest girl to translate. Then, she bent over and buried her head in my lap and sobbed. I stroked her shoulders, trying to comfort her, but it was not long before I joined her in the tears. The girl cried a bit as well, but from her expression and demeanor, I knew that she had been part of this same scene, over and over again. What must it be like for her to see her mother in such a state, not once but over and over again? The little girl who was always happily playing and singing had grown up since I last saw them. Her childhood was lost on the day her father left and now she was left to watch her mother's emotional writhing as well as dealing with her own grief. Did that man have any idea what he had done to his family? I assured them both that I would continue their sponsorship. We needed to establish a bank account. I brought them some money in cash that had accumulated since we last sent support. She was not expecting that and I enjoyed the relief in her face as she received it. I am sure it solved some problems for them. She invited me for dinner the following night and I agreed, but I told her that we would go to the grocery store too and she smiled. I could not solve her terrible problem, but I could do a few things to relieve the immediate stress. On previous trips, when I was staying in their home, we would always go to the grocery store on the first night. That way, I could buy some things that I wanted to eat and she could buy some things to cook—and it did not affect their budgeted support. So that is what we did. The next day, we went to the same grocery store as always. She put a few things in the basket and I put a lot of things in the basket—milk and eggs, canned vegetables, frozen meats, toothpaste, laundry detergent, boxes of pasta. Then we went to dinner. We laughed and talked. Life will never be the same, but it does go on.

Ministries grow and flourish and they fail. The joy of seeing a ministry successfully plant and then go on to function as it should is incredible. When they fail, especially when a good one fails, it can feel like the death of a family member.

The Ometepe ministry was almost another failure. I had no contact information with anyone except the one partner who was now "off the grid." His wife did not have any contacts with the island either. My plan was to make a trip to Nicaragua, find a way to get to the island and look for one of our churches. All of the pastors knew each other. If I found one, I could find them all. But once again, as He has many times, the Lord intervened. Our former partner's wife left the church where her husband had pastored. She was attending a different church with her daughters, when one morning she saw one of the pastors from the island! He was on the mainland for some reason that Sunday and was visiting in the same church. He was not just "one of the pastors," but he was the oldest, most senior of the group. He had planted one church and now was nurturing another. She took his phone number and sent it on to me. I still had the problem that none of the men on the island spoke English and my Spanish is not worthy of boasting. I was excited to receive the number. Now I had a connection once again with the island. When I called the senior pastor, he was on the boat returning to the island. He understood who I was and he called for an English speaker to help with the call. The Lord provided one. A girl's voice, in perfect English, came on the phone and we had a wonderful relay talk. Yes, he was willing to meet me when I came to Nicaragua. Yes, he could contact and gather all of the pastors who were in our program. Yes, he was willing to be responsible for the money and distribute it to the others. No, he did not have a bank account. This was a problem, but it was a problem that could be solved. I knew it was going to work—and it did. After meeting with our (fallen) partner's family, this pastor moved in and managed very well the logistics I needed. All of the Ometepe pastors were gathered when I arrived and I entered the room to enthusiastic applause. One after the other of the men expressed through our hired translator that he thought I would never return to the island, thank you for coming, and many thoughts along these lines. Of course, they were glad that their sponsorship money would continue and they were excited to be getting the back funds that had not been possible to send in the last few months. I was excited about it too. I already had sponsors of the children's home who needed some explanation of the events and needed to be transfered to another child. I had a list of sponsors for the island children too, who now could just continue on as usual. The island ministry would continue. Ometepe is just a little volcanic island of poor agrarian people in the country of Nicaragua. It is not a very important or "strategic" place by any standard of man. But it is one of the uttermost parts of the earth and it is one that the Lord placed in front of us to work.

When I returned to the United States, I immediately contacted a couple who had taught the pastors and wives on the island in the past. I knew they were waiting to plan their next trip and now the way was open once again. It was a special joy when they left once again for the island and the ministry continued.

Ministry does continue—even through my failures and those of others. Even if we were not able to return to the island, what we already invested continues. What we already invested in the prostitute ministry continues. The Lord uses all of it and I am so very grateful for the truth of that.

Amazon

An opportunity came to see a ministry in the Amazon, a place that has fascinated me since childhood. The contacts came in the best way, through someone I knew well who knew the potential partner well. The ministry area was on the Amazon River in the place where Colombia, Peru and Brazil all come together. The best way to enter was through Colombia and I would need to return in the same way.

When I stepped out of the airport in Bogota it was my first time on the continent of South America. As I remember, it seems as if it should have been a reason to pause and acknowledge the event, but at the time, my only concern was to find my pick up. I have seen enough airports that all I really want to do when I land is get out of it. A young girl in a taxi came by, after a time. She had been held up in the traffic, which is heavy in any capital city, especially around the airport. I enjoyed seeing the city as we drove nearly an hour to the place where she lived. Bogota is a beautiful international city with high rise buildings and all the usual signs of affluence. We stopped by an older brick building and moved inside the security gate to a stairwell. As I feared, it was a long way up. Walking and climbing lots of stairs are common activities in every one of our countries. We came to a small flat occupied by a set of parents, three adult children and one guest in addition to me. I love to be with the people of the land, especially when I am first getting to know a new country. A hotel can be more comfortable in many ways, but the rich experience of a home is very valuable and memorable. I loved being with this family and getting a glimpse into their lives. When I could remain awake no longer, they showed me to a tiny room, not much larger than the single bed, and I collapsed into a sound sleep.

Next morning, there was another short flight and I landed in Leticia—one of the most interesting and unique little cities I have ever visited. The culture seemed very much like that of the Central American cities, but there was one major distinction. Leticia is a city of three countries and two languages. Actually, each country has its own name for the city and borders are marked on the streets with yellow lines and speed bumps. There is no process involved in moving from country-to-country other than stepping across the line. My flight landed in Colombia. My hotel was in Brazil. We walked a very short way to a restaurant for breakfast in Peru. One confusing issue is that each country has its own currency and prefers to be paid in its own. Another confusing issue is that Peruvian people often live in Colombia or Brazil, and of course, any of the other combinations. A person living in any of the three countries might be indigenous, and he may or may not speak Spanish or Portuguese. Leticia was also the most secure city I have been in. I constantly marveled that the partner left important things like camera or lap top cases in our open moto-taxi, sometimes for an hour or more while we went inside a home or a restaurant for lunch. When I questioned this, he explained that on these streets the residents and shopkeepers knew one another well. He would be more careful to secure things at night, but in the daytime, someone would certainly see and report any theft—and there was no place for a thief to go. There was very little crime of any kind. The small city was surrounded by heavy jungle. The only way out was by boat or flight. It was an "uttermost part" of the earth.

I had arranged to visit two potential partners and accepting both of them was a definite possibility. The first one was a pastor with a wife and one child. His daughter was visiting with grandparents in Lima. His house was almost submerged underwater due to the recent flooding and so the two of them were staying in the hotel with me. He took me to see his house. It was on pilings, but the water had risen almost to the roof line. Wow! I do not know how many of his belongings had been salvaged or what he was going to do for living space in the near future.

The hotel was a small, modest building, but I did have air conditioning and a bathroom, both very nice amenities. The pastor's wife was already moved in to sleep in my room and they seemed to be concerned about whether I would be happy with the arrangement. A man had come from the United States to translate for me. He arrived the previous day and was already in a room shared with the pastor. The little hotel was also home for the family that owned and managed it. It seemed that the family used at least half of the guest rooms. We walked through their kitchen and living room to get in and out from the street. All of this worked for me.

The next day we went "out on the river." This involved hiring a boat from one of the merchants who crowded the river bank. To get to the launching point, we walked across a very single lane wooden slat bridge and a little aggression is necessary to gain the right of way. At the slightest hesitation, someone else will step forward and claim the bridge. This is not much problem, if both people are going in the same direction. However, it could just as well be a huge man with a load on his back, coming towards a smaller person. When I went across the bridge, there was an obstacle course of loose, moving boards to negotiate in order to reach the pier. I found a seat on the pier while the men haggled over the boats. There were several different kinds of boats. Those with a cover were preferable because of the protection from both rain and sun. When entering the boat, we had to do a balancing act to reach and settle upon a seat. Someone revved up the motor, and away we went.

The river looked very much as I had imagined it. Near the city there were homes built along the shoreline on pilings. Some of the homes had decks or walkways that connected them to one another. There were stores built in the river. For those who lived "on the river" in a stick house or a house boat, they could tie up at a dock and get many of their living necessities without ever going to the land.

The pastor had planted several churches. He took me to his current one, built on pilings like most other buildings, where now more than a foot of water stood over the floor. We did not get out of our boat, but I could clearly see the inside of the church through the open windows.

We continued on to the little school building, which was nearby and was the flood alternative place for the church to meet. The school was a dock with a few rooms built upon it. As we entered, the children were at their desks, evidently expecting us. The pastor and wife did a Bible session with the children—public school children—complete with songs, prayer, Bible lesson. It was all in Spanish, but it was easy to see their style and confidence and their obvious experience working together. When the school day was finished for the children, they filed out of the classroom as any children would. Then they loaded into the small hand-cut boats that were tied to the dock. These were *little children*, probably none older than ten. Some boats held only one child. Some carried two or three children. But they were all paddling off in different directions on the Amazon River towards home. I pictured an alligator turning over one of the tiny boats and the piranha fish eating the children. But I suppose the children of the Amazon know their environment just as country children in the United States know the wooded trails that lead them home.

As we continued on through the day, we passed homes where the people were perched on table tops because water completely filled their homes. Some homes had a second floor that was still dry, but the situation was very sad. Everything they had, which was not much, was piled up in the remaining dry areas. Each home had a boat tied up to it, therefore, they were not trapped, but probably had nowhere else to go. We saw cows huddled together on a tiny patch of land still dry, surrounded on all sides by the river. A short distance away, a group of chickens were similarly stranded. The water was expected to be high *for several more months*.

The pastor showed me the place where he hoped to plant the next church. He had already started some work there and had a young Bible-trained assistant who would move in to be the pastor as the church grew. The "village" was only a few homes on pilings. More were nearby, out of sight.

At one point, a small boy came zipping out from the shore in a boat similar to ours. After some Spanish conversation, I came to learn that the owner wanted our boat back for some reason. We were going to have to transfer ourselves to the other boat, the one that the boy was in. This was no issue at all for the Amazon people; however, it was a bit of a problem for me. Balance was of the utmost importance as one was stepping from one boat to another. They were not big boats, but it was impossible to step from one hull to the other. One must stand for at least an instant on the side of one and the side cross piece of the other before settling down into a secure place. I love water and I love boats—both attitudes that helped a lot in Amazon work. I successfully made the transfer as did the others and our original boat was soon heading back to port with its little boy pilot. We continued on down the river.

We saw both beauty and struggle for life as we motored along the river. Houseboats floated along, probably containing everything the family owned. There were some larger boats, but they were few. I was surprised at the lack of parrots and tropical birds that I was looking forward to seeing. Farther back in the jungle was the explanation for their absence. All of the birds close to the river had been trafficked for sale in the United States. We did see some fresh water dolphins and we sailed along beside them for a while. Occasionally, we saw monkeys in the trees. We came to one little island that had become a tourist stop because there were so many tiny monkeys, that is, a certain breed of small monkey, not babies. They were wild—not pets of any sort—but had become fairly tame because of the frequent tourists. We paid our money and the handler called. Here they come! Monkeys ran to us from every direction to get the food that was being held up to them. They jumped on our shoulders and heads, ran along the deck rails, swung from any branch. It was truly amazing and fun to experience for those of us who enjoy animals. I suppose it could have been frightening to one who did not want to be jumped on, crawled on, and have monkey hands going through their hair. It was also a good idea to have anything loose, such as sunglasses and jewelry, securely inside a bag. It might have been recreation for us, but it was serious food and shiny object accrual for them. If your shiny object was carried off into the trees, it was gone.

In the evening, we went to see a child who lived on the mainland in the city. The church was meeting that night. I rode my hired motor bike which was an adventure in itself. I love motor bikes and ride them in some situations in our countries. I am not an expert rider, but I have survived thus far and had no hesitation to venture out in Leticia. However, I did expect a bike in a reasonable state of repair. The one I got was so bad that I asked the partner to take it back and exchange it the next day. He did so, but the second bike was worse than the first. It was very difficult to start. It creaked and groaned in all kinds of unnatural ways. The engine shut down whenever I needed to idle, such as at an intersection. The steering was very loose. I could go on listing its deficiencies, but the bottom line was that I just did not feel safe on that bike, yet it was the only way to get to the place I needed to go. In the dark South American night, I was struggling through the streets to follow the partner on his bike ahead of me. If I lost sight of him, I would be alone—really alone—and that was not a good idea. I tried hard not to get in a situation where I needed to idle, but some were unavoidable. I bumped across international boundaries at least twice during the trip and had no idea which country I was in when we finally arrived at the church. We found the pastor and his daughter quickly and completed the Allow The Children work for them. We joined in the fellowship with the people for a little while before time to make an equally harrowing ride back to the hotel. I do not become afraid very easily and that trait has served me well many, many times. This night was one of those times.

On my last day with this partner, he gathered the daughter church pastors together at our hotel and I took the photos and histories for about six children. This program would not be big as it started out, but it would begin securely.

That evening, I moved to the care of the second partner. I met Jonaton in the United States and had several meetings with him before planning the trip to the Amazon. He was Colombian and had grown up on the Amazon, but life had now brought him to the United States. He was studying for a degree and taking some pilot training, preparing for mission work back in his own country. His family had been ministering in a variety of ways. His father was a pastor and would be able to contact many village pastors along the river to connect with our ministry. His cousin, Gonzalo, was involved in digging wells as a means to help a village and build a strong relationship with the people, which would then lead to sharing the gospel. It was a good idea. We do not know how important water is until we do not have it. Amazon people seem to have too much water, not a scarcity of it, but one cannot drink from the river. Like villages everywhere I go, they had containers on top of their houses to collect rain water. This worked well during rainy season, but when the rains stopped, thirst did not. When Gonzalo and his team spent the days working with the men in the village to dig a well with his equipment, they had a strong relationship and they were ready to hear the gospel. Small church fellowships had been planted all along the river and more were in planning.

We took a high powered public transportation boat to his place. We went to the dock, bought tickets and took a seat. The boat would leave when all of the seats were sold. It might be five minutes or two hours. When the time came, we were called to board. Life jackets were non-optional. We put them on, settled into a seat and we were soon zipping along at an impressive speed.

We spent the night in Gonzalo's home and the next morning set out "on the river." We traveled through an area so wide that the land seemed miles away (though it really was not that far) and also through places where the guy in the bow of the boat had to cut and push a way through the foliage. Several times, we needed to back out and try a different way. The canopy of the jungle blocked out the world and we paddled along exactly like many a movie I have seen. Gonzalo kept the river map in his hand held GPS device and I wondered what would happen if he should drop it… We had made so many turns through watered pathways that all looked exactly alike. There was no hope that I would ever find my way out and he as well seemed very dependent on the device. As we traveled, sooner or later we would come to a village and Gonzalo would park the boat and we would all disembark. We left the boat, full of our night time gear and went about whatever we were here to do in the village. He was checking the wells and meeting with different people. Jonaton and I would go to meet the pastor and do the intake on a child. The plan was that we would sleep in whatever village we happened to be in as night was falling. We were in one village having lunch when a storm quickly approached. It was fascinating to see the speed of the dark clouds and the beautiful day turn from sunny to menacing in literally seconds. We were all standing out on a porch watching when the drops started to lightly fall before what was obviously a deluge on the way.

Suddenly, Gonzalo shouted, "The boat!" and started running towards the river. Our boat had a cover, but it was no match for what was coming. Everything we had in there would be soaked and sitting in inches of water. I guess he had a tarp and he must have sheltered under it himself because we did not see him again until after the rainstorm. By the time I finished our Allow work and we returned to the boat, everything looked exactly as we had left it.

That night we slept in a village that was….. I have no idea where it was, but it was quite far "down the river" and into the jungle. They were indigenous people. They did not speak Spanish (or English) and none of our people spoke their language. Only the pastor spoke both and he was not there when we first arrived. Since it was clear that we could make it no farther that night, we began carrying our things into the church and setting up for the night. I had a pop up mosquito net tent. The men had hammocks that they suspended from the roof and hung a mosquito net over top. We had a bite to eat and then we each settled in to sleep. I loved the jungle night. It had all of the sounds that I would imagine. Some birds were screeching. A dog was barking. It was hot, but cooled down to comfortable when the sun was down. I could see a lot from my mosquito tent. I could look about at the men in the room with me, in their hammocks, and the village life through the church windows. It was not my first jungle village. The circumstances were very ordinary in many ways. From another perspective, it was anything but ordinary.

Not for the first time, I pondered the fact, *that God lets me do this.* I am a most ordinary woman, finishing out my fifties in reasonable, but not amazing health.

I am eligible for no awards in education or fitness or any other area. But there I was, on a continent without any family member or anyone that I knew well, sleeping in a jungle village church along the Amazon River in ….not sure what country. I think it was Brazil. It was one of the uttermost parts of the earth.

In Acts 1:8, the Lord called us to be witnesses to Him, listing a few specific places and then He said, "…to the uttermost part of the earth." What country or area or circumstance would be "the uttermost part of the earth?" We are running as hard as we can to keep up with what the Lord lets us do to reach the people in the difficult places.

Section IV

THE CHILDREN OF ALLOW THE CHILDREN

Allow The Children has touched the lives of many children over the years and they have touched ours. Each one is as unique as each of us are in the Lord's creation and plan. We want to bring you up very close and personal, to meet some of the precious treasures as we know them. We hope that you will be encouraged as we are, when you see just what He has privileged us to do and why we do it. *(Some names and identifying details have been changed for privacy.)*

The night that Simon fell from the roof

On one trip to Nepal, one of our pastor/partners gave me history sheets on several new children that he hoped to enroll in the sponsorship program. The children were not officially enrolled in our program until I had met them, confirmed their information and taken a photo. On this occasion, we made a plan to meet again in two days to see the children and to complete the process and I returned to the hotel.

I went downstairs to the hotel desk on the same evening about nine pm on some errand, perhaps it was to get another bottle of water. While at the desk, a phone call came for me from the same pastor I had been with earlier in the day. He told me about a meeting at the church. As the adults met inside, the children played in the church yard. Some of them scrambled up a stairway that was usually kept blocked, to the flat roof of the church. Simon, five years old, somehow fell from the roof and sustained a head injury. His family was very poor and unable to pay for any medical care. The pastor took some of the church funds and taxied the child to the hospital.

In Nepal, one must pay up front before any medical care is received. The money the pastor brought was enough for an x-ray and an exam, but the doctor determined that surgery was needed. Yes, the child needed surgery, but no surgery would happen until the money for it was paid. It did not cost nearly what it would in the United States, but it was past closing time for the banks, and few Nepalis carried so much cash. This was the patient and family's problem. The hospital would not meet the emergency need and wait for payment during business hours the next day. No money, no surgery. This practice might make one feel badly towards the hospital, but the policy is unfortunately necessary. Hospitals in developing countries simply do not have the money to give care and supplies away, no matter how great the need. If they would give care and wait for payment, they would be quickly overwhelmed and there would be no hospital for anyone.

The pastor called me at the hotel, asking that I come and bring some money for the surgery. I would have agreed to help any child, but this was actually one of the new children coming into our program. His history report was up in my room. At this point, a series of seemingly random circumstances began to occur that worked together in a beautiful tapestry—woven by God to provide for the needs of one little impoverished boy. The Lord does these things for all of His children, but so often we fail to recognize His hand. On this night, it was incredibly clear to see and I loved that He allowed me to be a part of it.

The employee, who usually manned the desk, had already left for home. The (adult) son of the family owners of the hotel was there in the lobby and he overheard the conversation. I handed the phone to him, asking that he get the name of the hospital from the pastor and write it in Nepali for me to give to a taxi driver. He took the phone, spoke briefly with the pastor in Nepali and hung up.

Nine o'clock is quite late at night for Nepal. Most businesses close by that time. Most city lights come from businesses and as they close, the streets grow dark. Taxis are few at night and one might have to wait for some time on the street before one comes along. Crime on the streets is not too bad in Kathmandu. I feel very safe in the day light, but the night time is different. There may be less crime because of less opportunity. Culturally, it is unusual to see a Nepali woman out alone at night and even less so a foreign woman. Most women would not be carrying a lot of money, but the opposite would be assumed for a "tourist" woman. Everyone involved knew that coming to the hospital at night placed me in a vulnerable position—both to street dwellers as I waited for a taxi and even the taxi driver as well. Handing the driver the note, written in Nepali, to communicate where I needed to go would also inform him that I did not know the way. He could easily take me to some secluded place and put me out of the taxi without my shoulder bag. Really, I did not even think through these things while the events were unfolding. I only thought of getting to the hospital with the money for Simon. Had I taken the call in my room, I might have popped out to the street without anyone at the hotel knowing where I was going. But the hotelier was present as I took the call and fully understood the situation. As he replaced the phone receiver, he said, "Okay. I am going to drive you to the hospital." This met my need and got me to the hospital faster and securely. It would have been kind of him if he had simply dropped me off, but he parked and came inside with me.

I found Simon on one of about a dozen gurneys in the emergency ward. He was unconscious, bruised and bleeding from several places about his face and skull. His mother was sitting silently beside him, stoically enduring the tragedy. What could it be like to see your five-year-old child seriously injured and have no means to help him? Knowing he needed surgery must have been frightening for her, but what about watching him wait for the treatment he needed—with the chance that he might not receive it at all—because of money. I quickly handed the pastor several large bills and he hurried towards the business office. He returned almost immediately with still another problem. I had plenty of money, but it was in American currency. The hospital wanted Nepali currency. This was just too much. They knew that the dollars could be exchanged for rupees as soon as the bank opened. They were crisp new bills in perfect condition. The child needed surgery and could die while they continued delaying, but the hospital held the power. They were not going to operate until we met their requirements. *What could we do?*

The Lord had the answer. Most Nepali men would not carry large sums of cash in their pockets, but at least on this day, the Buddhist hotel man who had come with me had the needed cash. He changed my dollars for Nepali currency and off the pastor went to the business office again.

This time it worked. We had the authorization for the surgery, but there were a few other steps to be accomplished. We were in a fairly large hospital in the capital city, but they did not have the supplies needed for the surgery, things like IV fluids, blood and medications. The hospital gave the list, and it was our job to go about to other hospitals and pharmacies to collect everything and pay for it. We exchanged more money. The hotelier drove the pastor in his car. Several other men from the church set off on their motor bikes.

I stayed with Simon and his mother. He was unconscious and laying at an odd angle. He was crusted in blood and still oozing from several places. I positioned him a little better. I wanted to work on cleaning the wounds, but that would require gauze and bottled water, neither in evidence. They would clean him up in surgery (I hoped). If we were in the United States, he would have an IV line in, his vital signs would be checked at intervals and at least his face would be cleaned of blood. But we were not in the United States. An IV cannot be started if the supplies are not available. The room was packed with people on gurneys waiting for attention. Some were sitting up with a hand on the painful body part. Some were stretched out and looked worse than our boy. One man was dead. A man right next to us slowly and painfully stood, dropped his pants and relieved himself into a plastic container. Sounds of moans and coughing, struggling for breath and regurgitation filled the room and I am not even going to try to describe the smells. My nursing background meant that the child's condition was the only source of stress for me. The rest of it was only anecdotally interesting.

Eventually, our men returned with an impressive spread of supplies. In a very few minutes, a nurse collected our supplies back into the bags they came in and carried them away. Someone came to roll Simon away and the pastor told me that I should leave with the hotelier. He would stay through the surgery with the mother, but I was no longer needed. It was several hours after midnight as we pulled into the hotel. I was so thankful for the car and driver that the Lord had provided for me, thankful that I had the opportunity to help in this situation, thankful for a warm shower and a clean bed. I was suddenly very tired.

Three important things happened on this night. I did not make any of them happen. Even the money I gave was from the ministry, not my own.

(1) The life of a helpless, injured child was saved when the Lord drew a group of very different people, each one using his gifts and resources to meet the need. Simon recovered from his injuries and entered our sponsorship program. Today he is a strong high school student, diligent in his studies and very committed to the Lord. He came from a poor Hindu background, but is well on his way to becoming an educated Christian leader in his community. A good church has grounded him in God's Word, preparing him well as a witness in whatever walk of life he takes.

(2) The soul of Simon's Hindu father was saved about six months after this event. He became open to hearing the words of the pastor who had helped his son. He began attending the church with his family and the day came when he trusted the Savior.

(3) A wealthy Buddhist man was not saved, but a beautiful testimony was played out before him as he watched a Christian pastor from among his own people and a foreigner who had never even met the child showing compassion and real help for a child of a poor, uneducated family. He met and began a relationship with a Nepali pastor who can show him the Way—when his heart is ready to seek it.

The day that Ashish died

Nepal has a law which is common throughout Asia. If a vehicle hits a person, for any reason, the driver is at fault. If the driver is reckless in some way or if the accident was unavoidable, the consequences are the same. If the victim dies, there is a set amount to be paid in compensation to the family and then the issue is closed. If the person is injured, the driver could be liable for medical bills for years. Because of this situation, it is common for drivers to attempt to kill a person, if they are involved in an injury. Everyone can tell a story of someone they knew who died in this way. Of course, it is illegal to deliberately kill, but it is difficult to prove and worth a try. The professional drivers of the big trucks are especially likely to make the attempt, so I have heard.

I was already in a taxi, on my way across the city to visit one of our children's homes. When my phone rang, the voice on the other end was loud and fast with agitation and anguish. It was our house father trying to speak English in the midst of a crisis situation. I caught enough words to know that one of the children had been killed in an accident that had happened within the last few minutes. He knew I was on the way and he did not want me to come upon the scene unprepared.

I had about ten minutes to absorb the information, before the taxi dropped me. I would have been in a hurry if the child was only injured, but the report I had was that he was dead. No need for hurry. As I turned the corner on the road towards the children's home, I could see the accident scene. A large flatbed truck parked, still and silent, surrounded by police officers. As I approached, I could see that a police officer sat in the driver's seat and another at the passenger window. They were protecting a man, seated between them, presumably the driver. Other police in riot gear surrounded the truck. The villagers wanted to kill the driver and would do so, if not for the police. The people lined the sides of the road. Both the crowd and the tension were growing. Fires were burning on the road in both directions to prevent the truck from escaping. On the ground behind the truck was a small form covered with a cloth. I sank down in the dirt beside the body. I did not see anyone that I knew from the children's home. The police were keeping everyone else back, but no one prevented me from my place.

This was my child. He was as much mine as anyone's. Ashish was about six years old. He was an orphan from a Hindu family. An "orphan" might mean a child whose parents died or it could mean that the parents' whereabouts were not known. The effect for the child was the same either way—no support and often no one who cared about him. No relative had stepped up to care for this boy when he lost his parents. In fairness, they might be very poor and struggling to care for their own children. In any case, Ashish somehow came to us and we were his family. The leaders in the children's home were the ones who took care of him. I was raising the money that met his needs. We could not cure all of the hurts in his life, but things were better for him. He was going to school and getting enough to eat. He seemed happy with the other children in the home. His family was Hindu, but he was learning from God's Word every day.

This is what happened, as best we could piece the event together: Ashish was making the ten-minute walk from school to the home with a group of children. The road rarely had any traffic at all, but a truck had made a delivery today. It was parked alongside a three-foot- high retaining wall. The children hopped up and walked along the wall. Ashish leaned over from the wall and put both hands on the back of the truck. At that moment, the truck pulled forward, causing him to fall. There were several adult witnesses as well as the children who said Ashish was crying from the fall. Maybe he had a broken bone or some other injury, but he was not dead at that point. The truck driver did not know what happened. Evidently, he heard the crying and saw the reaction of the people. He might have assumed that he had rolled over the child. The testimony was that he threw the truck into reverse and deliberately backed over Ashish, then forward again. The crying stopped. His skull was crushed. A trail of brain contents was spread in a way that corroborated the testimony.

The people were angry and they were preparing to administer avengement. In the United States, we expect law enforcement to investigate these things and arrest the murderer who will then come to trial. In the developing world, the police might do nothing more than require the legal payment for a death. If the death was truly an accident, that might be allowed to follow through, but this was not an accident. News of what happened was spreading rapidly and more people were coming. When enough people gathered, they would move together and act, protecting one another so that no one would be individually blamed. They were going to kill the driver and burn the truck, not necessarily in that order. If the driver left the truck on foot, he had no chance. As long as the police could guard him, he would be alright, but the mob was going to rush the truck as soon as there were enough people gathered, and they were probably also waiting for darkness.

When the surge came, they would be going for the driver at the front of the truck. I was at the rear, and it was a big truck. Police with arms and riot gear were all around me, but it was still a little bit stupid that I stayed there for so long. If I were in the same situation again, I would not stay at all, but history is already past for this event and I am describing it as it was. I just did not want to leave Ashish.

The people did not know me, but they knew who I was. They knew that Ashish was from the children's home and that it was under American support. Connecting the dots, I must be the donor for the children's home. No one wanted to hurt me, but I was in a dangerous place. As I looked around, I was surrounded and blocked in by the crowd. I did not know how to get out or even which direction to go, but it did occur to me that I should get out of there. I silently asked the Lord to show me a way. Suddenly, a young man who worked with our children's home appeared from the crowd. He was not an English speaker, but his eyes were wild with anxiety and he thrust his hand out to me. I took his hand and stood. The crowd miraculously parted and allowed us through. As soon as I reached the back of the throng, a deafening whoop came from hundreds of voices as they simultaneously moved forward and then back again. It was starting and seemed almost as if they were waiting for me to reach safety before they began the advance. That might have been exactly what they were doing, either by their own choice or because of the unseen angelic protection around me.

We moved quickly to the children's home. As I entered the home, I joined the children who were huddled together on the floor of the sitting room. We had about thirty children in this home, ranging in age from infants to older teens. All of them were afraid, in anguish for their friend, and probably confused about what was happening around them. One from among them had died this afternoon and several of them had seen it happen. A man, trapped in a truck only yards away, was about to be killed and to move into Christ-less eternity. Someone handed me a Bible and I sat on the floor with them. As I spoke, one of the adults moved in to translate. What do you say to children in such a situation? I hope my words were comforting and reassuring as the crisis continued, but I knew that the single most important thing that I could do to help them was to model a calm spirit and trust for the Lord. In fact, I did feel completely calm. I felt sad and grieved and helpless, but the Lord gave me the grace and confidence I needed.

I wanted to stay the night with the children and it was just impossible to get a vehicle to any point near our building. But the home leaders wanted to get me out to a safer place. No one knew how the night was going to go. It was not appropriate to protect me over the safety of the children, but I cooperated with their instructions. The plan was for one of the mature men to walk me out of the immediate area to a place where I could get a taxi. Many of the streets were blocked off and traffic was in chaos. Everything was in chaos. We could hear the pings of rocks hitting the truck. People were running around me in both directions, some trying to get away from the rioting and some running towards it with sticks and rocks in their hands. Bonfires were burning on several roads both as demonstration and to provide light, I think. Roaring voices were coming from the direction of the truck. The police were lined up shoulder-to-shoulder with their shields. Someone was shouting into a bullhorn.

It is not proper in Nepali culture for a man and woman to touch at all when out in public, but my escort had my hand firmly in his as we moved along on foot as quickly as I was able to go. We were at least the length of a football field away when the police started shooting tear gas. My eyes and nose burned painfully and the children's home was much closer to the scene than I was. They were inside the house, but the windows did not close tightly. They had to be terrified, and I was ashamed to be moving myself towards safety.

Over the next few days, relatives of Ashish came from the village, wailing in grief. I have no right to judge them. Perhaps they were truly sorrowful to lose the child and it had nothing to do with claiming the compensation. We were allowed to have a short Christian ceremony for him and then the relatives took the body to the Hindu temple and followed the custom of a public cremation.

Ashish lived for about six years on the earth and then he died. He heard the gospel and he knew about the Savior who loved him. There are so many children in the villages living in terrible poverty who have never heard the Word of God. I do not know why the Lord drew Ashish to our children's home. Maybe if he had stayed in the village, he would not have died at six. Maybe he would have grown up and died in Christ-less eternity as the truck driver did. I do not know why the Lord allowed Ashish to hear the gospel and so many others never hear. He did not grow up to be a pastor or a missionary, but his family did come out of the village and crossed paths with believers because of what happened. He did not have years to "do something" with the education we were providing for him. His death will be a horrible lifetime memory for all of the children in the home, but maybe each one will hold life and heaven just a little dearer. His body was burned and ashes swept into the river like so many Hindus every day, but that does not matter. His spirit was already free. His short life reminds me that Allow The Children is not doing what we do for the glowing success story. We are blessed to have some of those and it encourages us. But that is not why we do this. We do it for one reason and only one. We are following and serving our Lord. He makes the choices. He uses each life as He chooses. We serve Him.

A little girl hiding from the rebel army

According to our records, Dona was eight years old when she came into our sponsorship program. She was very small and looked about six to me.

No parent was present, so it was Dona herself reporting her age. Most of the Nepali mountain people did not know their exact ages and there were few reasons to need to know. Most children in the city could state their full names and ages confidently, but when we did intake for new village children, a blank expression was a common response, even for parents. If the mother accompanied the child, she was more likely than a father to know the age, but less likely to know the surname. If she was from a different tribal group than the father, she might give her own tribe for the child's last name. When we next saw the child, perhaps for the annual update, the father might ask us to change the child's name to his tribal identity. His first name might change too, because they were calling him by a nickname, not the official name they intended him to have. The child might have been enrolled in school for the first time, because of our support, and listed a different age in their school records than the one given to us, so the parent might ask us to change that information too. If the child failed a year of school, which was common, his age might be kept the same for another year. For all of these reasons, I doubt that Dona had lived for eight years, even considering her state of malnutrition, which was also unfortunately common among our new children.

Dona was brought and stood before me while I was doing the annual updates for children in one of our sponsorship programs. A little brother held tightly to her legs and hid behind her as a small child might do with his mother—if he had a mother. The brother was said to be seven years old, but in my fairly experienced opinion, Dona herself was no older than seven and her brother five. Our partner for this area saw the little girl gathering sticks each day (for cooking) with her brother trailing with her. He found that they were barely surviving in an old wooden shack and there were never any adults around. He was asking me to take them both into sponsorship. If I agreed, he would enroll them in the school and give them the leftover for food and necessities. He had already alerted the church about them and some of the people had helped in small ways.

Give the leftover sponsorship fund to the kids? "Where are the parents?" I asked.

"They have parents, but not here," came the answer. I saw the adults glancing at one another.

"What? Well who takes care of them? Were they on their own?"

These two were unusual for several reasons. They were "loose," not connected to any of our partners or programs. Usually, a partner gave me new children who were from his church or a daughter church. Street children or abandoned children needed to go into a children's home, not a church sponsorship program. If we had a children's home in this area, that is exactly what we might have done, but these children were not orphaned. Their father was a pastor and they were not really abandoned, yet they were alone. If this is confusing to read, I was also confused as I learned their story.

Dona had an older brother, about fifteen years old. The three children lived with their parents in a remote mountain village, a place that was hours by foot from the nearest place that a vehicle could reach. A rebel military group had come through and captured Dona's brother and other teen boys, forcing them to join their ranks and train for military fighting. It was a communist group, armed, dangerous and illegal. They fought regularly against the Nepali army with heavy casualties on both sides. The rebels enjoyed a lot of village support because they were thought to be fighting for the cause and benefit of the poor man. The Nepali army, representing the government, was often assumed to be corrupt and funded at the expense of the people. As an American, any group connected with communism is repulsive to me, but the leaders I worked with had never taken the government/history courses that I have had. I was surprised to know that many of them expressed political neutrality between the two groups or were in favor of whichever one happened to be nearby, for fear of harm if any opposition was voiced. When I discussed the issue with a man, he usually did not want to share a strong stand for either side. He probably had friends or relatives in the Nepali army and also knew people in the rebel army. When I was alone with a woman who might be speaking completely freely, she often expressed that the rebel army was dangerous, but the Nepali army was also dangerous. Either group might come through a village and camp on private property, take animals or any kind of food, and capture (recruit) teen boys. Girls were not safe when either group was nearby for a completely different reason.

Dona's brother had escaped from the training camp and returned home. *Good for him*, most Americans would think, but his action put him in great danger and his whole family as well, if it was known that they helped him. Leaving the rebel army was not allowed. If he was captured again, he would be tortured and killed as a deterrent to the others. He could not stay at home. His father had to make some difficult decisions quickly. The boy had to go far away to a place where no one knew him and basically become someone else. He would hide his true identity until enough time passed that he might be out of danger. It would be years, but there was no other choice. Sending him to or near any relative was out of the question because it would connect him and possibly identify him, or the relative might even turn him in because of fear for his own family.

It was not completely clear why the father sent the two small children with the older brother. Maybe there were threats against the family. He must have thought they were safer away than if they stayed and could become victims of some kind of retaliation. He and the mother (or any adult relative) could not go along because their presence might identify the runaway, but the small children would not be recognized. It must have been and continued to be a horrific family crisis.

The teen boy brought his little brother and sister to settle in this place. He built a very minimal, crude shelter in a wooded area. He left each day to go to the market to get day labor jobs in construction or road work. He took his wages at the end of each day and probably spent all of it on the way home for food and whatever other urgent need they might have. There was no cooking gas. He burned the wood that Dona and the small brother collected during the day and cooked what he was able to provide. Of course, he knew that the small children were not safe alone during the day, but if he did not go to work, there was nothing to eat. The family of children had no support system here. They were trying to survive.

Allow The Children sponsored the two small children. The partner arranged for their enrollment in school. There was money left over each month that took some of the pressure from the young shoulders of their brother. The pastor and his wife, who sent these three off alone—their precious treasure—trusted the Lord God to provide for them. We were part of His answer and His church was part of the answer too. *What a privilege.*

Boys of Maranatha

Like most children in our homes, Pradeep's story begins with tragedy and loss. His mother died when he was very young. In the mountains of Nepal, losing either parent is a risk of survival for the children and the youngest are the most vulnerable. Both parents are critical in their roles to protect and meet the needs of the children. Somehow the father must have managed without family support because there was no one to step in when he also died suddenly in an accident of some kind. Pradeep was about eight when he came down the mountain with his younger sister. They were leaving everything they knew for a very different way of life. The woman who walked with them was called their "Aunty" and she might have been a relative or it may have been a courtesy title. She seemed to care about the children, but she brought them for the purpose of finding some other place for them. Once they were settled, she would return to her home in the mountains, probably never to see them again. She came to one of our churches, asked and received shelter and the pastor began looking for a family among the believers who might take two orphans.

The Nepali community does not have a strong middle class. There is a small group that could be considered financially comfortable or wealthy. The other two groups could be called poor and profoundly poor. The wealthy are not likely to adopt a poor orphan child who is no relation to themselves. The poor are struggling to provide for their own children. Taking in an additional child might mean more hunger for their own. If they have managed to pay the fees to have their child in school, taking in an orphan would probably mean that school, and all that education would mean for their child, was no longer possible. The pastor was looking for a family that would accept both children. Maybe a farm family would take a boy who was old enough to carry his share of the load, but Pradeep was not quite at that age. If his sister was only a little older, some family might take her for household help—washing clothes by hand, scrubbing floors, and cleaning up after meals. If the pastor was not careful, somebody might take her even now, anticipating the free labor in the near future. The most common fate of orphans without relatives was to become a field worker or a household worker. They would probably not receive any pay, only enough food to survive and work another day.

We had a sponsorship program with the church where the orphans were living. I had already visited the church and returned to Kathmandu, about six hours away. The pastor called to tell me of the arrival of the two children and asked me to take them into the program. Knowing that sponsorship support would be coming with the children might help find a family, and it would ensure that they were enrolled in school. I had already taken new children for this program and I normally required that I see children personally before we accept them, but this was an emergency situation and I agreed to include them. I sent some money for food and clothing.

I normally did not share much about one partner's ministry issues with another, but Maranatha Home was moving to its new building and would have more space very soon. Anand, the partner in charge of Maranatha, was with me in Kathmandu. I mentioned the orphans to him and he moved immediately to help. He called the pastor and learned that no family had yet been found.

The following morning, we were on the way to pick up the children and then take them to Maranatha. The children knew we were coming and that they would be leaving with us to go to a new home. Pradeep was excited to see us when we arrived, but his attitude changed quickly. It did not take long to "pack them up." They each wore a new outfit of clothing and each had a small bag with one change of clothes, all of it bought with the money I had sent earlier. The aunty seemed genuinely sorrowful at the parting, but the children were withdrawing emotionally before my eyes. They did not respond when the aunty hugged them, and they did not resist when the pastor led Pradeep and carried his sister to our jeep. Once again, they were leaving everything they knew with no idea what their lives would be like at the destination. They had probably never met or been close to a foreigner. The two of them sat in the back seat, close together. They clasped their hands in their laps and stared at them, stiff and unmoving. They were too overwhelmed even to cry and there seemed to be nothing I could do to comfort them. They did not understand my words and when I touched them, it only added to their fear.

Pradeep and his sister adjusted quickly to the home as almost all newcomers did. Getting good food at regular intervals, probably for the first time in their lives, helped to turn reluctance to contentment. They developed friendships, enrolled in school, and learned that they were safe.

Pradeep began to show leadership qualities quickly. He was well liked by the other children. He excelled in a lot of areas, including music, soccer, and social skills. He was absorbing spiritual things and was among the first to stand and recite Scripture. He was a good boy and he was growing into a good man.

Not all of the kids in our children's homes were orphaned and abandoned. Solomon was about the same age and size as Pradeep and also from a remote village high up in the mountains. The lives of the two boys before they came to Maranatha were probably very similar, and of course, they were growing up now, side by side. I hoped they would be lifelong friends and ministry partners.

Solomon's father was a farmer like everyone else, but he was also a church planter. They were a big family with at least five children. Allow The Children had gifted the family with some goats as we did for all of the pastors in our ministry. Goats were good for a pastor's family because they are low maintenance and provided a good income when selling the offspring. Solomon's father was a good church planter. He had started three fellowships and he faithfully walked the distance among them to lead and minister to the people. Walking was the only transportation possible because of the vertical terrain. He faithfully attended our pastor training seminars.

Schools in the remote mountain areas were free if they existed at all and worth every penny of it. The teachers were poorly paid and rarely supervised. Most of the adults were illiterate and did not consider education very important for the children. They would grow up to be farmers like the generations before them. Few of the children had a tablet and pencils for learning to write, so what they learned came from listening only. Classes would end at the fifth grade level. Children coming into our program from these mountain schools always struggled with sixth grade work in a "regular" school and usually needed to repeat the year.

Because the village education was so poor, the pastor asked us to allow his son, Solomon, to live and attend school at Maranatha. In his mind, he had found a "free" boarding school. From our perspective, we were educating a boy who would become a Christian leader among his people. Solomon might not choose to return to his mountain home after his education is complete. What we are doing also provides him with that choice—many wonderful choices in the world that our God has made for us. Wherever he goes, he will always be one of the mountain people. If his heart remains faithful, the Lord will use him.

Solomon's father returned whenever there was a school break to take his son home for a few days. I never visited his home, but I heard that it was a walk that could also be called a climb and a long way. Many of the children left during school breaks. Orphans often had ties with some relatives and it is important for them to nurture those relationships.

No one ever came for Pradeep and his sister. That is sad in its way, but not as sad as orphans all over the country in hard labor just to survive. These two are safe and together. They are going to school and they are being grounded in God's Word.

All of our children at Maranatha or any of our children's homes have their own unique stories. The Lord drew them to us in all different ways. Our work keeps this tool in place that the Lord uses in many different lives. I will write the line that I have said and thought so many times: *I cannot believe that the Lord lets me do this.*

Treasure from a Muslim village

In one of our ministry countries was a poor jungle village. Every family, except one, in the village was Muslim, as far as we know. One of our evangelists lived in the village. His children had experienced some abuse, when walking to and from school, because they were Christians. So at the moment, our sponsorship was paying for a teacher to come to their thatch house to teach the two children at home. The whole family were socially outcast because they had left their Muslim religion and come to faith in Jesus Christ. People did not understand this and they feared that the evangelist might try to draw others away. The Muslim leader of the village, the Imam, kept a close watch on him. If not for his family's land, he would already have been run out of the village, but he had a right to live on his land, and farm it for survival like everyone else. The evangelist had a difficult job. He could not share the gospel openly. He could not give out any literature, unless an individual accepted it secretly. He certainly could not hold any kind of worship and invite people to come. Any activity suspected to be an attempt to convert a Muslim would be very dangerous for all involved, but was his mission field, and he stayed. He could pray. He could carefully talk to men privately about spiritual things. He was the only light in this place, but one wrong move or even an accusation could result in personal injury, jail time for him or acts against his family. Evangelists working in strong Muslim areas cannot publish the number of "decisions" or any of the results of their work in a newsletter or website. No one outside the group can really know how much they are doing or how people are responding. For the sake of security, their accountability must be to God alone. So, we really did not know much about the status of this man's ministry, but our partner had significant confidence in him.

As we launched one of our children's homes, two children came from this village, sent by the evangelist. One was a nine-year-old boy named Tobid. He was probably wearing the only clothing he owned, which were torn almost to rags. He was one of six children in the family. His mother had died a few months earlier. His father "might" be a believer, the partner told me. He had been behaving the way a Muslim behaves when he is coming to faith. He stopped attending the daily prayers. This in itself would not draw too much attention. Muslims might be nominal, or devout, or anywhere in between in the practice of their faith and may fluctuate during their life, just as Christians do. He was also listening attentively to the evangelist, not openly responding, but without hostility. He had accepted a Bible. He was a very poor man, as they all were in this village, but he had an especially difficult struggle with six children and no wife. The evangelist had suggested that one of his children could go to our children's home and would be able to go to school. This would leave more food for the remaining children, which would not be a small issue. The father would also know that his son would be taught from the Bible and would practice as a Christian. Even a nominal Muslim man would not tolerate it. That he allowed the boy to go, was a statement of his Christian faith.

The circumstances of the girl were similar. She was ten years old. Her mother was a widow with two children. She might have been a secret believer as well or she could have been desperate for survival. We just cannot know with certainty.

The two children were with us for about a year, receiving both education and daily discipleship, responding well. When they made their first visit back to the village, the Imam "captured" and questioned the frightened children about the place where they had been living. The partner reported to me that "the Lord was pleased with the children's answers, but the Imam was not." He called Tobid's father and the girl's mother together with some of the other men in the village. They beat the man to unconsciousness. He had to be carried back to his house. The woman was not beaten, but she was severely threatened and intimidated. She must not allow her daughter to return to that Christian place. And so the partner's email to me reported that both of these children were lost to our program. The two families were being watched and could not leave the village. There was no way for the children to return. It was a great loss and a frightening one. We comforted ourselves in that the two children had heard God's Word for a year. It would not return void. If not now, then later, fruit would come in their hearts from what they had heard.

About a week later, the partner sent me a photo of himself with a brilliantly smiling Tobid. At nine years old, he had run away from a village that was hours away from the children's home. He had hopped a bus and returned to us. How he had found the way was a mystery to me. How had he ridden the bus without money? He had boarded with a group of others and the driver would assume that he was with some of the adults. Payment was expected when leaving the bus and the amount determined by the distance traveled. Tobid simply took off running and there was no chance of the driver catching him. I learned that it was a regular practice of young boys—but not girls. Tobid was back, but there was no chance of getting our girl back. She could not travel alone. We were all delighted to have Tobid. As children do in the third world, he understood clearly the difference education would make in his life and he had the chance to get one. He also told the partner that he was a follower of Jesus. He belonged here with us. What the child did came at great cost. He could never go home again. Everyone knew that he had run away. His father did not leave the village to get him and may have encouraged him to go. We do not know; but we do know that the father knows exactly where he is and had never come to claim him. He is growing up, strong in faith. He is a precious treasure. His one little life is worth all that we do.

The orphan in the counterfeit orphanage

Anyone who works in Haiti has heard warnings about fake orphanages. Americans will support orphans and it is a good way to make money. When the donor is coming, gather a bunch of children together, the more dirty and ragged the better. After the American leaves, give each parent a little money and they will be willing to send the child again next time. Because of this practice, it is risky for a ministry like us—with no staff presence in the country—to fund an orphanage that we did not birth and build ourselves. It all depends on the quality and reliability of the contacts involved and I recognized mine to be very good.

I first met Tania's orphanage when my main pastor/partner in Haiti asked me to go there and consider helping them. As we entered the metal gate, I saw a plywood box building on one side, an ancient car in the yard and trashy debris everywhere. Facing the building, it was open in the center, forming a hallway or a covered porch between two rooms, and it was set up for cooking. An entry to the left opened to the room where sixteen children and several adult women "helpers" slept. One of the adult women was a girl of about nineteen who had grown up in the home and simply had nowhere else to go. She was needed to help with the younger children. Another was the mother of one of the children and the wife of an abusive husband. She regularly stayed at the home "to help" and to escape her own situation. There may have been at least one other woman there, also with some problem story. There was a boy, named David, who needed a special school placement of some kind. He was mute, but not deaf, and seemed to have some other mental or emotional condition.

The second room was a bedroom for the house parents with an entrance on the far right side. I have rarely seen children in a poorer environment. Children in a village may have nothing materially, but at least they have the village. There are trees and animals, neighbors and all kinds of things to do, such as collecting wood for cooking, throwing rocks into a pond, bringing water from a common well or tending the vegetable garden. These were city kids, trapped inside a wall that was probably necessary for safety. They had almost nothing. Thin metal bunk beds with very little bedding lined the room. There were not enough beds, but most were small children who could easily double up in a bunk. Many of our children's homes did that. I have seen many poor children, and these seemed not only poor, but depressed and hopeless. I looked at them and I could see their need, but I really did not want them in our program. I did not feel ready to give them a lot of money and I should not do that early in the relationship, but I did not want children living at this level with our name on them. I immediately felt guilty about that. Let the hungry children stay hungry because of my pride?

I tried to find out what I could about them from the house father. He was Haitian, but had grown up in the United States and his English was excellent. He seemed to be in his late fifties, had served in the United States Marines and had retired back to his home country. He had adult children in the United States by a previous marriage. His present marriage was to a Haitian woman without United States citizenship. I tried to question him about faith-related issues and the man seemed to know the right answers, but I had a sense that he was not completely on the same page as I would wish. The pastor, who knew the wife, assured me that she was a godly woman who took the children to church and led devotions with them. The father was not as involved with the children. He was usually working.

The story was that this had once been a thriving children's home with a modest building and support from a specific donor who was no longer involved. Their building was lost in the earthquake four years earlier. He showed me photos of both the original building and its post-earthquake collapse. Many of the children had died. He pointed out several who had been among them at the time and survived. One child had crawled out on his own. Several were trapped for days. There were a lot of stories of that horrible time and they may have been true. Any child who was older than three had lived through that day in some way. They had managed to put the plywood building up as an emergency shelter. Some of the older children dispersed in various ways. Now the children's home was struggling along. How were they supported? Like many others, they got some government rations of rice and beans. The man worked part time in a security job. The pastor brought Americans here whenever he could, as he was doing on this day with me. These guests often left money and they were getting by day-to-day in this way. His wife, the housemother, was the main caregiver and the one who knew the most about the children, but she was currently in the hospital. The pastor verified that information. He had visited her in the hospital.

Tania was quietly sitting in a little chair off to the side of the porch. She occasionally glanced at me with deep brown eyes. She was an exceptionally beautiful three-year-old. Her story was that she was brought in as a very young infant, right after the earthquake and no relatives were ever found for her. I reached both hands towards her, expecting that she would probably respond negatively, if at all. I was a scary foreigner who she had never before seen. But as I reached for her, she flew into my arms and grabbed me around the neck and would not let go. I also did not want to let her go. I should not decide such important things on an emotional basis, but I knew in that moment that I was not going to leave this child and all of the others in such incredible need. This was going to be tough project and we were going to do what we could to help. I took photos of all of the children and the house father promised to send me the histories within a couple of days. I would have filled them in on site, as I often do, but he did not have the information in a readily accessible place, he said. His wife usually managed all of those things. She was expected to be discharged from the hospital the next day. They would get the history reports together and send them by email. It seemed to be a reasonable plan. I told him that he would need to form a committee for the home. My partner should be on the committee and the housefather's pastor should be a member, then he could choose a few others.

I did not get the reports and when I tried to contact the man by email, he did not answer. Especially early in a new partnership, if I do not feel that the communication is reliable and secure, that is a reason I might not continue. I know that it might be due to all kinds of third world issues and not the potential partner's "fault," but whatever the reason, we just cannot work if we do not have a good connection with the partner. My main contact, the pastor/partner, drove out to the children's home to discover what might be the problem. He found them having a funeral. The man's wife had died in the hospital. It was very sudden and unexpected. They had thought she was coming home. He had been involved in all kinds of tasks because of the death, as of course, would be expected.

About one week after the funeral, he received word that an adult son in the United States had died in a vehicular accident. I had no way to confirm the truth of this report, but certainly, it was possible. The next word that I had was that the housefather had contracted malaria and was in the hospital himself. This was confirmed by the pastor. The man was most definitely having a string of difficult events. I considered breaking off my relationship with him at that point. It was not working as I expected, and if a partner did not perform in the beginning, I normally did not extend patience for very long, but this situation was unusual. I did not have the materials I needed to make packets for sponsors and he still was not answering email communication well. But it just seemed wrong to drop the ministry in the midst of all of these other events. I kept thinking of Tania and the other children. What was happening to them?

When I traveled to Haiti again, after a few months, I was looking forward to moving the relationship along with the children's home. Tania ran to me and I held back tears as I held her. The housefather had the history reports done and ready for me. In answer to my questions, he was not attending any church and no one was taking the children. His wife used to do that, he said. He said he had been too emotionally spent because of the loss of family members, but I could find little evidence that he had ever been faithful or had much interest in spiritual things.

He had more children there—several older ones in school uniforms who did not have the sense of being children who lived there. They did not live there. His story was that they did live in the orphanage before the earthquake, but since the current wooden building was temporary and crowded, they were with relatives who had stepped in after the building was destroyed. They needed help and if a good donor was coming in, he would like to include them. I did not accept them into our sponsorship program and I was feeling guarded because he seemed to be trying to....maximize the sponsorship. I looked around at the small children and wondered if any of them were here "just for the day." I specifically asked him about each one and got the expected answer, but I still wondered.

I talked to him about the committee for the home, especially the faith affiliation of each member. The children attended a Baptist church with the housemother before her death. My partner knew the pastor of the church well and it was he who had originally asked for donor help for the children's home. But rather than invite that man to be part of the committee, as I had asked, the house father had changed to a different church and included the pastor of the new one. The former church was his late wife's church, he said, and the new one was closer to the home—an important issue because they had to walk. Both of these things were true, but my (main) partner did not know the new pastor and that was less desirable than the one with whom he had a close relationship.

Committee members of several non-Baptist denominations were included and I accepted those, but one was from a cult group. The most troubling issue about this was that the house father had no idea why I would object to this man, a good friend of his. It was certainly a warning flag and might have been a reason to pull out at that point, but little Tania was sitting at my feet. She had no say about all of this, but she was a helpless victim if I left her.

I was rationalizing... The housefather was not a pastor or a man of any Bible related training at all. He professed himself a believer, but like many Americans in the pew, had probably never examined doctrine to any depth. Active in the church for my entire life, I have my "list" of those whose affiliations are acceptable to me. I would quickly agree that not all Baptists are faithful believers and I am willing to work with many who see things differently than I do, but this group was not on my list. My partner stepped in and took charge at this point, as a pastor should, explaining carefully in both English and French why we as a ministry could not accept a committee member from his religious identity. Everyone seemed to understand and agree, but it felt like a classic "golden rule" situation—she who has the gold makes the rules—and it left me uncomfortable. Another rule was that the leader of an Allow ministry needed to be a mature believer, committed and faithful to the Lord, and I just could not fully qualify this housefather. So should I drop the partnership with the man who just lost his wife and has a house full of dependent children because his walk with the Lord is new and immature? Or should I trust the Lord to use all of the circumstances in this man's life and encourage him to take the next spiritual step that he needed to make?

After this trip, we did assign sponsors and began some minimal funding for Tania's home. It was reported back to me that the children of school age had been enrolled (with our funding) and the housefather sent photos of the children leaving for the day in their school uniforms. My partner was visiting the home regularly and it seemed to be working, even if less than ideal. For the sake of the children, maybe it would prove to be a worthy, if risky investment.

169

Maybe. I hoped that the day would come when I would be glad that I hung with them through a rough start. Hoped. I thought about watching Tania grow up healthy and safe, into a godly young woman serving the Lord. Did she have what she needed to be healthy? Was she safe? Did she have an example before her eyes of faithfulness to the Lord? I squirmed as I considered these questions, but there was still the truth that Tania needed Allow The Children to survive and if we abandoned her, it added more damage to the life of a child who had already suffered too much for three years. What would happen to her? I had to make her children's home work. In every other issue that I had ever faced, I had protected Allow The Children at all costs, even when it meant painful decisions. I insisted on our spiritual standards above anything else. I had bent a lot of issues this time and I did it (mostly) for one little orphaned girl.

During my next trip to Haiti, the partner did not specifically tell me that something was wrong, however I came to know that something had happened connected with Tania's orphanage. I was eager to see her, but there were four other ministries in Haiti. I needed to visit them all.

When we arrived at Tania's orphanage, my mind and heart were on her as I greeted several caregivers. One of the women was great with child. I had Tania's hand. I saw David peeking around the corner and the other children were gathered on the porch. They still needed many things, but they were going to school and we were sending enough for plenty of food. We walked around to the private porch on the side and settled down to talk. My partner and the housefather were making significant eye contact. I felt the tension as I waited.

First, the housefather started trying to explain some kind of legal problem that he had. I was confused, but I realized that the pastor had discovered it and the housefather assumed that he had told me. The pastor had not shared it with me, but now he was ensuring that I knew. And there was more.

"I am going to marry her!" he said suddenly with a nervous laugh. I was confused once again.

He began talking quickly and nervously. He could not marry her yet, he said, because of a variety of small issues. The information finally came that he had a relationship with one of the caregivers, who was now nearly ready to deliver his child. I held eye contact with him as he continued to speak, but I had nothing more to say. The pastor had discovered the situation and his presence now forced the housefather to disclose it to me. Repentance was not part of the discussion—only excuses and making light of the issue. I had rationalized some of the other issues more than I should have, but not this time. I could not continue a partnership with a man who was impregnating the staff.

My hand dropped down to stroke Tania's little head. I was not going to be able to make it work this time. I had come to take new photos of the children, but my camera stayed in my bag. In a few minutes, I was going to leave the property and leave this helpless little girl. I could not do anything more to help her. It was not my fault, but it felt like a failure. Her children's home was not going to work. What would happen to her now? The answer to that question was in the hands of the Haitian men seated with me.

I gave Tania a quick hug and stood to walk out to the pastor's truck. It was incredibly difficult to leave, yet at the same time I wanted desperately to be gone. As I walked, the housefather followed me anxiously.

"Sister, are we still partners?" he asked. He knew the answer.

I did not speak or slow my stride, just shook my head slightly. I did not want to talk anymore. I held it together until we drove away and then—I tried to keep it controlled—but I cried for most of the way back to the pastor's house. He did what pastors do. He tried to comfort me with words of faith. He also assured me that he would go back and help as the children's home dissolved.

After returning to the United States, I received an email from the pastor about the children's home. It was a fake. The real children's home was destroyed by the earthquake. Some group came in and built the temporary wooden building as an emergency shelter. Most of the children who survived were relocated to other homes. The housemother continued caring for a few children and all testimony is that she was a good, loving mother and a faithful believer. The nineteen-year-old girl and David, both true orphans, were from that time. Tania was orphaned by the earthquake as her history accurately reported. All of the others were children of the caregivers or fake "orphans" from the neighborhood and the histories I had on them were fictitious. The housemother (who died just as I became involved) was married to the man I met as the housefather for only a couple years. He was never part of the ministry. When his wife died, he saw a way to get some money. I was deceived and Allow The Children was deceived, but I take some comfort in knowing that a Haitian pastor was also taken in. Experience is the best teacher and the best protection from these things. Having the Haitian pastor beside me was the best defense I could have, but still it happened.

The pastor found a placement for David. All of the other children had at least one parent, except Tania. He took Tania to his own home and family, keeping her there until a new children's home for girls opened nearby. It is everything we would want it to be. It is a small home, for ten little girls, run by Christ-following women. Each girl has her own bed, good food, good clothing and toys. They go to school and church. Allow The Children still supports

Tania—only her—because it is not our children's home. Tania is growing up healthy and safe. She is well on her way to becoming a godly woman, serving the Lord. He had the answer.

The girl chosen by the Lord for our program

When we do updates on the children in the sponsorship program, a question that we often ask is, "What is your future aim?" Of course, many of the young children have not settled on a career direction, but it is interesting to see what the child will say. Young boys will often say "doctor" or "pilot," but occasionally they will say "pastor" and of course we want to encourage that. One time, a little boy told us that he wanted to be a "tourist" when he grows up, so we all enjoyed that answer. A little girl will say "nurse" almost all of the time, and in their teens many of our girls still hope to go to nursing school. In the developing world, there are very few life choices for a girl. Nursing is a way up and out.

Attaining a seat in a nursing school in Nepal is challenging and competitive. For a poor girl, just staying in school until the final exams is unusual. Her scores on the exams are critical in the application process and if she gets through that, she still has the nursing school entrance exams. These exams cost money and if she is accepted for one of the very limited seats, she needs to submit the admission fees within only a few days. If not, she will lose the opportunity and her seat will go to a girl who is on the waiting list. Schools are different, but the typical requirement is one to two thousand dollars up front and then about fifty dollars per month. Families might sell a piece of land to get the money. Less often, they might take a bank loan against their land. Even with a scholarship, nursing school is way out of reach for most girls in our program.

We had a donor who felt a special interest in helping a nursing student. We also had a girl in one of our children's homes who had been in our sponsorship program for years and had dreamed of nursing school. She worked hard and had top exam scores. Knowing that we had a reliable donor, I had already told her that Allow The Children would provide the fees. The donor did not have the information on this specific girl yet, but in my thoughts and plans we already had them connected. We also had a second girl in a different children's home who also hoped for nursing school, and I was praying about how to help her.

As we visited various areas for the sponsorship program, I received a request for some new children. I stepped out of my hotel room to meet a sad woman and her children. She was a new widow with little education and no job skills. Her husband had died suddenly in an accident. The children were all excellent students with high hopes and potential, but now they faced the likelihood that they would have to withdraw from school. Our usual practice was to take only one child from a family into sponsorship unless there were some special circumstances. The reasoning was to spread our help to as many families as possible and to be as fair as possible. Most of our children in family sponsorship (as opposed to a children's home) had siblings and many of the families were in desperate situations.

The family sitting before me had a boy about nine and Rani Maya, a girl who had just completed her exams with excellent results. Rani wanted to apply to nursing school, but her hopes disappeared when she lost her father. There was another son, aged somewhere between the other two, probably about thirteen. He was the family's oldest son. If any of the father's relatives helped at all, they would probably focus on the oldest son. Rani was too old to enter our sponsorship program. We had a maximum age for entrance. We stretched it quite often, but she was actually at the point where we normally stopped sponsorship. It looked like the youngest boy was the logical choice. I sat looking at them and they all looked at the ground. No one had made any verbal request that I do anything other than the usual practice, yet an unspoken request seemed to be in the air. This family was devastated by the loss of their father and sole support. I could not comfort their grief for their father, but the loss of income meant more suffering was to come. I was in a position to help with that. If I sponsored the youngest one, as the one most vulnerable, it would safeguard his education. I looked at the older boy. He would be responsible for his mother for her lifetime and he knew it. For now and the next year or so, his mother would try to manage, but he would feel the pressure to take responsibility for the family before his adulthood. He was an outstanding student and it would be tragic if he became a laborer. One sponsorship for the youngest boy would not leave enough money, after school fees, to make a significant difference for the rest of this family. Two sponsorships would secure both boys in school and the money left over would be about the same as one young teen boy could make as a laborer. It would alleviate most of the reason for the boy to withdraw from school. When he finished his education, he would be in the best position to lead and provide for the family. I snapped photos of both boys and took the histories. Rani would need a miracle for nursing school—but at least she had completed her basic education. I want to use our ministry in whatever way the Lord directs, but most of our efforts are to help young children who might otherwise have no chance at all to go to school.

I returned to the United States and learned through email that our girl, who was funded for nursing school, did not get a seat. It was surprising information because she had always been an excellent student, but the competition was too strong. She did well on the exam, just not well enough. I thought briefly of Rani Maya, but the funding really needed to go to the girl in the other children's home. She was in even more need than Rani. She had no family at all. I wrote informing the home leaders that their girl could apply for nursing school. I was surprised again when a reply came that this girl had changed her mind. She had chosen another job direction. Even when told that funding for nursing was available for her, she was settled in her decision.

The donor wanted to help a nursing student. We had no other girls in our program who were ready to apply for nursing. If we applied it for Rani Maya, it would make three children under support in one family, which was unusual, yet it clearly seemed to be the Lord's hand. It fit for the donor and it fit for Allow The Children. It was the Lord's answer and blessing for Rani Maya.

Rani applied and got the seat in nursing school. The family managed somehow for the three years she was in school. When she graduated, she found a job and helped with the family needs. As I look back on all of the events, it is so beautifully obvious that the Lord was directing the funds for this girl. From the moment she stepped in front of me, each step pointed to her. I simply followed what the Lord was showing us to do.

This and so many other incidents like it comfort me when I feel overwhelmed. There are many, many children who need the kind of help we give, but it is not my job to support all of them. I can trust the Lord to cross the lives of specific individuals with mine as He shows the plan for each one to follow. I have learned to be alert when I find a child in front of me who is not already part of our program. Is there a reason for the meeting, a purpose that the Lord will make clear later on? Perhaps so. My job is to be alert, to watch and to follow as the Lord leads.

Anita, Survivor of the Earthquake

Fourteen-year-old Anita woke to a normal Saturday morning in Nepal, but before noon on that day, an earthquake caused her house to collapse around her. Like thousands of others, she was buried in concrete and debris. Anita managed to crawl out of the rubble and she was not critically injured. Everything the family owned was lost and she was alone.

Anita's family was very poor. Her father wanted to work, however he had not been able to find a job. Like many other Nepali men, he went "outside" with a company that places men into jobs in other countries. Depending on the man's skills, he might be matched in a labor job or any of a variety of service jobs. The pay was better than in Nepal, but he had to cover his debt for his air ticket and placement. It was not uncommon for men to be away from home for three years or more. They give up being part of their family's lives during that time, in hopes for a better future.

Anita's mother was working as a seamstress and also attending a Christian training program. On the day of the earthquake, she stepped into the presence of the Lord with her younger daughter. Anita was left alone in the chaos of the capital city. Finding food and water were a challenge in those first days following the earthquake. Transportation was down. Communication was down. If Anita even knew how to reach her father, there was no way to do it in the immediate aftermath.

The ground continued to shake and some of the tremors were strong enough to bring already damaged buildings down. People were sleeping outside all over the city (and the country), even if their homes seemed safe. Anita was sleeping on the streets, as many others were as well. Other children were also orphaned, many of them younger and more vulnerable than she. Help in the way of food and water was coming, but it took some days for the city to organize and begin distributions. In the meanwhile, Anita dealt with the reality that her world was completely destroyed. The terrifying shaking continued almost daily.

When he heard about the earthquake, Anita's father left his good job and returned to Nepal as soon as he could. He found the ruins of his house and learned from someone that one of his daughters survived. He did not rest until he found her. Anita was fortunate. For many of the children, there was no one left to search for them.

The father and daughter faced huge difficulties. He would need to find a place to live and food to eat. He needed a job in a city where many places of business were flattened and hundreds of others were also looking. But at least these problems were on the shoulders of an adult and not a little girl.

The church family came together as the people of God should and were helping in many different ways. Someone who knew of the situation made a request to Allow The Children for Anita. We were privileged to take her into our program. Sponsorship would keep her in school and would meet a few needs besides. We are only one piece of the Lord's plan for her, but it brings a tremendous satisfaction to have a way to help after such a tragedy.

The Son of a Blind Mother

I was asked to return to one of our children's homes in Nepal to consider receiving a little boy with an unusual problem. Suman and his blind mother came from a remote mountain area, eighteen hours away. Along with the mother and son was a Brit who was not very happy with the situation. The man was the director of a residential program that provided job training for the blind. Suman's mother had been screened and accepted for the program. There was no husband and father. Gaining entrance to this program probably meant everything to this woman, maybe even survival. It was a chance to learn a skill and possibly an employment opportunity that would never have been possible back in the village. It was a chance to take care of herself and her son. Maybe they could have a better life.

The leaders of the training program arranged for the woman to come to Kathmandu by bus. Bringing her ten-year-old son along with her was not part of the agreement. There was a seat in the classroom and bed in the hostel for her, but not for the boy. He could not stay in the hostel with the women. He could not take a bed in the men's quarters. The program was for blind adults. They could not feed or house a child or pay for him to go to school. He could not stay. Why did she bring him? It was not part of the agreement. Some solution needed to be found.

I was unfortunately familiar with relatives, even parents, who wanted to "dump" a child in one of our children's homes. This was the first time a westerner had come with the same agenda. To his credit, he was trying to assure the boy's safety and well-being. He had met the housefather of our children's home at church and learned that the donor was in town. Maybe we could solve his problem. If we did not agree, his plan was to put the boy on a bus alone and send him back to the village.

Why did the mother bring him to Kathmandu? I could not know with certainty, but I could think of a few possible scenarios. Maybe the family back in the village was rejecting them, or was abusive and the mother could not leave her son in their care. She might simply have needed his help during the travel because of her blindness. But most likely, for her own reasons, she had no intention of returning to the village. She wanted to receive her training and find a job. She wanted a new life in the city and she needed to keep her son with her. She did not know how it would work out, but she was a believer and she must have prayed.

Now the request was before me to receive this boy into our children's home. If I said yes, we would support him and educate him, probably until he graduated. His mother would be about an hour away and they could visit regularly. If I said no, the Brit intended to bus him back to the village. He would be on his own, at the mercy of the extended family, and separated from his mother, very possibly to never see her again. With the help of the British training program, she might come to the point of making some income, but it seemed unlikely that she would ever be able to take custody of her son and meet the needs of them both. Suman was our boy—almost certainly until he graduated or until—as he gets older, the pressure to provide for his mother becomes so strong that he leaves school and takes some job. Either way, he and his mother needed help. We were grateful for the opportunity the Lord gave us to be part of the answer.

Manish stood alone for the Lord at the age of nine

Almost every believer in Nepal has relatives who are either Hindu or Buddhist. The relatives might be anywhere from nominal to devout in their beliefs and practice. The very poor are often too involved in daily survival to worry too much about other things. Manish's family was among the very poor. They lived in a house made of scrap materials in the slum of the capital city. At age eight, Manish could not attend school. He spent his days begging on the street and scavenging for food among the rotten things that the nearby shops threw away.

An evangelist, working with us, started a Bible club for the children in the slum. It was fun and different. Manish started attending. As best he could tell, Manish and several other children came to faith in the Lord. When his Hindu father came to know that Manish was attending a Christian meeting regularly, he was forbidden to continue. If he returned to the Christian meeting, he would be banished from the home and the family, he was told.

The family connection is so important in Asian culture. The family is the source of identity and protection from the hardships of life. Even adult children are expected to respect the opinions and instructions of the elders and to do otherwise is a great dishonor to them. The pressure to conform to the family is incredible. When a Hindu comes to the Lord, it is incredibly hard to take an independent stand that is different from the family's history and beliefs. To be disconnected from the family is just unthinkable and a huge sacrifice. For many believers, it means giving up their right to inheritance as well.

Manish chose the Lord and his father kept his word. Manish became a nine-year-old homeless child. Like the widow's mite, he did not have much, but he gave up everything that he had.

Manish and several other boys with difficult circumstances were the reason we started a new children's home. He came out of the slum to live in a modest flat with nine other boys. Breakfast and dinner came daily and he wore a school uniform instead of rags. We sent the whole group of them to a dentist and it cost a small fortune. After only a few months, the boys were independently carrying out their own evening devotion. They were ten boys, well on their way to a life of crime and drug addiction, but now they were studying and worshiping, preparing for a lifetime of ministry.

Difficult times were not over for the group. The 2015 Nepal earthquake destroyed the church in the slums. The boys' flat remained standing but the foundation was badly cracked. The building could no longer be occupied. Our children were back in the slums from whence they came, the pastor and his family (house parents) with them. Many others were building emergency shelters along with them and the earthquake left an abundance of scrap materials. Our sponsorship provided rent money for a place to live, but thousands of people were displaced about the city and many buildings were damaged. Finding a new place would seem to be an impossible challenge, but Manish and the other boys were about to have a life lesson in the Father's care.

Earthquake funds poured in and we gratefully wired them on to our partners in Nepal. The partner in charge of Manish's orphanage was one of four who received relief funds from us. We were all devastated by the news coming from Nepal, but it was good to be able to help. The partner found a small piece of land and quickly made plans to build an "earthquake safe" house. Many people in Nepal were afraid to sleep inside a concrete house. The ground continued to shake almost daily and another "big one" might come. The house was built in an amazing eighteen days. It was made from plywood and sheet metal. From the outside, it looked like a storage building, but the inside was surprisingly home-like and provided plenty of space. The best thing of all was the safety! If the structure falls on the children, they will find themselves under light sheets of tin and plywood, not concrete. The boys told us that when the ground shakes at night, the people from the surrounding buildings run outside with lots of shouting and commotion, but they happily stay in their beds.

Manish will probably not have a smooth, easy life. More challenges are sure to come. But he is learning to trust and follow the Lord. It is exciting to watch how the Lord trains him and to watch for how He will use Manish in the future.

A little girl called out for His Name

Kajol came to our children's home at the age of twelve. Her mother died and her father married again. The new wife did not want Kajol in the family and treated her unkindly. Some neighbors knew of her situation and recommended her for our children's home.

The same story is played out over and over in Asia. If a father remarries after the death of a wife, the family might function well for a time. The problems often come when more children are born and the resources of the family are stretched. If the father is frequently present and adequately provides, things might continue well. If the family is poor, he might spend all of his time as a day laborer. He needs to arrive at the market by daylight to compete for a job in construction or road work. If he gets work, it might be dark by the time he returns home and collapses into bed. The children are at the mercy of the stepmother. If there is not enough food for all, she might want to give more to her own children. If all of the children cannot go to school, she desperately wants to send hers. If her child is a son and those of the first marriage are daughters, the father probably agrees. It is also common to withdraw an older child, especially a daughter, from school in order to enroll a younger one, so that all can have a few years of education.

The home where Kajol came to live is high up in the mountains. The tribal people have had very little influence from the outside, still living the lives as they have for centuries. They survive with farming and animal raising, and survival also depends heavily on the family group. The young, the weak and the sick are cared for by the mature and strong. Family loyalty and responsibility are very serious matters. When the family system works, it works well. When it does not work, it is tragic. Kajol and others like her who lose their families are vulnerable to all kind of hurt and abuse. Losing the emotional support and safety of the family is disastrous even for an adult. Perhaps the children do not fully understand the ramifications, which might explain how they could possibly bear it. It is rare that we see any behavior problems in our children's homes. Most of our children are very grateful for good food and a safe place to sleep. That they go to school is not short of amazing. They will not risk their "seat" in the home.

Though we cannot know for certain, Kajol probably never heard the Name of Jesus before coming to the children's home. She comes from a remote and isolated place where anyone from the outside rarely penetrates. All of the children are orphans or half orphans like Kajol, and they all lack for family who would step in and help them. The Lord used the tragedy they suffered in life to bring them to Himself for eternity. Each one of them will know the way to eternal life in Jesus. Each one will be discipled and prepared as an able witness for Him in whatever walk of life she chooses.

How can we plant a church in the tribal mountains? It might start with a home formed of damaged and rejected children—a people called out for His Name.

Born in a toilet

A little boy in Burundi, Africa, stopped by in the early hours of the morning to use a community toilet. It was a ceramic "squat" toilet, which are common in Africa and Asia, and often very dirty. The odor of human waste saturates the air and the heat only makes it worse. As the child entered the rough structured stall, he saw the produce of someone who had been there before him. It was dark and moving…. He ran to call his mother. Nyishuyimana is an African name which means, "The answer of God." The baby had been born and abandoned in the toilet, left there in the filth.

A rescue center in Burundi, Africa, exists to help babies like Nyishuyimana. It is a place where abandoned babies can be taken for care. It is a place where a mother with AIDS, who knows she is going to die, can bring her children for care. The program matches orphaned and abandoned children with Christian widows who are willing to care for them, but may also be in significant need. We sponsor the child, providing the funds needed for the child's care. If a widow receives two or three children, the funding is enough to provide food for her as well. It is a foster care program, but a very special one. It takes two desperate situations and solves the problems of both. The center supervises the care and parenting of the children and follows them as they grow. They are brought in for regular medical exams and when the time comes, they are enrolled in school.

The School for the Blind in Burundi

Chanella has experienced a great deal of hardship in her young life. She became blind at six months of age, following an illness. Her mother died when she was four years old as a result of infection after child birth. Her father is very ill and unable to care for the two children. During school breaks, Chanella lives with an elderly aunt who is widowed and very poor.

Cedrique became ill when he was in the first grade. A traditional African doctor boiled water and added "medicine" which was applied to his eyes and caused his blindness. His mother then rejected and abandoned him. A pastor took him into his family for care, but he already had nine children.

Samuel was shot in the head at the age of six. He was left blind and with weakness in his left arm.

Dorcas' parents kept her hidden away because of the shame of having a handicapped child. She was given only a little food and care. A neighbor came to know of her situation and asked the school for help. The family willingly released her. She was frail and malnourished. She had only rarely been outside and had difficulty walking.

Falgenvine became blind as a sixth grader after suffering from malaria. Her father is a pastor. She wanted to be a teacher, but thought that hope was gone along with her sight. Now she is studying again and has a chance to reach her dream.

The school for the blind in Burundi, ministers to all of these children, and so many more. They are studying both academic subjects and learning music and crafts which may help them earn a living someday. The children are taught from God's Word daily and many have come to faith in Him. Though they have faced hardship and tragedies in their lives, they learn the way to eternal life with the Savior who loves them.

Over 1000 children

In 2015, our list of children under sponsorship passed one thousand one hundred names and continues racing towards the next landmark. Each one has his own special story. Some of their life histories are amazing and fascinating and some are too painful to share. We tried to share just a few of them here to show some of what the Lord lets us do. One of the blessings of the mission is watching the way the Lord draws many people together to accomplish His purposes.

Sometimes I scroll down through our children lists and wonder how it all happened and where it is all going. We will just need to wait and watch and keep working—*because the story of Allow The Children has not ended yet.*

ABOUT THE AUTHOR

Michael and Sue Cook left the business world to devote themselves to missions and ministry work. They began making short project trips to many different countries. This grew into a ministry life that they had not planned, but found the joy of a perfect fit for their hearts and their hands in the work that the Lord gave to them. With the blessing of business investments providing their personal support and travel expenses, they give their time to the ministry without salary.

Michael and Sue live in Lynchburg, Virginia, when they are not traveling internationally. Sue enjoys her grandchildren, dogs, ocean, thunderstorms, challenges, projects, Bible, praise music, chocolate, bare feet, September and late nights. Michael likes his grandchildren, Bible, lakes, mountains, fishing, the color green, navigating bureaucracies, jigsaw puzzles, news trivia, well laid plans, Virginia Tech football, *any* music, peach yogurt and early mornings.

BE PART OF THE STORY

Sponsor an orphan or abandoned child

Bring a Hindu, Buddhist or Muslim child into a Christian environment. The child is taught daily from God's Word and has an opportunity to trust the Lord as Savior. Most orphans still have extended family ties to which they will return some day as witnesses.

Sponsor a Pastor's child

Shoulder some of the load with a village pastor, meeting the needs of his family and enabling him to minister to others. It is a huge blessing to men who may be following the call of God with no salary at all.

Sponsor a child from an impoverished believer's family

Many Christian families are not able to pay the school fees for all of their children or may not be able to meet the basic needs of all of their children. Sponsorship might mean that the child can stay with his family instead of being surrendered to a children's home for survival. Sponsorship helps to produce an educated adult, well grounded in God's Word, to be a church leader and a witness in the community.

To sponsor a child, visit www.allowthechildren.org.

CONTACT US

By mail: Allow The Children, PO Box 15039, Lynchburg, VA 24502

By personal visit: 20883 Timberlake Road Lynchburg, VA

By phone: 434-525-8866

By e-mail: sue@allowthechildren.org

By website: www.allowthechildren.org

Made in the USA
Monee, IL
18 June 2021